Communicating with normal and retarded children

Communicating with Normal and Retarded Children

EDITED BY

W. I. Fraser

Senior Lecturer in Rehabilitation Studies
University of Edinburgh

AND

R. Grieve

Senior Lecturer in Psychology
University of Western Australia

Bristol
John Wright and Sons Ltd
1981

Published by John Wright & Sons Ltd., 42–44 Triangle West, Bristol BS8 1EX.

British Library Cataloguing in Publication Data

Communicating with normal and retarded children.
  1. Language acquisition
  2. Mentally handicapped children – Language
  3. Communication – Psychological aspects
  I. Fraser, William Irvine   II. Grieve, R
  155.4'5'28   P118

ISBN 0 7236 0572 6

Printed in Great Britain by
John Wright & Sons Ltd., at The Stonebridge Press, Bristol BS4 5NU

Preface

The starting point of this book is the way in which normal children acquire language and the mistakes they make. Several different professional perspectives are then given of how and why the mentally retarded get their communication wrong and what remedies can be applied.

The contributors have all recently collaborated in a wide range of studies of communicative development and disorders in the mentally handicapped. Each one is, at present, personally engaged in research into the speech and language problems of normal and retarded people, and is directly or clinically involved with the mentally handicapped in the collection of research data, and teaches some aspect of communication disorders to his own profession and other professions.

The aims of the book are twofold. First, to trace the common growth between professions in understanding of normal language development and the retarded person's language. Each professional gives his account of contemporary knowledge which has to be shared. Secondly, to encourage research (particularly of an interdisciplinary kind). Each contributor gives his own views of recent research and of studies that need to be carried out. Each professional presents some of his own research findings, often in little-explored areas or from a novel angle. These findings are usually the result of interdisciplinary effort and therefore do not readily fit into the mainstream professional journals.

It is hoped that this book will be of interest to academic and clinical psychologists, educators, linguists, advisors and tutors in nursing and social studies, child health doctors, psychiatrists and a range of therapists.

List of contributors

William Fraser MD, FRCPsych *Senior Lecturer in Rehabilitation Studies,* Gogarburn Hospital, Glasgow Road, Edinburgh.

Robert Grieve MA, PhD *Senior Lecturer in Psychology,* Department of Psychology, University of Western Australia, Nedlands, Western Australia.

Robert Hoogenraad MA *Lecturer in Linguistics and Modern English Language,* School of English, University of Lancaster.

Ivan Leudar BSc *Research Fellow in Psychology,* Department of Psychology, University of St Andrews, Fife.

Dace Ozols BSc *Research Assistant in Psychology,* Department of Psychology, University of St Andrews, Fife.

Chris Pratt MA, DPhil *Lecturer in Education,* Department of Education, University of Western Australia, Nedlands, Western Australia.

Ian Tierney PhD, Dip Psych *Research Fellow,* Medical Research Council Cytogenetics Unit, Western General Hospital, Edinburgh.

Sheila Wirz MEd, LCST *Speech Therapist and Research Fellow,* Department of Linguistics, Queen Margaret College, University of Edinburgh

Contents

SEPTEMBER
1976

Dear Mummy, you are the
kindest Mother in the World,
and I am gratefull to you, for what
you have done and looked after me!
I love you verry much, The
weather is not settled just now,
hand in hand in life and death,
with you Mother

your loving son.
S————

Spontaneous letter from a Down's adult in hospital.

Introduction

W. I. Fraser and R. Grieve

By way of introduction, we wish to consider an instrument. It is not a medical, nor a psychological instrument, such as a stethoscope or an IQ test, instruments which may help us check an individual's physical or cognitive wellbeing. It is a much more powerful instrument than either of these. In fact, it is a very powerful instrument indeed, for it can affect the way people think. It can also affect the way people feel. It can even affect the way people behave. Surprisingly, the instrument is not new-fangled. It has been used for thousands of years. Nor is its use restricted to a handful of experts. Everyone or nearly everyone, uses it practically every day in life. What is the instrument? It is, of course, language.

We owe this example to the psychologist George Miller, who makes us think, in an unexpected way, of something we are apt to forget. Namely, language exerts an enormously powerful influence on our thoughts, emotions and behaviour, both as individuals, and socially.

However, as we know, the use of language does not always proceed smoothly, and this book will be concerned with aspects of this fact. Mostly, it will be concerned with individuals who typically encounter difficulties in using language – mentally retarded individuals. But we will also be considering other individuals, ostensibly 'normal', who also typically encounter problems and difficulties in the use of language – normal children. Our title refers to children, but we shall mention adult communication too where it helps to clarify how language develops and can deviate.

But before proceeding to explain why we wish to consider communication problems in this way, and to explain the structure and introduce the contents of this volume, we first need to have some idea of what we are up against. What sorts of communication problems are encountered? Consider some examples.

A 5-year-old child lies immobile on air cushions, except for his face which flickers and blinks continuously. He is 'untestable' by traditional psychometric and psycholinguistic means. He smiles at strangers, at his parents who each week visit the special care nursery where he lives, and at the nurses who look after him. He does not seem to have much development beyond that of a five-month-old child. X-ray studies of his brain show that he has little cortex with which he might process language. He vocalizes infrequently, and when he does, it is difficult for a new careworker on the ward to know if he is in distress. Yet his mother seems to know what he wants.

A 10-year-old girl, again untestable by usual psychometric means because of behaviour disturbance, bangs her head five times every minute, pokes her eyes, and screams shrilly. She used to have some spoken language, but no longer has. She has been hitting her face and eyes for the past seven years, and in previous settings she has been trussed up to prevent injury. When she has been given behaviour therapy, she has proved too self-damaging for 'time out' to be continued. She has blinded one eye. What has gone wrong and how can we make contact with her now?

A 15-year-old boards the school bus. He is dwarfed, and his voice seems very low-pitched and grating. Something about his voice and manner suggests unhappiness. His movements look agitated, his voice sounds agitated, but precisely what is it about his movements and voice that says he is upset? He does not have the verbal capacity to tell in words. How can a more precise recognition of his emotional distress be made?

In a training centre canteen, two adolescents with Down's anomaly are chatting. They are obviously communicating, both verbally and non-verbally, more expansively with each other than they ever do with the staff, or usually do with their parents. Why are we, who are not handicapped, unable to do as well when we try to communicate with them?

A different contrast faces a social worker who has just left a hospital where several inarticulate, ageing Down's anomaly patients have spent their lives. She visits a 90-year-old genteel lady, living alone at home with her 60-year-old son. They are receiving no services or benefits. Her heart is now troubling her, but she looks as young as him. She says: 'You can't be old when you have a duty.' He looks very apprehensive (Who says the retarded are poor at detecting emotional leakage in others?), signalling this appropriately with his face. But politely and clearly, he says: 'Excuse me, would you like some comics for the handicapped children?' He recounts with pride that he was privately educated by a tutor, and inquires whether the social worker wants any further information. His writing shows no evidence of any ideomotor apraxia, topographical agnosia or abnormal movements (see Frontispiece). He says he would like to go to an evening class. When asked: 'Do you really want to go?', he says, with a hint of reproach: 'When I say "Yes", I mean "Yes".'

Now consider a 4-year-old, normal child. Presented with 2 sticks, one with 6 beads threaded on it, the other 4, he is asked to indicate which stick has less beads. Unfortunately, he does not know what the word 'less' means. Undaunted, he produces a response and selects one of the sticks. If he does not understand the language of the instruction, what determines the selection he makes?

Another normal child, also 4 years of age, is asked a question about collections of toy horses and cows. He is certainly wholly familiar with all of the individual words in the question, but he is not sure precisely which sets of toys the adult's question is referring to. Again, he produces a response, despite his failure to accurately understand the meaning of the question. In fact, young normal children of about this age will even answer questions that cannot be answered — that is, nonsense or bizarre questions.

What determines young children's responses in such contexts? Why do they typically produce responses? And what does an examination of such phenomena have to tell us about communication difficulties in retarded children? It is with problems like these that the present book is concerned — problems of communication, whether encountered by individuals who are normal or retarded. For convenience, the book is presented in a number of different sections. Section I is concerned with early vocal communication. Firstly, the chapter by Pratt describes what is known about crying in normal infants. After a review of various methods of analysing cries, a new 'cry index' is described, which permits the overall patterns of prolonged crying episodes to be considered, information that is especially pertinent to caregivers. In the following chapter, by Fraser and Ozols, some recent studies of crying and its analysis in retarded children are described, suggesting that mothers can teach professionals some facts about detecting distress in retarded infants. In future, it seems likely that the topic of what is, and can be, communicated through vocal cries will attract a considerable amount of empirical study, for many retarded individuals never reach the verbal level of communication. If we wish to understand and alleviate distress, we are going to be dependent on whatever signals, non-vocal or vocal signals such as cries, the individual can manage to produce. Learning about such a form of communication is therefore practically important, and the material in Section One provides an introduction to this area of study.

Section Two is concerned with verbal communication. The chapter by Hoogenraad is intended to provide a contemporary account of what is known about the normal course of early language development. In an area where the conceptual apparatus, methodological procedures and technological innovations are fast changing, it is difficult to keep up to date with the study of normal language development. However, we believe it is necessary to make this effort, for the recent emphasis in this area of study on social and pragmatic aspects of language and its use has direct relevance for the study of verbal communication in retarded individuals, as a subsequent chapter by Fraser attempts to illustrate. If clinicians cling to purely neuropathological concepts, they will mainly shunt about in side-tracks. Fraser shows that what must be taken note of is the main lines along which cognitive, linguistic and developmental ideas are quickly progressing. In the second chapter in this section, Grieve describes some recent studies of communication problems in normal children aged 3—7 years. Here it is shown that when children of this age are presented with questions or instructions, they typically produce a response even though they do not, or cannot, fully understand what these questions or instructions mean. The ways in which young normal children do this are described, and the implications of this work for obtaining a fuller understanding of the communication problems of retarded children are also briefly considered.

In Section three of the book, Leudar considers another aspect of communication — non-verbal communication — where emphasis is given to the transmission of meaning which is never made explicit. The grammar of posture (which the professional can be taught to recognize) may occur effortlessly between two handicapped people to lubricate communication, or it may occur intentionally between a defective person and a normal person to covertly achieve an aim. Leudar also describes the social origins of much non-verbal gesturing of retarded people.

The first three sections of the book are therefore intended to describe a sample of what is known about three important means of communication: vocal, verbal and non-verbal. Having introduced some issues, provided some information and described and discussed problems, it is then necessary to consider what is to be done about these problems. Therefore in Section four, the chapters by Tierney and Wirz consider therapeutic approaches to communication problems. Although these chapters stem from relatively traditional backgrounds — behaviour therapy and speech therapy, respectively — the chapters in this section are innovative in nature, indicating the need for radical changes in therapeutic approaches. Nevertheless, the changes suggested in this section have, to our mind, the air of practicality and common sense. For example, Tierney's concern that traditional behaviour therapy in language typically fails to generalize outside the therapeutic context in which gains may be made, is an issue of considerable importance. And his proposal, that we need to understand the cognitive basis that underlies communicative behaviour, and try to remedy that underlying cognitive base when it is deficient, certainly deserves continuing consideration and examination. Wirz's chapter is partly devoted to a consideration of how the roles of speech therapy, and speech therapists, might be most effectively defined, and is also concerned with how scarce expertise can be effectively deployed whilst ensuring staff and client satisfaction.

The chapters in Section four raise a general question. Namely, how does a wide range of personnel, representing a wide range of disciplines, effectively collaborate in understanding, and alleviating, communication problems? The issues here are not simply academic. They are concerned with policy matters — the nature of training of personnel, the nature and effective integration of different kinds of expertise, areas of responsibility, appropriate divisions of labour, and so on. They are also concerned with ideals, and with constraints on ideals, for example, lack of knowledge, and lack of money. In the final chapter of the book, the editors attempt to provide an overview of what the book as a whole is attempting to say, an indication of how some progress in understanding and alleviating communication problems might be sought, and why this is not only worthwhile but increasingly necessary.

The study of communication problems is a rapidly developing subject. It is reaching the limits of complexity beyond which practitioners lose control of their knowledge of related fields. The assessment and treatment of the mentally handicapped is also a rapidly expanding multiprofessional business. This book therefore attempts to identify aspects of linguistic failure, retarded language and communication deficit conditions, in such a way as to be useful to both educational and health care staff.

Early Vocal Communication

Chapter One

Crying in Normal Infants

Chris Pratt

Crying, the familiar sound of infancy, has been studied by authors from various disciplines. In recent years the bulk of research has been completed by paediatricians and psychologists. Paediatricians have tended to concentrate on the analysis of cries and the potential value of these sounds as a diagnostic tool for use with both normals and abnormals. There has been a long-standing recognition that the infant cry sound may be of great importance in aiding the identification of certain abnormalities. Indeed, in one instance, a syndrome has taken its name from the cry sound: the *maladie du cri du chat* refers to an abnormality in which one of the characteristics is a shrill cry, claimed to resemble the sound of a cat (Vuorenkoski et al., 1966). One of the main questions for paediatricicans, therefore, has been to find suitable methods of analysis which will reveal differences in cries that can be used in the diagnosis of problems in infancy.

Psychologists, on the other hand, with their interest in other aspects of infant development, particularly in parent—child interaction, have viewed the cry as an important infant behaviour which may communicate needs and serve as an attachment behaviour. Bell and Ainsworth (1972), for example, have carried out an extensive investigation concerning maternal responsiveness to infant crying, and the role of the cry as an effective attachment behaviour which maintains contact between mother and child. Others, including Morsbach and Murphy (1979), have examined the identification of different cry signals by groups of adult judges.

Yet despite the amount of interest shown in the area by these disciplines, and the importance of the cry signal as an indicator of infant states and needs, there remain considerable problems in analysing and interpreting cry sounds. The first aim of this chapter, therefore, is to present and assess previous work in the area in an attempt to examine the problems that have arisen in the course of studying infant cry signals. Following this, research carried out in England (Pratt, 1978) will be presented. This research adopts a different approach to the topic, and in so doing helps to shed some light on the complexity of crying behaviour and associated behaviours in infancy.

Although references to crying date back centuries, Darwin (1877) was

3

one of the first to refer to the differentiation of infant cries. He describes briefly the time of appearance of different cries representing hunger and pain, followed by the appearance of voluntary crying, as compared with neonatal reflex crying. Following the publication of his report numerous others appeared, perhaps the best known of which are the descriptions by Champneys (1881), Dearborn (1910) and Blanton (1917). But regrettably there is little consensus of opinion to be found in the writings of these authors. Indeed, all they seem to have in common is the subjective nature of the descriptions they provide. Blanton, for example, provides a zoological taxonomy of cry sounds referring to 'the potrack of the quail, the cry of the goat, the whine of the young pig and the wail of the wild cat . . .' (p. 46). These papers, therefore, clearly lack a satisfactory method of analysing and classifying cries which overcomes the problems of subjective interpretation. However, these reports do highlight the need to ascertain an acceptable means of describing infant cry signals – a requirement which has continued to raise problems for researchers in the area.

Little progress was made until the 1940s when a few attempts to find more satisfactory methods of analysing cry sounds were made. These included the work of Irwin and his colleagues (Irwin, 1941; Irwin and Chen, 1941, 1943; Irwin and Curry, 1941). Using a broad transcription of the International Phonetic Alphabet (IPA), as described by Fairbanks (1940), they attempted to transcribe the cries of young infants. But the IPA is a transcription device developed to record human *speech* signals in the written form, and in more recent years Lieberman (1973) has demonstrated that, because of the anatomy of their vocal tracts, infants are not capable of producing such sounds, even during a crying episode. Thus the success that Irwin and his colleagues report in using the IPA must result from some distortion of the sounds represented by the symbols. The authors do not report these distortions, and in fact attempted to avoid them. Consequently the system is not available for use by other researchers, even if it were a suitable one. Thus there still did not exist a sufficiently objective classification system for analysing crying behaviour.

This state of affairs continued until the sound spectrograph became available (Koenig et al., 1946). Although the spectrograph was developed to analyse speech sounds, particularly those of an adult male, Lynip (1951) pioneered its application to the analysis of preverbal utterances. In his lengthy monograph, Lynip demonstrated the potential of the instrument to depict the acoustical components of the cry in a form suitable for objective analysis. But the technique was not used to full advantage until twenty years later, when Truby and Lind (1965) provided a detailed analysis of infant cry sounds. Working as paediatricians, these authors were aware of the diagnostic potential of the cry, but were concerned that subjective expressions, such as 'weak', 'shrill' and 'wailing', used in case notes, remained ambiguous and of little value. Consequently they set out to analyse and classify the cries of normal infants. They used several techniques including sound spectrography and cineradiography, but in their report they concentrated on acoustical analysis based on the visual-acoustic display represented on spectrograms. Their analysis of cries, elicited by giving the infant a 'pinch', revealed the existence of three different cry sounds which the authors initially labelled as the 'basic cry', 'turbulence' and 'shift'. Subsequently, the authors referred to them as 'phonation', 'dysphonation' and 'hyperphonation', respectively.

Briefly, *phonation* (the basic cry) is heard as a periodic cry during the egressive stage of the cycle. *Dysphonation* (turbulence) is heard as a 'raucous' or 'harsh' cry, and results from extreme effort which overloads the larynx and produces a random distribution of energy. Finally, *hyperphonation* (shift) is perceived as a very high-pitched sound or a shift to a higher pitch during the cry signal. In comparison to descriptions of 'hunger' cries, 'angry' cries and the use of terms such as 'weak' and 'shrill', the acoustical categories described by Truby and Lind do provide a means of classifying cries, without imputing any intentions or emotions into the signal. Thus subjective interpretation is avoided, and the objective classification can be verified with spectrographic analysis. The authors also claim, that with experience it is possible to identify auditorily these three primary cry types with a reasonable degree of confidence, without necessarily having to examine the spectrographic evidence.

In providing such an analysis, Truby and Lind had concentrated on a very narrow field of crying – elicited cries of young normal infants. Subsequent reports by these researchers and their associates have broadened the scope greatly, however. The research that has followed has taken two directions. These are further studies of normal infant cries in different situations, and the study of the characteristics of abnormal cries. Wasz-Höckert et al. (1968), for example, have tackled the problem of acoustic identification of cries recorded in four different situations. They recorded vocalizations of infants just following the birth, following an injection or pinching the infant, at least 3½ hours following a feed, and finally the sounds that infants make when lying comfortably. Wasz-Höckert et al. labelled the vocalizations recorded in these situations as 'birth cries', 'hunger cries', 'pain cries' and 'pleasure sounds', respectively, although they acknowledge that these labels cannot be taken to necessarily imply the infant's experience at the time of recording. In a sequence of intensive analysis of the acoustical attributes of these sample cries, followed by statistical analysis, the attributes which differentiate the cries in the four categories were determined. They found that for the samples from infants up to 1 month, two criteria were sufficient to identify the cries and assign them to the appropriate category. The criteria were 'melody type' and 'length of signal'. For the cries produced by older infants (1–7 months), three attributes were found to be sufficient for identification of the cry type. These were 'melody form', 'nasality' and 'shift'. Depending on the way different variations in these attributes are present in any specific cry, it can be assigned to the appropriate category. Thus the cries from each of the four categories were differentiated acoustically, and further, on the basis of two or three attributes, depending on the infant's age, the cries could be labelled correctly as one of the four types.

Wasz-Höckert et al.'s analysis appeared therefore to provide a sound basis for the continuation of work on infant cry signals. It lent itself to the study of the cry as a possible communicator of different infant states (Wasz-Höckert et al., 1964a, b), where the ability of groups of individuals to recognize the different cries can be assessed. Their work also provided a large body of data against which the characteristics of abnormal cries could be compared.

Lind et al. (1965), using the same methods for analysis as Wasz-Höckert et al. (1968), compared the cries of brain damaged and normal infants. They found that the melody form of the abnormal group was predominantly rising–falling, compared with falling in normals, and further, that a much higher percentage of abnormal cries featured hyperphonation. Similar studies by Lind et al. (1970) of infants with Down's syndrome, and by Vuorenkoski et al. (1966) of infants with *maladie du cri du chat*, also revealed differences between these groups and normals.

Yet despite the objective nature of these studies of cry sounds and the promising findings which result, the work of Wasz-Höckert, Lind and their colleagues has not been used to the full, either in the field of medicine or psychology. Other studies have followed, including the work by Müller et al. (1974) and Morsbach and Murphy (1979) on the auditory recognition of cry sounds. These have only led to conflicting and confusing results, however, with some studies demonstrating high levels of auditory recognition and others revealing identification at chance level only. Even attempts to approach the topic from a slightly different angle, for example, using a behavioural classification system (Stark et al., 1974), have been limited in their use. Hence, despite these types of studies appearing to give hope to those interested in infant crying behaviour, there remain certain problems which have prevented work proceeding at the rate of progress which could be expected from the amount of research that has been carried out. These problems centre on the following three issues:

1. the restrictive nature of spectrographic analysis;
2. uncertainty concerning the underlying cause or causes of the cries;
3. over-simplification of the situation being considered.

Regarding the first problem, studies such as those referred to above by Wasz-Höckert and colleagues have provided detailed analysis of several acoustical attributes of the infant cry. Yet the use of the sound spectrograph to enable such analysis involves a great deal of time (Crystal, 1973). The sound spectrograph analyses 2·4 seconds of cry at a time, but to transfer this length of sample on to the machine, then wait for the print-out, takes some 2–3 minutes of time. Consequently, to analyse in full a 10-minute sequence of crying, or alternatively 250 samples from various cries, would take between 8 and 12 hours. This time refers only to the production of the pictorial representation of the cry. Analysis of this representation, in terms of pitch, melody type and such like is in addition to it. Thus, although the spectrographic analysis enables detailed study of the cry form, it does so at considerable cost in terms of time. Also, because spectrographic analysis is so detailed and is restricted to very short samples (2·4 seconds maximum), it breaks up the overall patterns of the cries and prevents full consideration of these patterns. The method of analysis available has therefore determined the samples selected for analysis, rather than consideration of those aspects which may be relevant. Hence, because the spectrograph provides excellent details of very short sequences of cry, but poor detail of the overall form of an entire episode, researchers have concentrated on sampling short sequences. And despite attempts to ensure that these sequences are representative of the sequences found in the whole episode, there is still the problem of the failure to take into account the form of the episode. For example, if one takes a crying episode of 10 minutes' duration, it may consist of 250 cycles or sequences. The researcher may then select 25 of these for analysis such that the 25 form a representative sample of the population of 250. But no matter how much care is taken in selecting the sample, the form of the episode, that is the way in which the 250 sequences fit together to form a complete pattern, cannot be represented by this method of analysis. As a result, the form of the episode has generally been ignored, although observations have revealed that in practice small components of the cry are not used meaningfully by those concerned with infants. Instead, the characteristics of the entire crying episode, and the way in which the cry form develops over time, have been found to be of greater importance. For these reasons, spectrographic analysis is not entirely suitable as the only method of analysis for the continued study of normals in various situations, nor for the study of the differences between groups of normals and infants with abnormal cries.

The second problem, concerned with the uncertainty regarding the underlying reason for crying, is one that raises difficulties in medical and psychological research on crying. Lacking the power of language, infants cannot effectively communicate their state. Further, although lack of food, for example, leads to a definite psychological imbalance, the infant's psychological experience of this imbalance is far from clear. The problems that arise from this lack of knowledge of the infant's experience vary, depending on the researcher's focus of attention when studying crying. Thus the investigator, who is interested in the ability of groups of judges to identify cries emanating from different contexts, is restricted to consideration of differences in the situation. He cannot be sure that the infant is experiencing different states, and consequently producing different cry sounds. Similarly, if a researcher is concerned with mothers' sensitivity to the demands of their infants, he has problems in determining whether a given response by a mother to a cry matches the infant's needs. The fact that a mother may be successful in calming the infant does not necessarily indicate that her response was linked to the cause of the cry.

Another aspect of the second problem involves a difficulty especially pertinent to the field of paediatrics: namely, problems are found to arise in the comparison of cries of different groups of infants. Wasz-Höckert et al. (1968), through selecting very different situations (pain, hunger, pleasure and birth), showed that the normal infant's cries do vary from one time to another. But they also acknowledge that the labelling of the situations results solely from consideration of context, and cannot be taken as a definite indication of the infant's state. Thus we are presented with the case where there is an awareness that cries of normals do differ at times, but without knowing exactly when or how they differ. This means that in the comparison of cries of normals with abnormals, great care needs to be taken to ensure that the cries stem from similar situations. In certain cases, for example the *cri du chat* syndrome, the problem does not arise as the cry is consistently different. But in other cases, where a paediatrician suspects that an infant has an abnormal cry, then great care has to be exercised in selecting a cry sample for analysis which is contextually comparable with the cries of normals, so that if differences are found to exist, one can be sure that these differences do not simply result from different situations. In practice, one must therefore avoid haphazard sampling of cry signals for comparison, and select for comparison samples from specific situations, including, for example, elicited cries, where one can be reasonably confident that no other differences in context occur. The diagnostician is further restricted because of the first problem. If he requires fairly quick feedback concerning the possible abnormality of the cry, then he cannot select too many samples to analyse given the time-consuming nature of the analysis.

The third problem is concerned with the tendency to oversimplify the situation being considered. Although it is necessary at times to severely restrict the situation in the pursuit of detailed knowledge of certain aspects of crying, this approach on its own can lead to other equally important factors being overlooked. For example, although spectrographic analysis has provided valuable insights into the acoustic quality of cry signals, it does not tell us anything about the influence and relative importance of these attributes on the activities of caretakers concerned with the infant's welfare. Further studies of auditory identification of cry types may tell us whether or not judges can identify the different cries, but they fail to tell us whether the same judges normally make these identifications in the daily caretaking routine, when a variety of other cues are available. The intention here is not to denigrate the importance of these studies. Sound spectrography in particular has greatly enhanced our knowledge of certain aspects of crying. Rather, it is intended to question the scope of these studies in dealing with all the complexities of crying and associated behaviours of infants and adults. In the study of crying there is a great deal more to consider than the constituent parts of the cry signal, and whether judges can detect differences in isolated sequences of cries. It is to these broader aspects of crying that we now turn.

In a naturalistic study of infant crying in the home environment, Wolff (1969) revealed that there are many factors which influence the infant's cry and maternal reactions to it. In his investigation, Wolff describes changes in cry with age, and associated changes concerning maternal responses and interpretations of cries. Further, in a series of related ad hoc experiments, he revealed that certain assumptions relating to the causes of infant cries are probably false. In one instance, in an experiment on crying and the changing of wet nappies, he found that there was no difference afterwards in the behaviour of two groups of infants where one group was changed from wet to clean, dry nappies, and the second from wet nappies back into wet ones. Infants in the second group stopped crying as often, and fell asleep as readily, after the change as those who were changed into the clean, dry nappies. Thus Wolff questioned the assumption of certain caretakers that infants cry because their nappies are wet. In studying the infants for long periods of time, Wolff also found that the cry frequently labelled as the 'hunger cry' is in fact the basic cry which infants produce in a wide range of situations. This reveals problems in the approach taken by Wasz-Höckert and colleagues, where they selected only a small range of specific situations for sampling. By failing to take into account the entire range of cries that infants produce, they did not ensure that cries resulting from one particular situation, say hunger, do not also arise in other situations. Wolff's study thus raises a number of issues for researchers interested in studying infant crying behaviour.

Consequently, the problems that have been encountered in the past suggest three major changes in emphasis in the study of infant crying. First, the analysis of the cry sound should be less restrictive, in order that the form of an entire episode may be coded. Secondly, because there remains a great deal of uncertainty regarding the exact causes of infant cries, greater care is required in assigning cries to specific categories, especially when these categories are labelled with such terms as 'hunger' and 'tiredness', labels which carry with them implications regarding the infant's experience. It would be more advisable therefore to shift the emphasis away from these categorizations. Finally, research into crying behaviour should avoid oversimplification, and the researcher should shift his emphasis in order to maintain a fuller awareness of the general context in which crying occurs.

With these considerations in mind, a naturalistic study was recently undertaken (Pratt, 1978, 1980). The study involved 27 mother–infant pairs living in Oxfordshire, England. Four visits at 4-weekly intervals, were made to each mother–infant pair for the purposes of recording the mothers and infants, and discussing crying behaviour with the mothers.

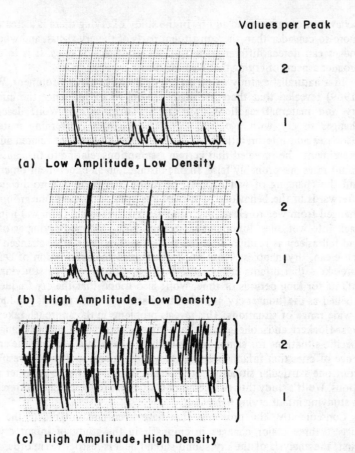

Values per Peak

(a) Low Amplitude, Low Density

(b) High Amplitude, Low Density

(c) High Amplitude, High Density

Fig. 1. Three examples of pen recordings.

The infants ages ranged from 3–50 weeks of age at the time of the first visits. During each visit to the homes, video and audio recordings were made. The recordings concentrated on the infants' cries and other related aspects of the context, including maternal caretaking activities. No attempt to control the situation was made. Consequently the sound recordings included the speech of the mothers and background noises in addition to the cry sounds. Following the data collection period in the homes, the data were analysed in the laboratory. The sound recordings of the infants' cries were coded using a 'cry index' which was specially developed for the analysis. The index is computed from amplitude tracings of the cries produced by a single channel pen recorder (*see Fig.* 1), and it takes into account two acoustical components of the cry – the amplitude and density.

The *amplitude* of the cry corresponds to the loudness. There is a minor complication, however, in so far as the physical strength of the signal decreases with increased distance between mother and infant (the inverse square law). Consequently the amplitude of a signal at the point where it reaches the mother is considerably less than the level at the source, i.e. the infant. Nevertheless, as a result of the perceptual constancy phenomenon, mothers are able to perceive the signal with a reasonable estimate of its strength at source. Consequently the amplitude component can be measured on a scale which reflects the amplitude produced by the infant.

The *density* of the cry refers to a different characteristic. It is a measure of the amount of time spent crying per unit of time. Low density crying is represented by a few vocalizations separated by periods of silence, whereas high density crying refers to continuous crying where there are only small inspiration breaks in the sound output. Units of 10 seconds were selected for the computation of the density and the amplitude. This length of unit is sufficiently short to be sensitive to important variations in the cry, without being too short and therefore oversensitive to very minor fluctuations. Furthermore 10-second units enabled a sufficient number of cry sequences to be selected which were free from other sound sources, including voices and background noises. However, with regard to the length of unit chosen for analysis and the calibration of the amplitude and density described below, these could be adjusted to suit the individual requirements of other investigators using the index in different settings. In the context of this study, the amplitude was scored on a nominal scale. As shown in *Fig.* 1, high amplitude peaks which led to a pen deflection greater than half the scale were designated as high amplitude peaks, and assigned the value 2. Those leading to a pen deflection which was less than the midpoint of the tracing were labelled as low amplitude peaks, and assigned the value 1.[1] Finally, a numerical value is calculated for the amplitude during a 10-second sequence according to the following formula.

$$\text{Amplitude Value} = \frac{(2 \times \text{Number of high amplitude peaks}) + (1 \times \text{Number of low amplitude peaks})}{\text{Number of peaks in the sequence}}$$

---

[1] A more precise calibration of the amplitude peaks was not possible in the context of this study as the distance between the infant and the microphone varied slightly during the recording sessions. This led to minor variations in the strength of the recorded signal in addition to the variations that result directly from the amplitude of the cry. By adopting a twofold clasification system the potential error in misclassifying peaks is minimized to less than 5 per cent (*see* Pratt (1978) for full consideration of this). In future, however, investigators may choose to control the recording situation such that the distance between the microphone and infant is constant. This would enable a more precise calibration of the amplitude peaks. However, in studies of the type described here, where it is not possible to keep the distance constant, the index as described provides a sufficiently accurate and sensitive measurement.

This leads to a range of values for the amplitude from 1·0 to 2·0. A figure of 1·0 would represent a sequence composed entirely of low amplitude peaks, whereas 2·0 would consist of high amplitude peaks. Intermediate values, for example 1·8, would refer to varying combinations of high and low peaks, in this case mainly high amplitude peaks.

The density of the cry is measured as the percentage of time spent crying per unit of time. Therefore, if the total time spent crying during a 10-second unit is 3 seconds, the density would be 30. This would represent a low density value, whereas a figure of 80 would indicate the high density of a full cry. The density ranges from 0 (silence) to a maximum of 90. The figure of 100 is never reached because there are always brief periods of silence during the ingressive phases. Finally, the cry index is calculated by multiplying the values of the two components, amplitude and density, together such that:

$$\text{Cry Index} = \text{Amplitude} \times \text{Density}$$

In practice, the index covers the range from 0–180. A 0 score represents silence, and a score of 180 (amplitude 2 × density 90) would reflect a full blown cry.

A major advantage of the cry index is that it provides a method of efficiently summarizing entire cry episodes, in contrast to the sound spectrograph which makes consideration of the overall form of the episode difficult.

By sampling 10-second units of crying across the range of the episode, it is possible to calculate index values, and represent the changes in these with time, in graphical form. Then, through studying the variations in the index values, the changes in crying can be related to aspects of the original situation which influence the index level. The cry data from the 27 infants were analysed in this way, with the index values being calculated for each episode. This revealed three main aspects of the situation which influence the cry signal. They are:

1. the internal state of the infant;
2. the age of the infant;
3. the situation in which the infant is involved.

The variations that result from each of these factors can now be considered in turn. These variations, however, remain as abstractions from the data base. They are abstractions because they consider the influence of each factor in turn, whereas in reality, all three factors influence the final cry forms that are observed.

1. THE INTERNAL STATE OF THE INFANT

This is probably the main influence on the form of the cry, yet unfortunately the infant's state and his experience of it are factors about which little can be said with certainty. As has been stated above, the lack of knowledge concerning the infant's state will continue to present problems to the researcher. Inferences made by investigators regarding the infant's state at any point in time are drawn from considerations of context. Usually such factors as time of day, time relative to the infant's routine, and the infant's general behaviour, are taken into account. Previously, however, these have lead to very specific labels such as 'hunger' and 'pain' (Wasz-Höckert et al., 1968), which carry with them specific implications concerning the infant's experience. These attempts to specify exact causes

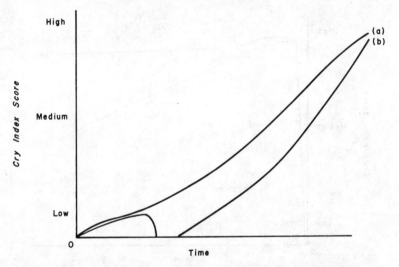

Fig. 2. The first cry form, showing a gradual rise in the cry: *a*, cry continuous; *b*, cry interrupted.

increase the likelihood of misinterpreting the situation. Consequently, in the discussion that follows the variations in cry forms are associated with broader infant experiences of changes in physiological state.

It is essential to stress, therefore, that more specific labels which are provided in the text remain only as suggestions of possible occasions when these cries may arise. The labels serve the sole function of helping to relate the discussion to situations which are more familiar to researchers in this area. It is not the intention to equate these labels, including 'hunger', 'tiredness' and 'pain', with the cry types described.

The first type of cry form appears on those occasions where the infant is in a state of physiological imbalance, such that the imbalance increases with time. In these cases, the cry appears at low values of amplitude and density, then rises gradually with time until it eventutually reaches maximum values (*see Fig.* 2). This change in levels may take up to 20 minutes, especially in the case of older infants.

In practice, continuous development of the cry form resulting from such states of physiological imbalance is observed fairly infrequently, as it arises only when infants are left undisturbed with nothing to distract them. More frequently, one finds an alternative form where the cry will again start at low values, then rise before subsiding temporarily due to some distraction or attention being provided. However, if an appropriate response is not forthcoming from the caregiver, then the cry will start again and continue to rise. This type of cry form is seen in such situations

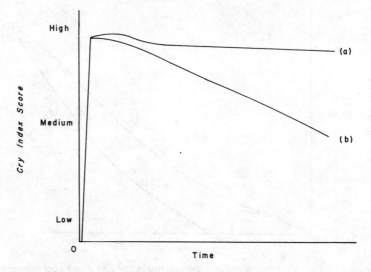

Fig. 3. The second cry form, showing the sudden rise in the cry to maximum values: *a*, cry continues at high values; *b*, cry begins to drop in value.

as those where the infant is assumed to be hungry, or where the apparent reason is tiredness. In these specific cases it can be assumed that the imbalance will increase with time, and produce examples of the general cry form that has been described.

The above variations of the same cry form differ markedly from those occurring in another set of contexts where sudden changes occur. In adult terms, examples of these occasions are when pain, shock or a sudden startled reaction would result. Regardless of the infant's actual experience, it would seem reasonable to assume that in general, very sudden physiological changes occur, and again matching context with this knowledge, the characteristic cry form can be determined. In these cases there are again two variations, depicted in *Fig.* 3. In the first of these, the cry starts very suddenly and at high index values. It then continues at these high levels, perhaps dropping slightly but not subsiding to any great extent.

This cry will then continue, but usually because of the dramatic initial rise it is not allowed to continue for any great length of time, because a response will be forthcoming. The other variation of this cry form is similar in so far as it also starts at high levels, but instead of continuing at very high levels it subsides to intermediate amplitude and density. It can only be assumed that the first variation occurs in situations where the cause has a long-lasting effect. Such situations include injury which will continue to produce pain – for example, a fall sufficiently severe to leave its mark. The other variations occur when, say as a result of a minor fall, there is no great damage done, and following the initial minor painful stimulation, the cry subsides.

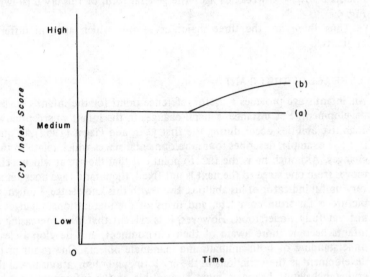

Fig. 4. The third cry form, where the cry rises to medium values: *a,* cry continuous at these values; *b,* cry shows a further rise.

Finally, there is a third cry form which presents itself as the most difficult one to deal with as far as the infant's internal state is concerned. This is because, as far as can be found from context, the cry appears to result from psychological factors rather than physiological ones. There may indeed be some physiological change that occurs but this has not been determined. They are psychological cries to the extent that they would be labelled as ones resulting from anxiety, frustration, annoyance and the like. In these cases the cry gives the definite impression of being switched on. It starts at what may be termed 'appropriate' levels of amplitude and density, such that the cry is intermediate in level. Frequently the cry then continues at this level with only minor fluctuations, but on occasions it may rise to higher levels, though not in the same predictable manner as the first cry form described above. Again, the cry will continue until some intervention occurs. The term 'appropriate' is used as the cry appears from the outset to be pitched at a level which is sufficient to attract a response. Admittedly this is speculative, but is supported by the observations. One instance where an infant is unable to reach a toy illustrates this. The infant is sitting and attempting to lean forward to grasp a toy, but cannot quite reach it. This leads to the onset of the cry, but as soon as someone intervenes and gives the toy to the infant, the cry immediately subsides, compared with other cry forms which take longer to decrease. These cries appear to be deliberately produced and are not observed in very young infants below 4–6 weeks of age. The general form of this cry is shown in *Fig.* 4.

Thus there are the three major cry forms which arise in different contexts.

2. THE AGE OF THE INFANT

An infant's age provides a useful reference point for the infant's stage of development. For instance, general changes in the infant's perceptual and cognitive abilities occur during the first year, and Piaget (1952), to quote but one example, describes four developmental stages which relate to these changes. Although he is the first to point out that the age at which a child moves from one stage to the next is not fixed, the infant's age does act as a very useful indicator of his abilities. Even with this knowledge, though, the picture is far from complete, and many of the maturational changes are not yet fully understood. However, it is evident that with increasing age infants become more aware of their environment, and develop a clearer understanding of both animate and inanimate objects. One result of this development is the variations in the cry form, and observations reveal that crying behaviour becomes more susceptible to the influences of others around the infant. As mentioned above, the cry which appears to have psychological origins does not occur in young infants. Therefore this form of cry does not appear initially. Once the cry does appear, it then changes with age, becoming more and more geared to the requirements of the situation. The extent to which it appears to be controlled to suit the situation increases with age.

Perhaps the most noticeable change in form with age arises in the cries which are of the first type described above. These cries start at low values and then increase with time until they reach maximum values. But the time they take to rise and the speed at which they do so depends on the infant's age. These variations are shown in *Fig.* 5. It can be seen that for infants aged less than 10 weeks , once the cry starts to rise it does so more quickly than for older infants. In the case of the younger infants there is very little crying at intermediate values, whereas infants over 10 weeks spend more time crying at intermediate values. It is difficult to ascertain the cause of this difference, but one suspects that the older infants have more control over their crying behaviour than the younger ones. Further, although the change takes place around 10 weeks, it does not occur suddenly. Indeed the change is quite gradual.

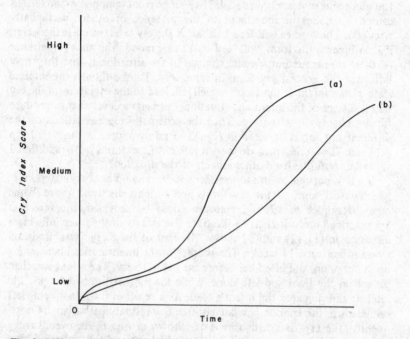

Fig. 5. Differences in speed of rise of cry with age: *a,* younger infants — cry rises more quickly; *b,* older infants — gradual rise in cry.

3. THE SITUATION IN WHICH THE INFANT IS INVOLVED

This heading covers a host of possible situational variants including the different positions of the infant, and the many events that take place around him. One obvious change in the situation would appear to be the actions of the mother, yet the actual behaviour of the mother does not always influence the cry form in a predictable manner. Although one might assume that a response from a mother would typically lead to a reduction in the level of crying, an analysis of the cry form immediately before and after the mother's response reveals that while 76 per cent dropped as would be expected, 24 per cent of all cries continued at the same level or rose to higher levels following the mother's response. Further, with reference to (2) above — the age of the infant — it was found that 40 per cent of the cries of infants less than 14 weeks old continued or rose to higher levels following the mother's response. For infants older than 14 weeks the figure drops to 20 per cent. Hence, although the mother's initial response to the infant often leads to a reduction in cry level, this is not always the case.

Other factors which influence the cry form and result in variations are too numerous to describe in detail. They range from temporary distractions caused by noises or movement to the presence of others, particularly strangers. The former will lead to a fall in the cry level, whereas the latter, if it influences the form, will lead to it being raised. The main importance of these numerous but specific changes in the situation is that they may influence the general cry form in some way. Thus, although the internal state of the infant is the factor which will lead to the overall form the cry takes, the age of the infant and situational variants will interact to produce further changes to the form. Thus the schematic representations of the different cry forms depicted in *Figs.* 2–5 rarely appear in the pure form depicted. The cries that do occur reflect these forms with additional variations resulting from other aspects of the situation.

It is now possible to turn to consider specific examples of crying episodes which reveal some of the cry forms and variants discussed above. While many examples of specific episodes could be provided, the few that are described are sufficient to illustrate the effects of the three influences discussed in (1), (2) and (3) above. The first of these cries was produced by an infant aged 11 weeks. The mother of the infant noticed her waking up in her pram, and lifted her before she began to cry. The infant was then placed on the floor and left alone, while the mother finished tidying the kitchen and prepared the infant's feed. As a result of the infant being left on her own, the episode is relatively free from situational variants. Consequently, the cry rises with time as is shown in *Fig.* 6. An overall rising trend can be seen, characterized by an initial rise and fall, followed by a steady rise to high values. At the final peak value the mother intervened and picked up her infant, which resulted in the complete abatement of the cry. Although the actual cause of the cry cannot be determined, the infant had not been fed for well over 4 hours, and consequently hunger would seem to be a likely reason. In the second example, shown in *Fig.* 7, the context is very similar, and indeed the general cry form is also similar except that now there is a very definite drop in values to 0 (no crying) 2 minutes after the cry started. This drop resulted from the mother picking up the infant and changing his position. But following this, the infant was again left alone which led to the sharper rise in cry values until they reached a peak when the mother intervened again and fed her infant.

The third example, of an infant aged 10 weeks, comes from a different context (*see Fig.* 8). On this occasion, the infant fell over on to her face at a time when her mother was in a different room. Prior to falling over, the infant had been sitting contentedly for some time. With the fall, the cry started abruptly at high values, but it did not continue for long as the fall

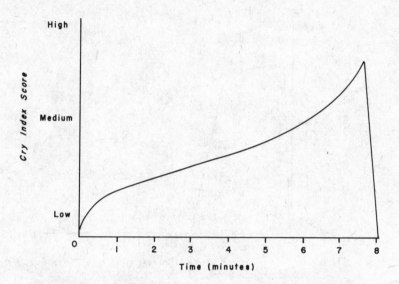

Fig. 6. Cry produced by infant (aged 11 weeks) following waking up.

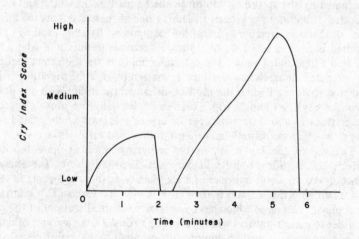

Fig. 7. Cry produced by infant (aged 6 weeks) following waking up. Note the drop in the cry at 2 minutes when the mother picked up the infant.

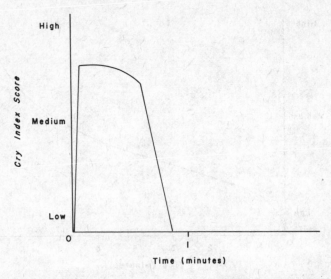

Fig. 8. Cry produced by infant (aged 10 weeks) who had just fallen over. The cry reduces in value following the mother's response.

was only minor, and the infant's mother came into the room, picked her up and managed to console her.

The final example, taken from an infant aged 38 weeks, reveals a case where the mother's action leads to the infant's cry. The infant had been fascinated by the recording equipment being used in the study, and made repeated attempts to approach it. During one of these attempts the infant was deliberately removed from the equipment by the mother. This resulted in a short sequence of crying, 12 seconds in duration, where the cry had a high index value. The original amplitude tracing shows that the cry occurred immediately the infant was removed from the equipment, and that it stopped when the mother distracted the infant with one of his favourite toys, a spinning top. These examples therefore provide specific illustrations of the different types of cry that infants produce, and also reveal the effects of situational variants on the final form of the cry.

The use of the cry index in the analysis of cries as presented here reflects the significant shifts in emphasis discussed above. The analysis concentrates on whole episodes of cries, classifying these according to type and examining the variations that arise in the cry forms. This contrasts with previous research which has considered only small sections of the cry. In order to concentrate on whole episodes, a considerable amount of detail concerning such acoustical components as pitch and type of phonation, has been lost, but the important characteristics of amplitude and density have been retained. These are seen as important because they are the components of the cry which are most relevant to mothers and other infant caretakers (Pratt, 1980). Further, there is a move away from specific labelling of cries to adopting a broader perspective, in line with Wolff's (1969) discussion of the basic cry. The cry index enables a more objective description of the cry forms, however. The shift to a broader perspective seems justified for two reasons. Those concerned with infant cries rely on the sound of the cry more as an indicator of general distress levels, than as a cue to specific causes. In addition, given the uncertainty of identifying specific causes of cries, avoiding such labelling greatly reduces the potential error margin.

The use of the index has been described in relation to a study of mother–infant interaction. The question that now arises relates to its potential for future studies of the infant cry sound. Clearly, the index will be relevant to studies akin to the one described, that is in studies concerned with aspects of mother–infant interaction. As well as providing an apt description of the cry, the index also serves as a means by which the effects of mothers' behaviours can be assessed. Thus it has been shown that mothers normally respond before extremely high values are reached. The reason for this may be considered in terms of payoff for the mother. Once the infant is screaming at maximum values it is very difficult to quieten him. By leaving the infant crying too long before she intervenes, a mother encounters the situation where her response is less effective than it would have been if introduced earlier, and she now has to spend more time calming the infant than on those occasions when she responds before top values are reached. One specific area of study which requires investigation at present is the cause of mothers complaining that their infants cry excessively, and fail to respond to their caretaking activities. It may be that in some of these cases the timing of the mother's response is inappropriate. In general, mothers who encounter these problems may leave the infant to cry too long before responding. Thus one possible study would be to compare the timing of mothers' responses to their infants, relative to the index value of the cry at the time of response. If mothers who complain of excessive crying are found to respond at higher levels than normal, then some remedial advice could be offered.

With reference to the cry as a diagnostic tool, the potential of the cry index has still to be examined. It may well be that in the case of certain syndromes the overall form of the cry is different from that of normals. At present, however, this remains only a possibility, as no research has been carried out in this area. But if differences in crying are found to exist, then not only would it be useful for future diagnosis of infant problems, but also helpful in providing a basis for advising parents on the specific characteristics of the cry. This latter point can be explained with an example. When discussing infant crying behaviour with a mother of an infant with Down's syndrome, the mother had been most concerned that she was not sure how to respond to the child. The cry had been so different to that of a normal child that she had found great difficulties in using the cry as an indicator of distress. Consequently, if differences between normal and abnormal cries could be documented, then more detailed advice to parents could be provided.

In conclusion, this chapter has centred on an alternative method of cry analysis. This new method has definite advantages in studies of mother–infant interaction, and in coding lengthy sequences of cries. Its potential as a diagnostic tool has yet to be determined, and it may be that the cry index will provide useful information additional to that which can be obtained by other means. However, the index should not be considered as a replacement for other techniques, such as spectrographic analysis. The two approaches complement each other, by concentrating on different aspects of the cry. Sound spectrography provides finer detail on short periods of crying, while the cry index that is described here provides more global information on the overall patterns of cries. While the utility of the index in clinical settings has still to be determined, it can be observed in the meantime that the more global information provided by the cry index is especially pertinent to caretaking and its problems.

References

Bell S. M. and Ainsworth M. D. S. (1972) Infant crying and maternal responsiveness. *Child Dev.* 43, 1171–1190.

Blanton M. G. (1917) The behaviour of the human infant during the first thirty days of life. *Psychol. Rev.* 24, 456–483.

Champneys F. H. (1881) Notes on an infant. *Mind* 6, 104–107.

Crystal D. (1973) Non-segmental phonology in language acquisition: a review of the issues. *Lingua* 32, 1–45.

Darwin C. (1877) A biographical sketch of an infant. *Mind* 2, 285–294.

Dearborn G. V. N. (1910) *Motor–Sensory Development: Observations on the First Three Years of Childhood.* Baltimore, Warwick and York.

Fairbanks G. (1940) *Voice and Articulation Drillbook.* New York, Harper.

Irwin O. C. (1941) Research on speech sounds for the first six months of life. *Psychol. Bull.* 38, 277–285.

Irwin O. C. and Chen H. P. (1941) A reliability study of speech sounds observed in the crying of newborn infants. *Child Dev.* 12, 351–368.

Irwin O. C. and Chen H. P. (1943) Speech sound elements during the first years of life: a review of the literature. *J. Speech Disord.* 8, 109–121.

Irwin O. C. and Curry T. (1941) Vowel elements in the crying vocalization of infants under ten days of age. *Child Dev.* 12, 99–109.

Koenig W., Dunn H. K. and Lacey L. V. (1946) The sound spectrograph. *J. Acoust. Soc. Am.* 17, 19–49.

Lieberman P. (1973) On the evolution of language: a unified view. *Cognition* 2, 59–94.

Lind J., Wasz-Höckert O., Vuorenkoski V. et al. (1965) The vocalization of a new-born brain-damaged child. *Ann. Paediatr. Fenn.* 13, 56–63.

Lind J., Vuorenkoski V., Rosberg G. et al. (1970) Spectrographic analysis of vocal response to pain stimuli in infants with Down's syndrome. *Dev. Med. Child Neurol.* 12, 478–486.

Lynip A. W. (1951) The use of magnetic devices in the collection and analysis of the preverbal utterances of an infant. *Genet. Psychol. Monogr.* **44**, 221–262.

Morsbach G. and Murphy M. C. (1979) Recognition of individual neonates' cries by experienced and inexperienced adults. *J. Child Lang.* **6**, 175–179.

Müller E., Hollien H. and Murry T. (1974) Perceptual responses to infant crying: identification of cry tapes. *J. Child Lang.* **1**, 89–95.

Piaget J. (1952) *The Origins of Intelligence in Children.* New York, International Universities Press.

Pratt C. (1978) A study of infant crying behaviour in the home environment during the first year of life. Unpublished doctoral dissertation, University of Oxford.

Pratt C. (1980) For crying out loud – I need some attention. In: *Proceedings of the Australian Association of Speech and Hearing Convention.* (In press.)

Stark R. E., Rose S. N. and Benson P. J. (1974) Classification of infant vocalization behaviour. Paper given at the American Speech and Hearing Association, Las Vegas.

Truby H. M. and Lind J. (1965) Cry sounds of the newborn infant. In: Lind J. (ed.) *Newborn Infant Cry. Acta Paediatr. Scand. (Suppl.)* **163**.

Vuorenkoski V., Lind J., Partanen T. J. et al. (1966) Spectrographic analysis of cries from children with maladie du cri du chat. *Ann. Paediatr. Fenn.* **12**, 174–180.

Wasz-Höckert O., Partanen T. J., Vuorenkoski V. et al. (1964a) The identification of some specific meanings in infant vocalization. *Experientia* **20**, 154–155.

Wasz-Höckert O., Partanen T. J., Vuorenkoski V. et al. (1964b) Effect of training on ability to identify preverbal vocalizations. *Dev. Med. Child Neurol.* **6**, 393–396.

Wasz-Höckert O., Lind J., Vuorenkoski V. et al. (1968) The infant cry: a spectrographic and auditory analysis. *Clinics in Developmental Medicine, No. 29.* London, Heinemann.

Wolff P. H. (1969) The natural history of crying and other vocalizations in early infancy. In: Foss B. M. (ed.) *Determinants of Infant Behaviour, IV.* London, Methuen, pp. 81–109.

Chapter Two

'He Sounds and Looks Sore...'

Professionals' Evaluations of the Profoundly Handicapped Person's Pain and Distress Signals

William I. Fraser and Dace Ozols

Introduction

Confronted by the vocalizations and grimaces of a profoundly handicapped person, and an anxious mother or nurse suggesting illness, the medical practitioner is often at a loss where to start. The doctor without special knowledge of the mentally handicapped is increasingly likely to have to face this problem as community care expands. The literature on the subject is of little help, and the widespread notion that the mentally handicapped are insensitive to pain is downright misleading. Although there has been considerable research into infants' distress, including cry analysis to identify syndromes, little research has been carried out with older age groups of mentally handicapped populations.

Spectrographic Cry Analysis

In the previous chapter Dr Pratt has traced the development (and limitations) of the spectrograph. In 1976, Sirvio and Michelsson found spectrographic abnormalities in the crying of premature and asphyxiated babies; the greater the prematurity or the asphyxia the more abnormal the cry characteristics. Abnormal cries associated with congenital abnormalities, chromosomal aberrations, brain disorders and metabolic disorders were documented subsequently with increasing precision.

Abnormalities have been found particularly in the pitch, by which is meant the measurable height of the fundamental frequency as presented on a spectrogram; and the latency period, that is the time between the stimulus applied to the child and the onset of the crying (usually between 0·5 and 3·5 seconds). The latter is a very reliable indicator of abnormal cries. Some features in infants are now clearly correlated with distinct diseases; for example furcation, the split in a fundamental frequency of a strong cry into a series of weaker ones; biphonation, a double series of the fundamental frequencies; and noise concentration, a single energy peak at over 2000 Hz. Furcation occurs in newborns with jaundice, biphonation

24

in central lesions and noise concentration in infants with brain infection due to herpes. Abnormalities have also been found in melody type, which in a normal infant is of a rising–falling type. Brain damage caused by meningitis or hydrocephalus causes (as paediatricians are well aware) a shrill cry and a rising–falling configuration; *cri du chat*, a prolonged cry and high pitch; and Down's syndrome, a low pitch (although this is disputed). Lind and his co-workers (1970), in their study on spectrographic cry analysis, considered that Down's pitch was lower than average, but not strikingly so (mean minimum pitch 270 cps, normal m/mean 390 cps). Lind also considered that the melody of Down's was similar to that of the *cri du chat* syndrome, and that both cries were longer than normal pain cries and were 'tense', with a stuttering characteristic. Taken together these features seemed to constitute a 'Down's voice profile', which seemed to differentiate rather well between Down's and normal pain cries, and staff could readily be trained to recognize the Down's cry.

The Spectrograph and the Detection of Emotional States

Although there are more powerful ways (e.g. clinical examination, chromosome analysis or urinary chromatography) to diagnose syndromes, cry analysis does add something. It helps towards saying 'The cry of X disease is such and such . . .', and from this base-line we may learn to decide that 'the message of this (such and such) abnormal cry is . . .'. After all, the infant and the very retarded have few ways of conveying emotion. Pain cries (internal pains) are the least definable, yet they are the most variegated. Wasz-Höckert and his colleages (1968), as Rosenhouse (1978) has pointed out, were studying not pure pain cries but pain/alarm vocalizations. Rosenhouse has shown that pain, hunger and alarm cries have some features in common, and that 'illness' cries share, with the cries of infants who are premature or brain damaged, a high-pitched quality, and low amplitude in the long pauses between cries. Of course, the child has to be very ill to sound like this. The hunger cry has most intensity in the middle frequencies, and its tempo gradually increases to 'frantic'. The intonation is rising–falling. There may be some similarity in the sensations of the baby for all discomfort situations so that parts of the cries are not specially 'marked', and produce a 'general discomfort' pattern.

Caretakers' Abilities to Detect Emotion

Ricks (1975) gathered a series of cry messages (e.g. frustration, hunger) from normal infants and young autistic children, and asked their mothers to identify their own children and the messages in the cry of others' children. Mothers of normal children could identify the message of loud infant cries, but not easily their own child. Mothers of autistic children unerringly identified their own child, and messages in the cry, but not in other autistic children. Babies' cries were not only precursors of language but also had a 'true language' function with different forms for definite messages and functions. The problem is that in brain damaged children, messages in cries are not so easily recognizable. The medical literature is of little help; Fraser and Ozols (1980) could find no references to the subject in a linked retrieval over 20 years of papers on pain detection in the profoundly handicapped. In a series of studies, the authors first asked profoundly mentally handicapped children's parents (being most experienced, and the people staff turn to first anyway) to explain, by giving them a multiple choice questionnaire with a chance for them to amplify, for instance how they detected earache, toothache, colic, vague discomfort; and asked them what action they took. We also asked nurses, experienced with the same children, the same questions.

Parents and nurses agreed on how pain and distress were shown; distress being mainly signalled by crying, facial expression, aggression and gross motor 'fussing'. Although there was no overall significant difference in the utilization of one of these behaviours over another, twice as many parents utilized facial expression as nurses. Pain, it was agreed, is mainly conveyed by crying, the character of the cry, the facial expression, self-aggression and gross motor activity, and cries identified as being unusual by nurses and mothers were those where the pace, the cycle and the sequences of the cry seemed different rather than the pitch or the intensity. Twice as many parents as nurses thought their offspring's cries did not sound unusual. Where parents and nurses differed was that nurses did not detect a consistent behaviour pattern in pain whilst mothers did. Interestingly, parents thought that their offspring were less sensitive than normal, and that they underacted in a painful situation, whilst nurses considered the subjects had a normal reaction or over-reacted in pain. Parents felt that pain was the main cause of crying, and to a lesser extent frustration and fear, whilst nurses felt frustration was the primary cause of crying with pain a secondary cause. Here it is worth recollecting Pratt's (1977) conclusions that younger infants cry for psychological reasons and older infants for physiological reasons. Perhaps parents' recollections dated more from infancy and nurses' perceptions were of more mature infants. Nurses considered that the more children cried, the more alternative causes for crying there might be; and conversely, the less they cried, the more heed the nurse would pay to the possibility of pain when crying occurred. So there was considerable agreement between parents and nurses about means of identifying pain and distress. Both sought medical professional help less often as the child grew older, preferring to observe him for longer continuous periods. Both nurses and parents thought the mentally handicapped became less sensitive to pain with age. Parents thought crying became less common with age, while nurses thought crying diminished with time spent in hospital.

Most importantly, parents considered there was consistent behaviour associated with pain and that they could detect non-vocal signs signalling pain. The cries and vocalizations seemed largely alarm signals.

One problem is our perception of the handicapped and his signals. We may not recognize the situation as potentially distressing, or our pre-conceptions, attitudes or visual cues may mislead us.

This was evident (Fraser and Campbell, 1978) in studies of the language characteristics of individuals exhibiting de Lange 'Amsterdam Dwarf' syndrome. This syndrome is a constellation of mental retardation and growth failure, and there is a characteristic hairy facial appearance with thin lips and various limb malformations. With regard to language, most definite cases of the syndrome are said to have low-pitched voices and little spoken language. However, in examination of six cases, Fraser and Campbell found that perceived low pitch was not low pitch at all. In fact, the average fundamental frequency of sustained 'ah' vocalizations was 208 cps, *above* that for an average adult male. However there was a vocal 'fry'

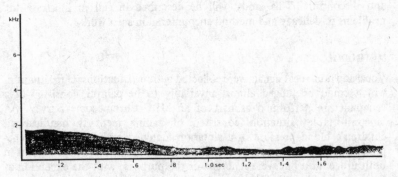

Fig. 9. Narrow band pattern of portion of vocalization showing vocal fry 1·4—1·8 seconds.

present (*Fig.* 9), which could explain the harshness and dysphonia charac-teristic of the dwarf throughout his life. (The possibility of recognizing the syndrome from the vocal fry on the sonogram print-out deserves to be studied further.) What is of particular interest is that the listener was distracted by the individual's appearance; because the speaker was dwarfed, a slightly higher pitch than normal was perceived as low. (One might also speculate to what extent the self-mutilating behaviour commonly found in this syndrome results from social reaction to the dwarf's typically un-attractive, even menacing appearance.) A finding such as this emphasizes the importance of bearing in mind that our normal adult's perception of the mentally handicapped individual's language may not be veridical, as we are tempted to suppose.

Both parents and experienced nurses in Fraser and Ozols' (1980) study were drawn to the possibility of pain and distress by the changing cycles and sequences of cry episodes, rather than the pitch and intensity of the cry. Parents claimed that the cries of their offspring in pain did not 'sound' unusual.

Wasz-Höckert et al. (1968) had shown that certain features of cries of normal infants in pain could be identified and taught to staff. A search for such features in 149 pain cries (Fraser and Ozols, 1980) from the first cry episode after venepuncture of 394 moderately, severely and profoundly handicapped persons did not, on a Siemen's AB Mingograph and a Kay Electrometric Spectrograph (measuring pitch, friction, harmonics, glottal activity, configuration of cries and other factors), reveal any recognizable 'markers' of pain, nor were there any features which distinguished pain cries from matched utterances of discomfort or neutral utterances which could be taught to staff.

The next step therefore was to observe how parents and professionals evaluate vocal and non-vocal signals in real life settings of unavoidable pain and discomfort. This study will be described in full to illustrate the problems of delicacy and method encountered in such work.

METHODOLOGY

Vocal and non-vocal signals were collected in three situations. One situation, which could be judged almost invariably to be painful, consisted of a venepuncture performed as part of an MRC Chromosome Survey. An 'uncomfortable' situation consisted of taking mentally handicapped children's blood pressure in a situation matched with that of the venepuncture as closely as possible. Staff familiar to the subject were present in both procedures but were ignorant of the purpose, with the exception of the person taking the blood sample who, on each occasion, was a stranger. Several weeks elapsed between the taking of the respective samples, but accurate balancing of the order of the blood sample and the blood pressure sample was considered as ethically unreasonable. A 'neutral' situation was obtained at play and after bathing. The population consisted of 29 'children' (16 males, 13 females), whose chronological ages ranged from 3–22 years (mean 11·3 years), without any speech, and whose social ages ranged from 0·06 to 1·78 years (mean 1·20 years), as measured on the Vineland Scale of Social Maturity. Subjects who had clinical syndromes which have characteristically abnormal vocalizations were excluded, for example autism, de Lange Amsterdam Dwarfism, hypothyroidism, Down's and *cri du chat*. A video film was made of the facial and bodily expression during the blood sampling, the blood pressure estimation and the control situation. Before either the blood sample or blood pressure was taken, the subject was pacified and not in pain or discomfort. In the blood sample condition the portion of film showed the complete facial/body expression from 5 seconds before the needle was inserted in the arm, during the period when the needle was in the arm, which varied, until withdrawal of the needle or 15 seconds had elapsed. Likewise, the blood pressure condition showed facial/body expression before the cuff was applied and continued during the measurement.

A composite film was constructed of 57 sections of randomly assorted film taken from 19 subjects, so that there were 19 pieces of film of blood sample, 19 of the blood pressure condition and 19 of a 'neutral' painless situation. One half of the screen was masked by a blank screen so that it was possible only to see the child's facial expression and bodily movement, without seeing which procedure was being carried out. Each section of film lasted 15 seconds and was followed by a blank screen of 10 seconds' duration before presentation of the next section of film. This film was shown without sound to 5 groups of caretakers (all females). This constituted Condition I.

Group 1: 4 nurses who had close personal contact with the children in the film.

Group 2: 4 nurses who were experienced with mentally handicapped children but not these children.

Group 3: 4 teachers working with the mentally handicapped in a school unit within the hospital who had close contact with the children in the film.

Group 4: 4 postgraduate students of psychology without previous experience with the mentally handicapped, but highly trained observers.

Group 5: Mothers of children who appear in the film; this group consisted of 16 parents of 11 children in the film. The parents had been carefully appraised of the circumstances and the limited objectives of the study.

Each group was shown the film separately and each participant asked to choose which of three situations for each section of film was being shown, on the premise that a blood sample would be acutely painful, the blood pressure uncomfortable and the painless condition would be neutral. The mothers were not shown the whole series of 57 film portions as it was thought that they might find this distressing, and were shown instead 9 film sections of 3 children, including their own child, in each of the three situations.

An audiotape of the children's cries accompanying the various conditions was presented to groups 1 and 2 without the film (Condition II), and then presented synchronized with the film 1 month later (Condition III); they were again asked to identify the situation. A rating scale devised by Stengel et al. (1955) was used to assess the amount of facial expression and bodily movement. Three female postgraduate students, experienced in observing on videofilm, rated the amount of expression and movement on the 57 film sections.

RESULTS

There was no significant difference between the total scores and percentages obtained in each group in identifying visual pain, discomfort and neutral situations (Condition I) between groups 1–4 (*Table* 1). Each group was able to distinguish the blood sample more accurately than the blood pressure or control situations, whose scores could have been obtained by chance.

Table 1. Correct Identifications of the 3 Experimental Situations on Videotape Presentation; Visual Cues only (Percentage Score).

Group	Blood Sample	Blood Pressure	Neutral	Total	χ^2
1. Nurses (acquainted)	55%	35%	35%	42%	8·5 P <0·02
2. Nurses (experienced)	61%	36%	35%	43%	11·7 P <0·01
3. Teachers (acquainted)	57%	40%	37%	43%	8·3 P <0·02
4. Psychology students	62%	37%	37%	45%	12·5 P <0·01
5. Mothers	56%	35%	26%	39%	8·3 P <0·02
Total	49%	36%	28%	38%	

Table 2. Correct Staff Identifications of 3 Situations; 3 Modes of Presentation (Raw Scores).

	Blood Sample	Blood Pressure	Neutral	Total	χ^2
Video alone	41	12	11	27·3	< 0·001
Video + audio	47	18	16	22·3	< 0·001
Audiotape alone	30	19	17	4·5	N.S.

The greatest number of correct identifications were of the blood sample, and the most common incorrect identification was the blood pressure being mistaken for the neutral situation. Mothers were best at identifying the blood sample (100 per cent correct) in their own children.[1] The professional groups could not distinguish blood sample utterances from blood pressure utterances or neutral utterances by ear, on 15-second, randomized audio samples (Condition II). When the audiotape was presented synchronized with the videotape (Condition III), no improvement occurred in identification (*Table* 2).

[1] Interestingly, fathers failed to differentiate the blood sample from the neutral condition or blood pressure. The number of fathers was insufficient, however, to firmly condemn their incompetence.

When facial expression (as measured by the 5-point rating scale: 3 raters, inter-rater reliability 0·86) was compared with correct and incorrect judgements, there was a positive correlation between correct identification of the blood sample and the amount of facial expression, and a negative correlation between the neutral sample and facial expression ($r = 0·80$, $P< 0·001$ and $r = 0·61$, $P< 0·001$, respectively). There was also a positive correlation of neutral samples, which were incorrectly identified as blood samples, with the amount of facial expression ($r = 0·71$, $P< 0·001$). The amount of bodily movement (as measured by the 5-point rating scale: 3 raters, inter-rater reliability 0·81) was also found to correlate with correct blood sample identification, but there was a negative correlation between incorrectly identified blood pressure and bodily movement ($r = -0·62$, $P< 0·001$). Again there was a positive correlation between the amount of bodily movement and neutral samples incorrectly identified as a blood sample ($r = 0·53$, $P< 0·05$).

DISCUSSION

The way a child reacts to a new situation is not a reflection of just one set of feelings such as pain or fear. The evidence is to the contrary (Bretherton and Ainsworth, 1974). We should rather view distress signals as adaptive behaviour important to the child's survival, and as part of a 'comforting system' (Dunn, 1977). These profoundly handicapped persons were no longer infants and were doubtless stultified in their adaptive potential, by their own cognitive deficits, and also by their experience of idiosyncratic comforting at home and in hospital. The common causes of distress in infancy — hunger, temperature changes, evening crying and sudden stimulation — could not be accurately investigated, retrospectively. Interview methods have severe shortcomings. Nor could the more common non-acute forms of pain be observed. Observational studies have sampling limitations and ethical constraints. It is possible on the basis of infant cries alone to distinguish pain (or more likely pain plus alarm) from hunger in normal infants.

In our study, the visual cues of profoundly retarded children appeared to be the most decisive factors in such distinctions. Auditory cues did not provide additional help, seeming largely to be alerting signals; the continuous form of the signal in a given environmental context being more crucial than discrete features of the cry (such as pitch, intensity or rising—falling configurations), just as Pratt suggests is the case in normal infants.

Pain in these profoundly handicapped persons was identifiable using both facial expression and bodily movement as measures on a quantitative scale, but uncomfortable and 'neutral' situations were not. The ability to judge seemed dependent on a level of individual experience with each mentally handicapped person, which was best reached by the mother in this study, and even nurses with experience of a large number of mentally handicapped children and of the subjects observed did not identify emotions better than the untrained or inexperienced. This is not surprising in view of the tiny amount of time available for individual care by nurses (Oswin, 1977). A special fear of parents when their child is admitted to hospital is that nobody will know when he is distressed. They would be reassured by precise requests for their knowledge of their child's pain and distress signals at the admission interview.

As regards these profoundly handicapped subjects, it was clear that the ease of identifying a painful situation increased with the amount of facial and bodily expression shown, and conversely any emotion displaying a large amount of facial and bodily movement was perceived as a painful situation.

Clinicians will not usually have access to means of calibrating cries over periods of time (e.g. Pratt's cry index). They must rely on their skills as observers of the context in which the suspected communication of pain (e.g. crying) is occurring, paying particular heed to the caretaker's special knowledge of the subject's idiosyncratic non-vocal signalling, and regarding crying in the profoundly handicapped as a continuous rather than a discrete means of transmitting information.

Acknowledgements

This research was funded by the Mental Health Foundation (Burmah Oil Fellowship) and Fife Health Board.

References

Bretherton I. and Ainsworth M. D. S. (1974) Response of 1-year-olds to a stranger in a strange situation. In: Lewis M. and Bosenblum L. A. (ed.) *The Origin of Fear*. New York, Wiley.

Dunn J. (1977) *Distress and Comfort*. London, Owen Books.

Fraser W. and Campbell B. (1978) A study of six cases of de Lange Amsterdam Dwarf syndrome: with special attention to voice, speech and language characteristics. *Dev. Med. Child Neurol.* 20, 189–198.

Fraser W. and Ozols D. (1980) Cries of pain and distress in the severely mentally handicapped. In: Mittler P. (ed.) *Proceedings of the 5th Congress of the International Association for the Scientific Study of Mental Deficiency.* Jerusalem. (In press.)

Lind J., Vuorenkoski V., Rosberg C. et al. (1970) Spectrographic analyses of vocal responses to pain stimuli in infants with Down's syndrome. *Dev. Med. Child Neurol.* 12, 478.

Oswin M. (1977) *Children Living in Long Stay Hospitals*. London, Spastics International Medical Publications.

Pratt C. (1977) A study of infant crying behaviour in the home environment during the first year of life. Unpublished doctoral thesis, University of Oxford.

Ricks D. M. (1975) Vocal communication in preverbal normal and autistic children. In: O'Connor N. (ed.), *Language, Cognitive Deficits and Retardation*. London Butterworths/IRMMH.

Rosenhouse J. (1978) A preliminary report. Analysis of some types of baby's cries. *J. Phonet.* 5, 299.

Sirvio P. and Michelsson K. (1976) Sound-spectrographic cry analysis of normal and abnormal newborn infants. *Folia Phoniatr.* **77**, 161–173.

Stengel E., Oldham A. and Ehrenberg A. S. C. (1955) Reactions to pain in various abnormal mental states. *J. Ment. Sci.* **101**, 52–69.

Wasz-Höckert D., Lind T., Vuorenkoski V. et al. (1968) The infant cry: a spectrographic and auditory analysis. *Clinics in Developmental Medicine, No. 29.* Spastics International Medical Publications in association with Heinemann Medical Books Ltd.

Verbal Communication

Chapter Three

Original Sin and Original Virtue

A Study in Approaches to Normal Language Acquisition

Robert Hoogenraad

> You have been taking my advice too literally, king. To dis-
> believe in original sin, does not mean that you must believe in
> original virtue.
>
> (T. H. White *The Book of Merlyn*)

Academic disciplines are ever subject to extremes, and the study of normal language acquisition is no exception. Nature advised us that language is unique to man, so we believed that language must be part of the essential nature of man, an inborn or innate capacity that will out no matter what the circumstances. (I exaggerate a little for effect, but not much, as we will see.) Some of us disbelieved in this 'original language', so we had to believe, per se, in innate inarticulateness, in language being coaxed slowly out of a blank slate or *tabula rasa* (again the exaggeration for effect is less extreme than you might think).

For those concerned with language handicaps (language pathology, broadly conceived), the question is of more than academic interest. If it is original sin — language tightly and specifically genetically predetermined, essentially the innateness hypothesis discussed below — then there would seem to be little hope beyond surgery or genetic engineering for any language handicap that has even the hint of a genetic abnormality in its aetiology. If it is original virtue — man infinitely malleable, with language impressed on the malleable clay by environmental factors, essentially the behaviourist position discussed (*see* Language as Original Virtue) below — then we are bound to conclude that successful intervention in language pathology is a simple matter of manipulating the environment; we could call it 'environmental surgery'.

Original sin or original virtue? Neurosurgery or environmental surgery? You will recognize it as a question about the nature of man, as Chomsky (1972 and elsewhere) has rightly framed it. Man fixed and limited but creative, or man unbounded but with nowhere to go; language innate or learned; heredity or environment; nature or nurture; mentalism or behaviourism; rationalism or empiricism; mentalistic or mechanistic; creative or deterministic? Whether it is good or bad, virtue or sin depends on which factor you decide to emphasize. But I hope to show that with respect to normal language development at least, we have taken king nature too literally. Although both answers are attractive in their different ways, because they define conceptually simple views of language acquisition (shades of Occam's razor), the truth (neither sin nor virtue) is conceptually much more difficult to deal with, and forces us to come to terms with a contingent fact: there is, for one reason or another, a great deal of variation in how language is acquired normally.

Language as Original Sin

Campbell and Grieve (forthcoming) have presented the historical evidence for a fascinating series of experiments — the so-called 'isolation experiments' — that are reputed to have been carried out in a variety of cultures, from the 7th century BC until the 16th century AD, to determine the original language of mankind. The answers reported by the less cynical chroniclers, based on the first words of the children brought up isolated from speech, should not surprise us; they closely reflect the ideology of the teller of the tale (not, however, his nationality or politics, a salutary reminder that ideology does not equal nationality or politics). In these experiments the holy grail was *the* original language (using language in the particular). It will one day prove to be a fascinating glimpse of prevailing ideologies of our own age that for a decade and more research was directed at a similar holy grail: to establish that language (language in general this time) is original with man, in other words to establish that language is innate.

The innateness hypothesis of language is due to Chomsky (*see*, in particular, 1959; 1965, chap. 1; 1972; 1975, chap. 1), though its application to language acquisition studies was first suggested by McNeill (1966). For a decade or more it biased the approaches of even those investigators who did not overtly accept the innateness hypothesis. The prevailing concern until very recently has been to search for various kinds of invariants or universals in language acquisition, presumably on the often unspoken assumption that if language is innately specified, then like the embryo developing in the womb, apparently oblivious to all external, extrinsic influences, so language also ought to develop along a narrowly determined track. Since the innateness hypothesis has been astoundingly influential as a guide or a goad to research, depending on whether the investigator was convert or agnostic, I will attempt to give a brief resumé of the hypothesis.

I must begin by admitting that, having studied Chomsky's considerable output on the innateness hypothesis, I am still unclear as to its precise content. With this disclaimer, the hypothesis as I understand it is essentially as follows. When the child reaches a critical stage of maturation, language acquisition begins *de novo*, without essential reference to other cognitive factors. Under innate constraints that are specific to the language faculty of the mind, the child constructs a grammar (a system of rules or constraints) that best fits the data (the sentences to which he is exposed), using a process of hypothesis formation and testing (hence the view of the child as a wee linguist (McNeill, 1966)). The possible form of the grammar is determined on the one hand by these data, and on the other by the innately specified structure of the language faculty, perhaps implemented through prior limitations on the form of the hypotheses.

There is essential reference to only two kinds of factors, one endogenous, the other exogenous, in this hypothesis. The endogenous factors are the innately specified framework and processes which constrain the form of the grammar; the exogenous factors are the sentences to which the child is exposed. In particular, there is no essential reference to any other kind of experience, either prior to language acquisition or concomitant with the sentences he hears. This view of the independence of the language system from other cognitive processes (not to mention social processes) comes out clearly in the following reply by Chomsky to a question about the relation between thought and language posed by the ethologist W. H. Thorpe.

I think one could design an automation which never thinks but which has the capacity to acquire any specific human lauguage in a rather short time from a small amount of data.

I would want to put into the automaton an initial specification of what kind of operations, what kind of mechanism, it has, and leave the automaton just enough leeway so a small amount of data could select one of the possible languages. Having acquired this language, the automaton could produce sentences and assign them semantic interpretation.

(Chomsky, 1967, p. 84.)

The process of language acquisition is seen as one of fitting a system to data under prior constraints, without any necessary reference to the facts of language use and accompanying experience. There is, for instance, nothing that I can find in Chomsky's work to suggest that the child, given adequate care and attention, could not learn language by being exposed to tape-recorded sentences, of the appropriate sort but unrelated in any way to his current experiences. We have here a new variant of the isolation experiments referred to earlier.

Language as Original Virtue

Chomsky's (1959) review of Skinner's *Verbal Behavior* (1957) set the cat amongst the behaviourist's pigeons (though in fact Lashley (1951), and even Harlow (1953), had already cast doubt on the behaviourist programme, albeit less stridently). Chromsky's criticism was not, as is sometimes supposed, that pigeons are not human (presumably obvious even to the pigeons), but that language is not for pigeons. Briefly, Chomsky (1957, 1959) purported to demonstrate that human language displays characteristics that do not make it accessible to the behaviourist's stimulus–response mechanism, and that presuppose an innate specification for language. It should be pointed out, because it is often overlooked, that Chomsky did not prove that behavourist theory is inadequate to the task; he merely demonstrated that it could not give a simple account, granted certain intuitions about the structure of English that are not accepted by all reasonable men.

The behaviourist account of language is conceptually simple, and hence appealing; learning language is essentially learning the contingent associations between utterances and the responses they produce in the hearer. Here is the account by Bloomfield (1933), by way of illustration.

Suppose that Jack and Jill are walking down a lane. Jill is hungry. She sees an apple in a tree. She makes a noise with her larynx, tongue, and lips. Jack vaults the fence, climbs the tree, takes the apple, brings it to Jill, and places it in her hand. Jill eats the apple (p. 22.) Instead of struggling with the fence and the tree, she made a few small movements in her throat and mouth, which produced a little noise. At once Jack began to make the reactions for her; he performed actions that were beyond Jill's strength, and in the end Jill got the apple.

Language enables one person to make a reaction (R) when another person has the stimulus (S). (p. 24.)

The gap between the bodies of the speaker and the hearer – the discontinuity of the two nervous systems – is bridged by the sound-waves. (p. 26.)

Bloomfield is rightly venerated as a linguist, but he is no great shakes as a psychologist. It is not that what he says is untrue, but that it is merely banal, and simply does not do justice to the great subtlety of the phenomenon of language use. It does not even stand up as an account of the kind of situation in which children learn language. Skinner (1957) presents a much more elaborate and subtle behaviourist theory of language ('verbal behaviour'), but as Lyons (1977) points out:

The most striking feature of any behaviourist theory of meaning so far proposed is its inadequacy to deal plausibly with more than a very small fraction of the utterances of everyday life. And this is true not only of the earlier theories of Watson, Weiss and Bloomfield, but also of the more sophisticated and more highly developed theory of Skinner. An enormous leap of faith is required before one can accept that the apparatus sufficient to account for illustrative utterances like 'I'm hungry', 'It's raining', 'Water!' or 'Pass me the salt, please' is in principle capable of accounting, without further theoretical extension, for the full complexity of language behaviour. (p. 133.)

Even without such an extension, it would seem that the behaviourist account of language explains too much; pigeons do not learn language. Why not? Well, a possible explanation might be that they cannot articulate speech sounds due to (the accident of?) the physiology of their vocal tract.

('What of parrots?', I hear you ask. What of parrots indeed?) But a range of higher primates, whose vocal tracts are also deficient in the relevant respects, have now learned versions of the indigenous sign languages of the deaf and dumb (usually using a behaviourist methodology to teach them!) with various degrees of success. Arguments continue about whether these have, or have not, demonstrated that apes can learn human language. In any case, it will be argued that the higher primates are phylogenetically close to man, so that allowing them to join the club (with qualified membership, no doubt) will be held to prove nothing one way or the other about the innateness hypothesis. It needs someone to persuade a parrot to learn language (to ape rather than parrot language).

The behaviourist seeks the essential factors of language acquisition in the environment, i.e. in the context of speech, in utterances and the contingent responses to them. They can surely not be faulted for paying attention to such observables; where they fail is in reducing the endogenous factors to simplistic drives and stimulus—response arcs. Recently there have been strong temptations on the part of investigators of language acquisition to turn to contextual variables as the sole, or overriding explanation of language acquisition. Explanations have been sought, for instance, in the linguistic input to the child, for example in terms of the adjustment in their speech by the child's caretakers ('motherese') and in its changes during the course of the child's linguistic development. Explanations have also been sought in the responses to the child's utterances, for example in terms of expansions and corrections of his ungrammatical utterances. Fletcher and Garman (1979, pp. 328—329) and Wells (1979) stress the danger inherent in either ignoring such exogenous factors or of overemphasizing them to the exclusion of endogenous factors

Nature's Advice

The acquisition of language involves both endogenous and exogenous factors, and I take it as axiomatic that the endogenous factors must include an ultimately genetic basis that is properly described as innate, in the sense that it is given at conception (note, not birth) and is species-specific. The only real questions are about the nature and extent of this innate specification, and how it is implemented in the process of language acquisition.

Normal language acquisition begins at birth, unfolding slowly from behaviour that is at first non-verbal and largely non-vocal, that is apparently without communicative intent, and that involves primarily affective, emotional interaction between mother and infant. Language develops out of a basis so unlike language in all important respects that we are only slowly coming to recognize it as relevant to language acquisition at all, as descriptions of the continuities from these early primitive stages of interaction to the subsequent flowering of the child's language in the second and third years of life are gradually being elaborated in painstaking research. There are still those who start from the premise that language acquisition begins *de novo* in the child's second year, with the onset of articulated words, but these do not number amongst them many investigators of early childhood language. While there is still a great deal of room for disagreement, not only about descriptive details but also about profound theoretical questions, it is now generally agreed that we cannot adequately understand language acquisition if we ignore its continuity with early communicative development.

Such considerations suggest that Chomsky's innateness hypothesis ('language as original sin') and the notion that language is moulded into a plastic organism ('language as original virtue'), although intelligible, are wrong. Work on mother–infant interaction from birth (*see* Stern, 1977; Schaffer, 1977) and on the early stage of language development (*see* Halliday, 1975; Carter, 1979) has provided strong, if as yet not conclusive, evidence of the continuity of the process of communicative development and language acquisition (*see* Grieve and Hoogenraad, 1979). Such studies suggest that the acquisition of language depends crucially on the fact that the infant and his caretaker(s) have a strong propensity to take an interest in each other's subjective states from birth. This has been termed 'intersubjectivity' (Trevarthen, 1974; Newson, 1977), and the evidence suggests that language development builds on earlier subjective development. The language of the adult, in this view, is the culmination of a long process of communicative development that begins at birth (and, incidentally, has no well-defined point when it is finished).

Consider the endogenous and exogenous factors involved in the child's communicative development. At any stage of his development, the child's intersubjective interactions depend not only on the endogenous structures that underlie his behaviour and the way he experiences his environment, especially his social environment, but also on exogenous factors, including the way others interpret his behaviour and the way they behave towards him. In the process of these interactions the infant develops new ways of experiencing (undoubtedly with concomitant changes in his endogenous mental structures), thus changing his communicative needs and his perceived environment. The process of development consists of adapting to these new needs and modes of perception, by adapting or redeploying his extant modes of intersubjective behaviour, and recruiting new modes of behaviour into the process. But, and this point is crucial according to recent work (*see* Trevarthen, 1977a), the exogenous factors do not remain constant; for instance, throughout the infant's development the mother constantly adapts her behaviour to the infant's changing behaviour. Thus to understand the process of communicative development we must take account not only of endogenous factors and the way in which these change, but also of exogenous factors and the way these change.

The process of communicative development, in this view, is a continuous process of mutual adaptation of factors of both endogenous and exogenous origin. Clearly there are essentially innate constraints; for instance, there is the infant's extraordinary interest in human faces. Just as clearly, these do not exercise their influence independently of other constraints that may be exogenous in origin; for instance, there is the biologically given, extraordinary mobility and expressiveness of the human face. While it is not excluded that some of the changes in endogenous constraints are initiated by immediately genetic mechanisms, it seems that more often changes are the logical outcome of a confluence of factors which include both changes from within (changes in the infant's experiencing and behaving) and changes from without (changes in the behaviour of others towards the infant, which may itself be ultimately grounded in a genetic prespecification). We may have to go back to early stages of development (before birth?) to find the first (innate) emergence of many of the constraints on the process of language acquisition.

Simplicity or Complexity: Sin, Virtue or Truth?

We linguists are frequently exhorted to the banner of this theory or that hypothesis with the reassurance that all sciences need to idealize. Just so. But, to paraphrase Chomsky (1975), some idealizations are more conducive to conceptual convenience than to scientific understanding. The study of language acquisition, like any scientific enterprise, must learn where simplification is justified and where it distorts the very phenomena under investigation. This is particularly important where practical application of the findings from language acquisition studies is envisaged; half-truths are worse than no truths at all, however conceptually (or ideologically) appealing. In particular, there can be no room in a mature discipline for results that are based on value judgements (whether aesthetic, moral or ideological); we need truth, not sin or virtue. Later in this chapter I hope to show that what is complicated about language acquisition is not so much the process itself, as stripping ourselves of our preconceptions about language – our language – communication, and what is 'easy', 'reasonable', 'obvious' and so on (see the chapter by Grieve on communication problems in normal children in this respect).

One of the chief stumbling blocks in the study of language acquisition is that language has two arbitrarily related aspects: form and meaning. There are the noises (or signs, or scribbles) that we make to communicate on the one hand, and the meaning we wish to convey on the other, and there is no necessary relation between them. If the child says 'Mommy hit Kendall' he might mean 'Kendall hit Mommy' (see footnotes to various tables in Braine (1976) for other examples from the literature); if the child says 'office' she might mean 'aeroplane' (see Grieve and Hoogenraad, 1976); and the child who says 'chuffa stúck' (with rising intonation) might not mean 'Is the train stuck?' but rather 'The train is stuck; do something, respond' (*see* Halliday, 1975, p. 76 *et passim* for examples). In other words, the fact that a child says something does not guarantee that he means by this what we understand by it. Saying, meaning and our understanding are different things when we are studying the child's language, and this becomes increasingly true (and more urgent as a problem for the investigator) the earlier we go back into the child's developing communication, even when we go beyond language (verbal communication) to prelinguistic (non-verbal and even non-vocal) communication.

In the early 1960s studies of language acquisition were apt to study the child's utterances without worrying overly about their meaning, on the grounds that since language is innate the child is in possession of the underlying structures (the 'deep structures') of sentences, which determine their meaning (their 'semantic interpretation'), before he produces the fully fledged grammatical utterances (the 'surface structures') of the language he is learning. But no one who has studied child language in depth can long escape the conclusion that children do not always mean what they superficially appear to mean. The method of 'rich interpretation' (Brown, 1973) was intended to overcome the problem by drawing on contextual information and, especially, the mother's interpretations of the child's utterances, in order to arrive at the child's purported intended meaning. Mother knows best! The method is based on the assumption (almost certainly false, though *see* Campbell (1979) for an influential contrary opinion) that the young child, in the early stages of language acquisition, communicates his intentions accurately. Doubt is thrown on the assumption by the not uncommon observation that older siblings are often more successful at interpreting the young child's speech than are parents or other adults.

The method of rich interpretation (or 'Mother knows best') is in error in so far as it confuses intended meaning with the interlocutor's understanding. It is a moot point how often they coincide for adult interlocutors; for young children a modicum of mismatch may well be vital if the child is not to enter the vicious circle of a private language — perhaps this is why twins are sometimes extremely slow to reach adult competence, unless they are separated (cf. Luria and Yudovitch, 1971). But ultimately meaning must come from interpretation; utterances (or any other communicative acts) do not come with their meanings neatly pinned to them, let alone with the meanings of their parts and the arrangement of those parts separately identified. We would seem to be in a cleft stick; meaning does not equal interpretation, but only interpretation yields us meaning.

The solution is methodological eclecticism. The rationalists/mentalists are correct in insisting that meaning is a property of the mind, more properly, a process of the mind. The empiricists/behaviourists are correct in insisting that, in language acquisition at least, meaning can only be interpreted from external, non-mental factors: observable behaviour (utterances amongst them only if their meaning is not in doubt), contextual information pertinent to this behaviour and background information on the child (preferences, propensities, personality, previous experience and the like). The mentalist's theory, the behaviourist's methodology. There is good reason to believe that introspection, the mentalist's catch-all method, will not work with the child (see Macrae, 1979, p. 167). Whether it is a viable and reliable method in the study of the adult's language is also open to question (see Labov, 1975), but in this context is beside the point. Instead the onus is on the investigator to gather his evidence where he can ('catch as catch can'), and then to interpret on the basis of his accumulated data. The advantage of this is that the investigator, if he does his work thoroughly, normally has the opportunity to sample far more evidence, and at a far more leisurely pace, than can the child's interlocutors in the hurly-burly of communication.

The method sketched out above is in fact the one used by most investigators at some time or another in their work, especially in observational studies. Its results erupt occasionally in those asides and footnotes that are the points of embryological rupture from which new ideas and new directions develop. It is most conspicuously absent in those experimental studies which base their conclusions on error scores, computed on the basis of the experimenter's expectations of what would constitute a 'correct' response. We might dub this the 'immanence fallacy', since it supposes that there is but one reasonable way of construing any phenomenon, that truth is immanent in the phenomenon and that the experimenter has privileged access to this truth (see Hoogenraad et al., 1978, and Grieve et al., 1977, for a discussion). Eclectic interpretation works because language in use in communication works interactively with what, for want of a better term, we might call 'context' (see Hoogenraad (1978) for a critique of the notion 'context'). This is more particularly true for the language acquiring child who, being deficient in language, must perforce give greater weight to contextual cues (see Hoogenraad et al., 1978; Grieve, see Chapter 4). The resulting rich linking of utterances with information from other sources yields much data that bear on the formulation of informed inferences about meaning and communicative intent. It depends on an assumption which may well prove to be inapplicable in certain cases of language pathology; that the child tries to communicate, and that he is reasonably skilled in circumventing the deficiencies of his language, and that by and large he limits his communication to what he can effectively communicate

Normal Variation in Normal Language Acquisition

There is another fact that has given investigators of language acquisition problems, namely variation. Discussion of normal language development must start from the fact that there is very considerable variation, both in the course of development towards normal adult competence and in the rate of development of the various component skills and processes − both coordinated and subordinated components − that comprise the normal use of language. Everyone knows that no two children are alike, and parents know that individuality, implying individual differences, begins to be evident very early in the infant's life. Researchers into language development, when pressed by parents who (because too many of us, isolated in the 'nuclear family', have no prior experience of children growing up) worry about this or that aspect of their first-born's language, are apt to evade the question with the observation that there are many routes of normal language development and, by implication, no norms.

Yet a Martian reading the literature on language acquisition research could be excused for concluding that all humans follow much the same pathway through their language development; that they do so at different rates would be more evident, but this is considered an inconvenient irrelevance necessitating the adoption of some 'independent' variable other than age, for instance the popular 'mean length of utterance' (MLU) (*see* Brown, 1973, p. 77ff., and the critique by Crystal, 1974, p. 94ff.). Alternatively a Venusian, reading a somewhat different literature concerned with language, education and social class, could be excused for concluding that while there may be marked differences between social classes (there seem to be just two in the literature), children within the same social class follow much the same course of development in their language towards much the same end-point. Wells (1979), in an excellent review of the research, of the latter kind in particular, points out the difficulties in interpreting such data, particularly as data from his large-scale Bristol project suggest that while there is considerable variation along many parameters, there are no significant correlations with social class factors which are not evidently attributable to the fact that the children are learning different dialects. This is a timely reminder that there is no such thing as 'English', the Procrustean language that all English-speaking children learn.

It is evident that variation occurs in language acquisition, and we should ask why it has been ignored to such an extent. We can isolate two broad reasons, which correspond roughly with the 'original virtue' and 'original sin' orientations outlined above. On the one hand we have investigators who − normally for reasons connected with education and social policy − wish to establish norms of language development, often norms that differentiate groups along such lines as sex, intelligence, social class, race and so on. Such investigators are not usually interested in the normal variation within their samples, except for statistical purposes of measuring 'validity' or 'significance' (*see* McCarthy, 1954, for a review of the older normative studies; Garman, 1979, for a discussison of this and more recent work). In such work the reason for ignoring variation is clear enough: it would complicate and confuse simple conclusions. But that there is variation is evident. (*See,* for instance, the comparison of MLUs from two studies, McCarthy (1930) and Templin (1957), in Cruttenden (1979)). Within Templin's study, for which standard deviations are reported, standard deviations are as high as 30 per cent of the mean values (and with a normal distribution of results the mean ± the standard deviation should encompass approximately 60 per cent of the data), while between the studies differences are as high as 20 per cent of the means. This is hardly the kind of variation that can be ignored under the banner of idealization.)

On the other hand we have investigators who wish to establish 'universals' of language development — human norms, if you like — usually because they are attempting to present empirical evidence that bears on some theoretical question. Here it is often methodology that imposes some spurious semblance of uniformity on the results. First there is the choice of subjects. If you want to study semantic or grammatical development you want a reasonably loquacious child who articulates clearly, so that there will be no doubt about what he knows and what he is saying. And you do not want the precocious child who never makes a mistake on the way to adult competence, nor one who sticks interminably at one level of development. You do not want one whose mother has funny ideas about how children learn language, nor do you want an excessively experimental or imaginative child who is always playing with the possibilities of language construction, and so on. If you are studying phonological development, on the other hand, you want a child who pronounces his words in an interestingly childish way (which will make him difficult to understand), but who articulates clearly and consistently. In one case you want a child whom you can understand without too much groundwork, in another one whose grammar and vocabulary are irrelevant to you. The requirements of straightforward research are likely to make for highly selected samples, and it is possible to lose sight of the potential for variation in the population sampled.

In addition there is the analysis of the data. We have already touched on the validity of interpretations; it is always one reason to be very wary of accepting the conclusions of any study too readily. There is also the question of what portions of the data the investigator suppresses or does not use in the analysis. Smith (1973), for instance, is an honest and very thorough observer, but his actual analysis is based on data that conform to a rule system, and one of a particularly theoretical kind, namely generative phonology. It is a tribute to his willingness to leave himself open to refutation that he presents all his data (pp. 210–262), and from time to time presents intractable data in footnotes. Not all investigators are so open. The danger is always that the elegance, intuitive reasonableness or even the shock of a counter-intuitive conclusion will blind us to the limitations of the evidence and the amount of data that does not conform to the conclusions.

A more subtle problem can be illustrated from the work of the Harvard study, summarized and discussed in Brown (1973). I will use two extremely influential conclusions from that study, that subsequently have often been taken as facts about language acquisition. The first is that in the earliest stages of grammatical development – in the so-called two- and three-word stages – children learning a range of different languages use only a circumscribed and small set of semantic 'operations and relations' (between 8 and 15) (Brown, 1973, p. 287), i.e. the kind of meanings that are usually grammatically encoded in the adult language. These are, in order of frequency of occurrence, 'Nomination, Recurrence, Non-existence, Agent and action, Action and object, Agent and object, Action and locative (or location), Entity and locative, Possessor and possession, Entity and attribute, Demonstrative and entity, and another seven elementary relations' (pp. 225–236). These were gleaned from a number of studies (12) of children (18) learning a number of languages (6). The ordering and criteria for inclusion in the list are based on frequency, but it is overall frequency, computed across the children, studies and languages. It is clear from Brown's discussion, and from the data of the original studies, that there is very considerable variation in the occurrence of these various 'operations and relations' in the speech of different children, and this is reinforced by even a cursory glance at the data of more recent studies (for example, Bloom et al., 1975). It is also clear that the list (of 11 or 18) reported by Brown does not exhaust the range of semantic 'operations and relations' conveyed by the various children; they are merely the ones that occurred in most of the data fairly frequently. But there is no reason to suppose that frequency of occurrence is an interesting, or even a relevant, criterion. However, there is every reason to believe that it reflects purely pragmatic, non-linguistic factors (it is easily changed by manipulating the context in which you collect your sample, for instance by recording during the repetitive daily 'maintenance activities' such as bathing and feeding rather than during play or reading). There is certainly no reason to believe that mere frequency reflects linguistic competence (or even cognitive competence) in any interesting way.

The second of Brown's conclusions concerns the order of acquisition of the grammatical morphemes (suffixes such as '-s', '-ing' and '-ed', and grammatical words such as 'in', 'on', and 'to') of English. On the basis of the 3 children studied by Brown and his colleagues (p. 314), using frequency of correct use as the criterion for acquisition, he arrives at a 'mean order of acquisition' (p. 317). Apart from doubts about the use of frequency as a criterion for acquisition, this is beyond reproach so far. But soon the mean order is reified into the order of acquisition of the grammatical morphemes of English (see Matthews, 1975, for a critique). On the basis of 3 children showing (to my cynical eye at least) considerable differences in order of acquisition (compare *Fig.* 14, p. 314 with *Table* 38, p. 317) of the grammatical morphemes of just one lauguage, which happens to be rather poor in grammatical inflections (cf. the study by Burling, 1959, of a child learning a highly inflected language), and on the basis of data of doubtful validity on the set of semantic operations and relations acquired first by just a few children learning a small, and not necessarily representative, sample of the world's many and diverse languages, it certainly will not do to conclude that 'the order of progression in knowledge of the first language, both semantic and grammatical, will prove to be approximately invariant across children learning any language' (p. 456). The error is to move too easily from 'average' or 'normal' to 'universal'. It is only because Brown is extremely honest and self-critical that we are able to use his own writing to criticize his results. Others do not necessarily make the shortcomings of their conclusions so easy to uncover.

However, if we cannot use the results of language acquisition studies to construct meaningful norms — stages of development, orders of acquisition, rates of development and so on — what can we do with the data from all these forays into painstaking natural history? I will attempt to provide an answer (*see* Phonological Development, *below*), using phonological development as an illustration. But before proceeding to do this, I wish briefly to discuss what kinds of factors appear to give rise to variation in language acquition.

Varieties of Variation

Let us begin with extrinsic factors that affect variation, beginning with the most global one. Not all languages are equal in all respects, a century of universalistic ideology in linguistics notwithstanding. Hence children are not all learning the same system. What may prove to be a check on rapid mastery for many children in one language may simply not be present as a feature of another language. For instance, many children learning the familiar Western European languages go through a phase of simplifying the phonological structure of words. They simplify clusters by reducing them to a single consonant (e.g. 'teet' for 'street', 'pang' for 'spank'), they make syllables open by dropping final consonants (e.g. 'bo' for 'ball', 'mi' for 'milk'), they drop the distinction between voiced and unvoiced consonants (e.g. 'bee' for 'pea' and 'bee', 'do' for 'to' and 'do') and make consonants harmonize (e.g. 'guck' for 'duck', 'bap' for 'tap'), they substitute stops for fricatives (e.g. 'ting' for 'sing', 'tay' for 'say') and so on (*see* Ingram, 1979, for a summary). But not all languages have consonant clusters, fricatives or a voiced–unvoiced distinction, and some languages favour open syllables and consonant harmony. Clearly the language which the child is learning determines the kinds of simplification processes he might need to have recourse to, so that the potential for variation might be expected to vary from language to language.

The same point applies to other aspects of language structure. In the

Walbiri language of Central Australia 'there appears to be an almost endless number of suffixes. By means of numerous suffixes and tenses (*sic*) an almost limitless variety of shades of meaning is obtainable. As one advances in the age grouping, the use of suffixes becomes more complicated. There is a baby language, followed by that of the children, youths, adults and finally that of the elders (Reece, 1970, pp. 6–7.) For a language (or in a culture) like Walbiri, it would appear that language acquisition is a protracted process, extending into old age in a way that is more obvious than it is for a language like English. In case we should be tempted to conclude that complexity is the main determinant for this protraction, compare this with the rapid mastery of substantial parts of the complex morphology of Garo, a Tibeto–Burman language of Assam, by the child observed by Burling (1959). (This is a paper that has been almost totally neglected, a fact which is amazing, since it is one of the few studies of the acquisition of a non-Indo-European language.) The determinants are probably a combination of grammatical (morphological) and semantic complexity, coupled with the domain of use of the aspect of the grammatical system under consideration. Amongst the Walbiri, for instance, age groupings are one of the principal forms of social/religious/political stratification, affecting the kinds of topics typically discussed, and no doubt the subtlety of expression required.

For the child learning English there is a great deal of heterogeneity in the language and its use: dialects, varieties, registers, not to mention national variation (*see* Halliday et al., 1964; Quirk et al., 1972), and, perhaps more importantly as a determinant of variation in acquisition, different access to the stratified varieties and registers, which depends on such factors as the style of child rearing, the typical mode of interaction within the child's family and later outside it, the child's personality and his birth order within the family. While such factors may be affected by social class, they are certainly not determined by it (*see* Wells, 1979, on these points). Nor are such factors necessarily restricted to large-scale societies such as our own, as witnessed by Reece's observation on the 2000 or so strong Walbiri: 'It is surprising how some get by with a very limited vocabulary. They appear to use the basic forms of speech and vocabulary and leave out the seemingly redundant shades of meaning and varieties of sentence forms.' (1970, p. 7.)

Whether or not one chooses to use the meaning resources made available by one's language is a matter of personal choice and personal style. Bartlett (1932) was at pains to demonstrate the importance of orientation or interest in guiding cognitive activity (e.g. memory), factors that depend ultimately on a complex interaction of personality and the culture in which we grew up. What we notice and consider relevant in our environment, for instance, is dependent on our personality and our culture. It should not surprise us, then, that there should be individual (as well as cross-cultural) differences in what we require of our language, and there is no reason why this should not also be true of the child. Indeed, Nelson (1973) argues that the child's personality, interacting with that of the mother, accounts for the different 'styles' of development that she observed in a sample of 16 children, reflected, for instance, in the kind of vocabulary that the child tended to learn first ('referential' versus 'expressive'). (Compare in this respect, the very considerable distortion introduced into the account by Clark (1979, pp. 149–150) of early vocabulary acquisition because, she insists, against all the evidence – e.g. Nelson (1973), Edwards (1978) – that children begin by talking predominantly about objects. Yet evaluative words like 'good', 'bad', and 'nice' and other non-referential words like 'no', 'all gone' and 'want' abound in samples of early speech, especially if they sample across the various daily activities of the child.)

There are other intrinsic factors that operate in language acquisition: motor skills involved in articulation, for instance, and factors involved in general congnitive development, as well as perceptual skills and memory span. These are not identical for all adults, and there is also no reason to suppose that they should develop at the same rate in all children. And as language quickly becomes a factor in cognitive development, and as interpersonal communication from birth (including later verbal communication) affects such factors as personality and perception (*see* Stern, 1977; Halliday, 1975; Richards, 1974), we should not be surprised that in language acquisition, intrinsic factors like cognitive development and personality, and extrinsic factors like the language being learned, the culture and child-rearing styles, should all interact to produce considerable variation. This variation occurs across cultures and subcultures as well as within societies and families, in rate as well as in style of development, in the perceptual and in the production skills involved. It is also to be found in the various components of language organization, namely phonological (sound system), lexical (vocabulary), morphological (affixation and modification of words), syntactical (the ordering of linguistic elements), prosodic (intonation, stress, rhythm and voice modulation), semantic (the organization of meaning) and discoursal (the organization of linguistic resources in use).

The result? Some children never seem to make a mistake on the way to adult competence (useless subjects for the investigator of language acquisition), and they may develop rapidly (the precocious child), or they may remain taciturn until an advanced age and then suddenly come out with quite sophisticated utterances. (There is an anecdote about Macaulay, that he did not speak until at the age of 4 years (notably apocryphal) a guest spilled a cup of hot tea over him. Asked if he was all right, he is said to have replied: 'Thank you, Madam. The agony is by now somewhat abated.) Others go through a protracted, highly differentiated sequence of phases in one or more aspects of their language. Occasionally normal adult competence will never be reached in some aspect or aspects of the language, while some minor speech defects, such as the relatively common mis-pronunciation of English 'r' as 'w', may even become a regular feature of a variety, as, for example, in 'Oxbwidge English'. Finally we have the perfect subject for language acquisition study; the child who goes through a leisurely, but not too protracted, orderly development in the aspect of language you wish to investigate, but quickly masters any other aspects of language where immaturity might mask the aspect under investigation. However, there is no guarantee that such a child is typical.

Phonological Development

Keeping in mind the normal variation alluded to above, for research purposes an optimally protracted and differentiated sequence of phonological development can be characterized. I will use this to discuss the major principles that seem to be involved in phonological development. Since I am concerned here with broad principles, I will not discuss details. The reader is referred to chapters by Stark, by Menyuk and Menn, by Crystal and by Ingram in Fletcher and Garman (1979). I will postpone discussion of communicative implications of the vocal or verbal behaviour of the child until later (see Function and Meaning, below).

The configuration of the infant's vocal tract is quite different from that of the adult (Stark, 1979). This is also true for the perceptual apparatus, e.g. the position of the inner ear with respect to the outer ear and the skull (Romanes, 1966, p. 191). There is probably also a considerable difference in the neurophysiological characteristics of the relevant parts of the nervous system (Marshall, 1979). While we could discuss these as limit-ations of the infant, we should resist this easy interpretation. The infant's earliest sounds (crying, fussing, burping, swallowing, etc.) are not under his active control, and are limited. As he begins to produce more controlled noises (cooing and chuckling) in order to express contentedness or pleasure, these again are limited. But they are more complex in that they involve such factors as sequences of coordinated, fairly controlled movements of various components of the vocal organs. The coordination and control need not be very precise, however, since the configuration of the vocal tract restricts the potential scope for movements. So instead of being faced with the problem of trying to control everything at once, the infant has the problem reduced for him to a few simple parameters. We can view his 'limitations' as a kind of filtering device that simplifies the problem of bringing a complex interacting set of organs under control, and then gradually relaxes the constraints to introduce further parameters in a controlled manner.

Up to this point the infant has begun to use various articulators to produce primitive vowel-like sounds (in crying, fussing, etc.) and consonant-like sounds (in maintenance activity), and then to combine consonant- and vowel-like sounds into primitive syllabic sounds (cooing, chuckling), thus adding a higher level of control (i.e. integrating articulatory parameters into a composite structure that requires simple serial ordering and probably a degree of coordination and adaptation of the different kinds of articulations involved). In reduplicative babbling (that is the repetition of a more or less uniform sequence of simple syllables, e.g. 'adadadada. . . ') the infant begins to add serial ordering of these higher level units (syllables), but does not yet differentiate succeeding syllables. At the same time he continues to further differentiate the segments (consonants and vowels), implying that he is bringing further articulatory parameters under control, and coordinating them with existing ones. Next, in non-reduplicated babbling (e.g. 'badagagugudubu. . . ') and later in 'expressive jargon', in which a variety of prosodic patterns are superimposed on babbled sequences to produce utterances that sound like 'foreign speech', the infant begins to control the serial ordering of differentiated simple syllables. (Note that he cannot yet produce these on demand, to reproduce a given word, let alone a longer utterance.) He then adds another level of control when he integrates these into primitive utterance-like units under an intonation contour. (Again note that these are not produced to order; at the same time that he is producing 'expressive jargon', the same child is communicating with simple syllables or perhaps reduplicated simple syllables, like 'bo' or 'dada'.)

Little is known about the development of perception during these early phases. It is clear that infants discriminate speech from other sounds from a very early age, and that they are sensitive to the more global aspects of speech, i.e. tone of voice (voice quality) and, probably later, intonation. It should be noted that it is precisely these aspects of the speech addressed to infants that is marked and exaggerated, and it seems reasonable to conclude that it is adapted to the infant's perceptual abilities and preferences. At the same time the infant does not actively begin to reproduce the kinds of intonations that he hears until the 'jargon' phase. It has been established experimentally that young infants can differentiate a number of distinctive features of sounds that keep speech sounds apart, i.e. distinguish them in (not all!) languages − voicing (e.g. 'pa' *v.* 'ba' and 'ta' *v.* 'da'), place of articulation (e.g. 'ba' *v.* 'da' and 'pa' *v.* 'ta') and rising versus falling versus level intonation (Morse, 1974). However, it is not clear how pertinent such findings are, since what is at issue in phonological development is the infant's ability to use the discrimination, rather than identification, of such features to differentiate units (e.g. syllables or words) within speech, and to reproduce sounds that he hears. With respect to this last point, note the distinction between the infant reproducing aspects of sounds which he hears others make, and those which he makes himself. It is possible that these are very different perceptual processes for the young infant, since the former involves only air conduction of the sounds, while the latter involves primarily bone conduction. Perceptually, these could be radically different for the young infant. I suspect that during the first 6 or 9 months of the infant's life, the primary input for *phonological* development is the infant's own vocalizations, at first made without any communicative intent, and that the vocalizations of the infant's caretakers serve a function in *communicative* development, but not in phonological development.

We also know little, and need to know a great deal more, about the perception by the child of speech addressed to him at the stage when he begins to reproduce words from the adult language (the 'proto-language' stage – Halliday, 1975), which overlaps with the babbling stage. Waterson (1970, 1971) who, to my knowledge, has done the only thorough phonological study of this stage, points out, as others have done, how very repetitive are both the daily routine activities, and the language used in these, in the life of the young child. Utterances addressed to the child tend to be stereotyped, short and exaggerated in their enunciation, with marked rhythm, intonation and stress. Waterson surmises that the child has a very short memory span – perhaps a couple of syllables in sequence – and that he perceives only certain phonetic features of words, usually in stressed syllables, and depending very strongly on the phonetic context (e.g. clusters versus single consonants) in which they occur, and not necessarily phonemic (i.e. distinctive in keeping words apart, rather than being a redundant feature of the adult's pronunciation).

The child who, while babbling, may be producing fairly complex syllable sequences, which might occasionally reproduce recognizable adult words by accident, typically shows a great deal of variation in his pronunciation in producing his 'proto-words'. He shears these words down to a few controlled articulatory features, which may make them not readily recognizable as the words he is trying to reproduce. Nonetheless, this is not regression, for he is now *reproducing* rather than merely *producing* sounds. He has added another level of control, since he is clearly attempting to produce a sound for which he has a prior acoustic image or target, however much this may deviate from the actual adult acoustic form. (In truth we do not know if, for the child at this stage, the acoustic image is identical or quite different. In other words, we do not know how much of the mismatch between adult word and child proto-word is due to perception, and how much is due to immature control over articulation and its organization.)

It is generally agreed that at this early 'proto-language' stage, the child's proto-words are best regarded not as sequences of phonemes (consonants and vowels that recur across words of the vocabulary), but as holistic 'articulatory gestures' (of the speech organs) or simple synergies of articulatory features. But as the child's vocabulary increases, this places an intolerable load on the organization of his articulations, since each proto-word is a special case, using a coordination of features that is peculiar to it alone. A true phonemic system begins to develop, in which he uses a small recurring set of phonemes (speech sounds), using shared articulatory characteristics, although with strong constraints on where, and in what combinations, they can occur. This set of phonemes may fail to include sounds that the child produced earlier in his proto-words, and sequences and combinations that occurred in proto-words may now fail to occur. The result is pronunciations that can deviate very markedly from those of the adult, and that may continue to do so, while gradually approximating closer to adult pronunciation, until 4 or 5 years of age. Nonetheless, the child shows clear evidence that he has an adult acoustic image for at least most words in his vocabulary (Smith, 1973), that is he perceives speech sounds in an essentially adult-like way at this stage (but *see* Macken, 1980, for a different view based on Smith's data). Although the child may now mispronounce words which he pronounced correctly in the later stages of his proto-language phase, we must again resist the temptation of concluding that the child regresses at this stage, for he is now able to accommodate a large and growing vocabulary. He has extended control of the articulation of words to a higher, more abstract level. He is also increasingly able to produce longer sequences of words within the scope of a controlled prosodic (stress and intonation) system, which is coordinated with the incorporation of these words into increasingly complex grammatical constructions.

The process of phonological development as outlined above should bring home to us forcefully just how complex phonological production and perception really are, how many hierarchically organized levels of control they involve, and hence how complex the phonological system really is. What general principles can we extract? Abstracting from detail, I believe them to be very simple indeed. The infant tackles the bewilderingly complex task in a piecemeal fashion, bringing just one aspect under control at a time, beginning with the most basic (so basic that we are apt to forget that it is something to be mastered at all), and gradually working up the hierarchy of control until finally, perhaps a year and a half later, the complete phonological system is reached. (It may take another 2 or 3 years for the child to master all the intricate coordinations involved in producing all the distinctive speech sounds of a language like English.) In all this the child is helped (not hindered) by various (changing) endogenous and exogenous constraints (not limitations), such as the changing configuration of the vocal tract, changing perceptual propensities, changing neurological characteristics, changes in the characteristics of parental speech, changes in parental reactions to the infant's vocalizations, and finally the complex hierarchical organisation of language and the phonological systems (phonemic and prosodic).

It only remains to point out that during the last stage of phonological development not all words in the child's vocabulary necessarily conform to his phonological system (nor do all the adult's words for that matter, *see* Menyuk and Menn, 1979, p. 63). Typically, some words will be pronounced in a way that does not conform to the child's current system (and these may be pronounced correctly or incorrectly). Are these the leading edges in the gradual transformation of the child-like ('incompetence') system into an adult phonological system?

Function and Meaning

We have left the child with a system of communication, which however immature, is identical in principle to that of the adult. It has 'double articulation', i.e. between the physical medium of transmission (sounds, writing, etc.) and the meaning transmitted, there are interposed not one but two levels of organization: the phonological and the lexico-syntactic, the one organizing the (arbitrary, meaningless) medium, the other the (communicative, meaningful) message. And we started with the crying, burping infant.

The very first vocal noises of the infant are either concomitants of other activities (as communicative as the unintended burp), or they are a primitive, innate reaction to degrees of internal maladjustment. They become, by degrees, more 'mental' (the fretting of the bored infant), more overtly communicative (cooing and chuckling) and less predominantly merely indexical (feeding noises, exertion noises). Although the latter never disappear altogether, they are gradually inhibited and brought under increasing control. But this vocal behaviour is only a subordinate part of the infant's earliest interactive behaviour, a great deal of which depends on the eyes and face, and gesture and touch to communicate and regulate predominantly affective states (Stern, 1977; Schaffer, 1977).

But, interestingly, the next vocal stage, babbling, is not communicative behaviour at all; it is an activity that appears to have as its teleological (biological) function 'practice' of articulation extend to control, and as its immediate (psychological) function 'play'. The child appears to take pleasure in playing with his vocal organs, and in the noises he produces. However, communicative interaction continues, using predominantly non-vocal channels on the part of the child (though not on the part of the caretaker). Later some of these modes of interaction (e.g. the use of eye contact) become subordinated to verbal communication, but continue to be essential in regulating smooth verbal interaction in face-to-face discourse between adults. Indeed the whole course of communicative development, from birth to maturity, would seem to be a process in which the currently central mode of communication becomes more peripheral and is then subordinated to the primary mode of the next stage, without disappearing (Trevarthen, 1977b). It is integrated into communicative behaviour, rather than becomming a separate secondary mode of communication; nothing is wasted.

It is intriguing that babbling, which is the first recognizably language-like production on the part of the infant (and the source where proud parents find 'mama' and 'dada' long before the infant has such notions to communicate), rather than being communicative and hence on the lexico-syntactical line of development, lies on the arbitrary phonological line in the development towards the emergence of the double articulation, emerging as much as a year before the child finally begins to develop a fully-fledged phonemic system. Is the drive that starts the infant across this verbal desert towards the verbal oasis at the other end his desire to 'sound' like a human, long before he knows what these sounds can do for him? Or is it yet another example of the infant's interest in the products of his own solitary activities at this stage? Or is it a more 'blind' specifically linguistic, innate drive? Deaf children begin to babble, but this soon fades (Cruttenden, 1979 – since he does not distinguish cooing from babbling, it is in fact unclear if deaf children do in fact ever babble).

In any case, the child next begins to use word-like sounds ('proto-words') to communicate rather more global meanings that often need a sentence or more to gloss them properly (hence they have also been referred to as 'holophrases'). These meanings are often very difficult to define, and appear to be rather unstable in many instances (Halliday, 1975). Their function appears to be, broadly speaking, interactional rather than informative; in that respect they therefore carry meanings that later are largely carried by grammatical and prosodic systems and by subsets of grammatical vocabulary ('empty words'). During this 'proto-language' stage the child does not combine words nor, apparently, does he modify them, for instance prosodically. So at this stage, the transduction from meaning to sound is direct (remember that there is no level of phonemic organization). So although the sound is usually arbitrarily related to the meaning (*see* Carter, 1979, for the interesting suggestion that some of the proto-words may have their origin in earlier 'indexical' noises made by the infant), the proto-language does not have a true double articulation, and it is doubtful if it could simply continue to multiply meanings and corresponding holistic articulatory gestures. Sooner or later the system is bound to become unmanageable. As the child attempts to keep more and more of these articulatory gestures apart in sound and articulation, a phonemic level of organization becomes imperative and inevitable.

It has been claimed by Halliday (1975) that his child invented his proto-words. But using the evidence from Waterson (1970, 1971) (*see* Phonological Development, *above*), Carter (1979), my own observations and Halliday's own data (1975, p. 148ff.), I am inclined to agree with Carter and Waterson that the child takes both his meanings and his sounds either from his caretakers' speech or, occasionally, from his own earlier vocal behaviour that was reacted to as meaningful by his parents. The fact that these proto-words are not transparently like their adult 'equivalent', either in sound or in meaning, both explains the failure of many investigators to recognize any language-like behaviour before the child begins to pronounce words in a more recognizably adult-like way, and also raises an interesting question: do parents understand their child's proto-language?

My impression is that, excluding perhaps the odd word here and there, many parents do not. They much more often appear to interpret (sometimes correctly, sometimes incorrectly) on the basis of contextual and non-verbal behavioural cues, rather than on the basis of the proto-words themselves. The investigator, with his videotape, notes and a lot of time to pore over each episode at length and in minute detail, is often in a better position to 'learn' the child's proto-language than the parents are. But then the child learns to talk, so perhaps misunderstanding does not matter, provided it is done in good faith, and the (mis)understanding is contingent on the child's behaviour and on contextual cues also accessible to the child.

What of the child's own understanding of speech? As discussed in Grieve and Hoogenraad (1979), Hoogenraad et al. (1978) and Grieve et al. (1977), it is not easy to garner valid and unambiguous evidence for the child's understanding of words (or grammatical constructions for that matter), since reasonable speech is always adapted lexically, grammatically, prosodically and pragmatically to the context of situation, so that normally the child will perforce have many contextual cues that bear on the interpretation of utterances addressed to him. And if the speech is systematically stripped of these adaptive features, it will be so contextually odd that it is bound to lead to a breakdown of the social parameters that support communication. The evidence, such as it is (*see* Hoogenraad et al., 1978), suggests that normally the child will let contextual cues override linguistic cues even when he understands the linguistic feature in question (*see* Campbell and Bowe, 1978, for a situation in which the reverse appears to be true).

Prosodic and Grammatical Development

To round off this chapter are some brief and rather general remarks about prosodic development (involving stress and intonation), and a more detailed discussion of one aspect of the grammatical acquisition of English.

A summary and discussion of work on prosodic development is to be found in Crystal (1975, chap. 8, 1979). Intonation and its development are probably the most neglected and hence least well understood aspect of language, and yet intonation is the primary feature that makes speech situationally and interpersonally relevant. Ignorance and neglect abound in language acquisition studies; one too often hears, even reads, statements to the effect that an utterance 'carried no stress', or the assumption emerges that 'all questions have a rising intonation'. Neither statement is true. Virtually all utterances have at least one point of phonological prominence, i.e. stress, and many questions in English do not have a rising intonation.

It is reasonably clear that intonation is the earliest meaningful aspect of language that is reacted to and differentiated by the infant (excepting, of course, 'tone of voice'), but it is less clear what the child understands from the various prosodic features. Later, towards the end of the proto-language stage, when the child begins to use intonation as a controlled variable aspect of his proto-utterances, it is clear that some children at least do not use it with the meanings that are conventional in the adult language (*see* for example, Halliday, 1975). When the child begins to put words together, prosody appears initially to be an important means of marking simple grammatical constructions. It seems to be mastered fairly quickly after that, though some of the more subtle aspects of intonation may only be mastered much later. Occasional references have been made in this chapter to the changes in the intonation of utterances addressed to the infant, and to some of the possible functions of the intonation and stress of adult utterances in the child's developing perception, but little of substance seems to be known about these important matters.

Just as the child may at first use intonation in a way that is not standard in the adult language, so also children do not always use word order conventionally at first. In fact the data from various studies presented by Braine (1976) suggest that many children begin by using the simple fact of collocation to mark the semantic roles (such as agent, action and the like), and that word order is either arbitrary or it marks (or is determined by) a cognitive factor such as topicality. It would seem that many children only slowly induce the general principles that determine what semantic roles are fulfilled by the grammatical functions such as subject, object, indirect object, complement and complement of the various prepositions. It should be added that these principles are not really well understood even for a much studied language such as English (*see* Fillmore, 1968; Halliday, 1967—68). English uses few grammatical inflections, and relies heavily on the ordering of words and higher level syntactic units (phrases and clauses). This may explain the preoccupation with word order in the last decade or so (*see* Braine, 1976, for a discussion of the issues). It emerges from the only study known to me of a highly inflecting language, that of Burling (1959), that quite a number of inflections are mastered rapidly, suggesting that where inflections carry a higher functional (communicative) load than they do in a more nearly isolating (non-inflectional) language like English, their apparent complexity (to our jaundiced eyes) appears to be no disadvantage for acquisition.

Despite the considerable research effort that has been expended on grammatical development over the last two decades, there is still lack of agreement about the correct framework of description, and about the criteria that should be used to decide when a child has mastered a particular construction. In Fletcher and Garman (1979), there are excellent reviews of recent work in chapters by Griffiths, Macrae, Garman, Maratsos, Fletcher, Bowerman and Karmiloff-Smith, so I will not attempt a review here. Instead I will use one example of grammatical development in English (drawn from data in Klima and Bellugi, 1966) to argue that the general principle enunciated at the end of Phonological Development above, also applies to grammatical development.

Polar (yes/no) questions in English are formed by placing the first auxiliary of the verbal group in the sentence initial position ('John is eating'/'Is John eating?'), when there is no auxiliary, dummy 'do' is used ('John stood up'/'Did John stand up?'). Negation also uses the first auxiliary or dummy 'do' ('John isn't eating', 'John didn't stand up'), while in emphatic affirmation the stress falls on the same elements ('John is eating!', 'John did stand up!'). Since polar questions are a request for a yes/no answer, it is natural that they should use the verbal element that carries negation or strong affirmation, and it is also natural that in a question they should occupy the same sentence initial position (the position that marks the 'discourse value' of the utterance) as the 'wh-' word in a wh-question ('What is John eating?'/'Is John eating?') (see Halliday, 1970, for a fuller discussion). There is thus a natural logic in this grammatical system in English.

The data from Klima and Bellugi (1966) suggest the following pattern of development for the 3 children studied (there are no data on strong affirmatives, as the authors do not report on stress placement). In the first phase the children use no auxiliaries, and they negate utterances with 'no' or 'not', nearly always sentence initially, i.e. in the 'discourse value' position, or else sentence finally ('No play that', 'Wear mitten no'). Polar questions are not grammatically marked ('See hole?'). (Klima and Bellugi claim that they are always marked by rising intonation, but this may not be true.) In the next phase, the children introduce the negative modal auxiliary 'can't' and the negative dummy auxiliary 'don't' ('I can't catch you', 'I don't sit on Cromer coffee'), otherwise they continue to use 'no' or 'not' for negation, but now in the auxiliary position, or in place of the verb 'to be', or occasionally in sentence final position ('I no taste them', 'He no little', 'This a radiator no'). Polar questions continue to be grammatically unmarked. In the final stage to be considered here, further negative auxiliaries are added ('won't', 'isn't'), and we still get the occasional 'no' or 'not' in auxiliary position, but no longer elsewhere. For the first time (using Klima and Bellingi's data on wh-questions) non-negative auxiliaries appear ('How he can be a doctor?' 'What he can ride in?'). The child now has an opposition between negative and affirmative auxiliaries ('can't' versus 'can') and, hey presto, the first polar questions marked with an auxiliary in the sentence initial position appear ('Does the kitty stand up', 'Can't you get it?'). Notice, by the way, that both positive and negative questions now appear.

So, in this aspect of grammatical development at least, we see the child extending control over the grammatical system by adding one grammatical distinction at a time. From a beginning when the child neutralizes all the grammatical distinctions that the adult language makes (in one-word utterances), he gradually adds grammatical distinctions (using word order or grammatical words and affixes), and with it increases subtlety of expression. In this instance at least, the children do not appear to be merely making their speech more adult-like in grammatical form, rather they seem to be making their speech more adult-like in function; they add one function, and the relevant grammatical means of marking it, at a time (*see* Fletcher, 1979, for a more thorough discussion of function or meaning in grammatical development). Thus grammatical complexity is mastered incrementally, and it is mastered in order to adapt the (grammatical) means of expression to increasingly more subtle functional requirements.

Conclusion

Cruttenden (1979) provides an excellent recent introduction to language acquisition, directed specifically at 'those concerned with language teaching or language remediation', while an advanced text of review papers directed at the more advanced or specialized student of normal language acquisition can be found in Fletcher and Garman (1979). In this chapter, my concern has not been to provide an introduction or overview of language acquisition studies. Instead I have been concerned with a different goal: to demonstrate that while language acquisition is conceptually complex for the investigator, it is simple for the child — child's work, so to speak.

References

Bartlett F. C. (1932) *Remembering: A Study in Experimental and Social Psychology*. London, Cambridge University Press.

Bloom L., Lightbown P. and Hood L. (1975) *Structure and Variation in Child Language*. Society for Research in Child Development, Monographs Series, vol. 40. University of Chicago Press.

Bloomfield L. (1933) *Language*. London, Allen & Unwin.

Braine M. D. S. (1976) *Children's First Word Combinations*. Society for Research in Child Development, Monographs Series, vol. 41. University of Chicago Press.

Brown R. (1973) *A First Language: The Early Stages*. Harmondsworth, Penguin.

Burling R. (1959) Language development of a Garo- and English-speaking child. *Word* 15, 45–68.

Campbell R. N. (1979) Cognitive development and child language. In: Fletcher P. and Garman M. (ed.) *Language Acquisition: Studies in First Language Development*. London, Cambridge University Press, pp. 419–436.

Campbell R. N. and Bowe T. (1978) Functional asymmetry in early child language. In: Drachman G. (ed.) *Salzburger Beiträge für Linguistik 4*. Wolfgang Neugebauer.

Campbell R. N. and Grieve R. (forthcoming) Royal investigations of the origins of language. To appear in *Historiographia Linguistica*.

Carter A. L. (1979) Prespeech meaning relations: an outline of one infant's sensorimotor morpheme development. In: Fletcher P. and Garman M. (ed.) *Language Acquisition: Studies in First Language Development*. London, Cambridge University Press, pp. 71–92.

Chomsky N. (1957) *Syntactic Structures*. The Hague, Mouton.

Chomsky N. (1959) A review of B. F. Skinner's *Verbal Behaviour*. *Language* 35, 26–58.

Chomsky N. (1965) *Aspects of the Theory of Syntax*. Cambridge, Mass., MIT Press.

Chomsky N. (1967) The general properties of language. In: Darley F. L. (ed.) *Brain Mechanisms Underlying Speech and Language*. New York, Grune & Stratton, pp. 73–88.

Chomsky N. (1972) *Language and Mind*. New York, Harcourt Brace Jovanovich.

Chomsky N. (1975) *Reflections on Language*. London, Fontana.

Clark E. V. (1979) Building a vocabulary: words for objects, actions and relations. In: Fletcher P. and Garman M. (ed.) *Language Acquisition: Studies in First Language Development*. London, Cambridge University Press, pp. 149–160.

Cruttenden A. (1979) *Language in Infancy and Childhood: A Linguistic Introduction to Language Acquisition*. Manchester, Manchester University Press.

Crystal D. (1974) Review of Roger Brown's *A First Language: The Early Stages*. *J. Child Lang.* **1**, 289–307.

Crystal D. (1975) *The English Tone of Voice*. London, Edward Arnold.

Crystal D. (1979) Prosodic development. In: Fletcher P. and Garman M. (ed.) *Language Acquisition: Studies in First Language Development*. London, Cambridge University Press, pp. 33–48.

Edwards D. (1978) The three sources of children's early meanings. In: Markova I. (ed.) *The Social Context of Language*. London, Wiley, pp. 67–85.

Fillmore C. J. (1968) The case for case. In: Bach E. and Harms R. (ed.) *Universals in Linguistic Theory*. New York, Holt, Rinehart & Winston, pp. 1–88.

Fletcher P. (1979) The development of the verb phrase. In: Fletcher P. and Garman M. (ed.) *Language Acquisition: Studies in First Language Development*. London Cambridge University Press, pp. 261–284.

Fletcher P. and Garman M. (ed.) (1979) *Language Acquisition: Studies in First Language Development*. London, Cambridge University Press.

Garman M. (1979) Early grammatical development. In: Fletcher P. and Garman M. (ed.) *Language Acquisition: Studies in First Language Development*. London, Cambridge University Press, pp. 177–208.

Grieve R. and Hoogenraad R. (1976) Using language if you don't have much. In: Wales R. J. and Walker E. C. T. (ed.) *New Approaches to Language Mechanisms*. Amsterdam, North-Holland, pp. 1–28.

Grieve R. and Hoogenraad R. (1979) First words. In: Fletcher P. and Garman M. (ed.) *Language Acquisition: Studies in First Language Development*. London, Cambridge University Press, pp. 93–104.

Grieve R., Hoogenraad R. and Murray D. K. (1977) On the young child's use of lexis and syntax in understanding locative instructions. *Cognition* **5**, 235–250.

Halliday M. A. K. (1967–68) Notes on transitivity and theme in English. Parts 1, 2 and 3. *J. Linguistics* **3**, 37–81; **3**, 177–274; **4**, 153–308.

Halliday M. A. K. (1970) Functional diversity in language, as seen from a consideration of modality and mood in English. *Foundations of Language*. **6**, 322–361.

Halliday M. A. K. (1975) *Learning How to Mean: Explorations in the Development of Language*. London, Edward Arnold.

Halliday M. A. K., McIntosh A. and Strevens P. (1964) *The Linguistic Sciences and Language Teaching*. Harlow, Longmans.

Harlow H. F. (1953) Mice, monkeys, men and motives. *Psychol. Rev.* **60**, 23–32.

Hoogenraad R. (1978) The relation between language structure and the use of language in context. Unpublished MLitt. thesis, University of Edinburgh.

Hoogenraad R., Grieve R., Baldwin P. et al. (1978) Comprehension as an interactive process. In: Campbell R. N. and Smith P. (ed.) *Advances in the Psychology of Language: Language Development and Mother–Child Interaction*. London, Plenum Press, pp. 163–186.

Ingram D. (1979) Phonological patterns in the speech of young children. In: Fletcher P. and Garman M. (ed.) *Language Acquisition: Studies in First Language Development*. London, Cambridge University Press, pp. 133–148.

Klima E. and Bellugi U. (1966) Syntactic regularity in the speech of children. In: Lyons J. and Wales R. J. (ed.) *Psycholinguistic Papers.* Edinburgh, Edinburgh University Press, pp. 183–208.

Labov W. (1975) Empirical foundations of linguistic theory. In: Austerlitz R. (ed.) *The Scope of American Linguistics.* Lisse, Peter de Ridder Press, pp. 77–134.

Lashley K. (1951) The problem of serial order in behaviour. In: Jeffress L. A. (ed.) *Cerebral Mechanisms in Behavior.* New York, Wiley, pp. 112–136.

Luria A. R. and Yudovitch F. I. (1971) *Speech and the Development of Mental Processes in the Child.* Harmondsworth, Penguin.

Lyons J. (1977) *Semantics, Volume 1.* London, Cambridge University Press.

Lyons J. and Wales R. J. (ed.) (1966) *Psycholinguistics Papers.* Edinburgh, Edinburgh University Press.

McCarthy D. (1930) *The Language Development of the Preschool Child.* Institute of Child Welfare, Monograph Series No. 4, Minneapolis, Minn., University of Minnesota Press.

McCarthy D. (1954) Language development in children. In: Carmichael L. (ed.) *Manual of Child Psychology,* 2nd edition. New York, Wiley, pp. 492–630.

McNeill D. (1966) The creation of language by children. In: Lyons J. and Wales R. J. (ed.) *Psycholinguistics Papers.* Edinburgh, Edinburgh University Press, pp. 99–115.

Macken M. A. (1980) The child's lexical representation: the 'puzzle–puddle–pickle' evidence. *J. Linguistics.* **16**, 1–17.

Macrae A. (1979) Combining meaning in early language. In: Fletcher P. and Garman M. (ed.) *Language Acquisition: Studies in First Language Development.* London, Cambridge University Press, pp. 161–175.

Marshall J. C. (1979) Language acquisition in a biological frame of reference. In: Fletcher P. and Garman M. (ed.) *Language Acquisition: Studies in First Language Development.* London, Cambridge University Press, pp. 437–453.

Matthews P. H. (1975) Review of Roger Brown's *A First Language: The Early Stages.* *J. Linguistics* **11**, 322–342.

Menyuk P. and Menn L. (1979) Early strategies for the perception and production of words and sounds. In: Fletcher P. and Garman M. (ed.) *Language Acquisition: Studies in First Language Development.* London, Cambridge University Press, pp. 49–70.

Morse P. (1974) Infant speech perception: a preliminary model and review of the literature. In: Schiefelbusch R. L. and Lloyd L. L. (ed.) *Language Perspectives: Acquisition, Retardation and Intervention.* London, Macmillan, pp. 19–53.

Nelson K. (1973) *Structure and Strategy in Learning to Talk.* Society for Research in Child Development, Monographs Series, vol. 38, Nos. 1 and 2. University of Chicago Press.

Newson J. (1977) An intersubjective approach to the systematic description of mother–infant interaction. In: Schaffer H. R. (ed.) *Studies in Mother–Infant Interaction.* London, Academic Press, pp. 47–61.

Quirk R., Greenbaum S., Leech G. et al. (1972) *A Grammar of Contemporary English.* Harrow, Longman.

Reece L. (1970) *Grammar of the Walibri Language of Central Australia.* Oceanic Linguistic Monographs 13, University of Sydney.

Richards M. (ed.) (1974) *The Integration of a Child into a Social World.* London, Cambridge University Press.

Romanes G. J. (1966) *Cunningham's Manual of Practical Anatomy. Volume 3: Head and Neck and Brain,* 13th edition. London, Oxford University Press.

Schaffer H. R. (ed.) (1977) *Studies in Mother–Infant Interaction.* London, Academic.

Skinner B. F. (1957) *Verbal Behavior.* New York, Appleton-Century-Crofts.

Smith N. V. (1973) *The Acquisition of Phonology: A Case Study.* London, Cambridge University Press.

Stark R. E. (1979) Prespeech segmental feature development. In: Fletcher P. and Garman M. (ed.) *Language Acquisition: Studies in First Language Development.* London, Cambridge University Press, pp. 15–32.

Stern D. (1977) *The First Relationship: Infant and Mother.* London, Fontana.

Templin M. C. (1957) *Certain Language Skills in Children.* Minneapolis, Minn., University of Minnesota Press.

Trevarthen C. (1974) Conversations with a two-month-old. *New Scientist,* 2nd May, 1974, 230–233.

Trevarthen C. (1977a) Descriptive analysis of infant communicative behaviour. In: Schaffer H. R. (ed.) *Studies in Mother–Infant Interaction.* London, Academic Press, pp. 227–270.

Trevarthen C. (1977b) Basic patterns of psychogenetic change in infancy. In: Nathan H. (ed.) *Proceedings of the OECD Conference on Dips in Learning.* St Paul de Vence, March 1975. Paris, OECD.

Waterson N. (1970) Some speech forms of an English child – a phonological study. *Trans. of the Philol. Soc.* 1–24.

Waterson N. (1971) Child phonology: a prosodic view. *J. Linguistics* 7, 179–211.

Wells G. (1979) Variation in child language. In: Fletcher P. and Garman M. (ed.) *Language Acquisition: Studies in First Language Development.* London, Cambridge University Press, pp. 377–395.

Chapter Four

Observations on Communication Problems in Normal Children

Robert Grieve

Introduction

Those experienced in working with the mentally retarded are all too aware that retarded individuals, especially children, frequently encounter difficulties in communication. Yet in trying to understand the nature of these difficulties, an important fact is often overlooked; namely, 'normal' children encounter difficulties in communication too. While some of their difficulties are easy to notice, others are less obvious. This chapter will consider the nature of some of these less obvious difficulties, and examine how normal children go about trying to resolve them. The implications of such work may then be considered. In particular, what does it tell us about how communication proceeds in normal children, and, does the work possess any relevance for those interested in trying to enhance the level and quality of communication in the mentally retarded?

The communication problems of very young children are readily apparent. The young child aged 1–2 years has a limited amount of expressive language in the first place, and the gaps in his linguistic knowledge, or the mistakes he makes with the knowledge he has, are relatively easy to spot. With a particular word, for example, he may be uncertain as to its correct pronunciation, he may regularly mispronounce it or he may forget what word it is that he wants to pronounce (Grieve and Hoogenraad, 1976). Even if his articulation of words leaves nothing to be desired, we may observe clearly and correctly pronounced words being used by the child in ways that are distinctly non-adult-like. The young child's early use of 'Daddy' to refer to any adult male, or his use of 'dog' to refer to any animal resembling a dog (e.g. cats, sheep, horses, pigs), etc., are relatively commonplace (Clark, 1973; Greenfield, 1973). When we also observe the young child producing utterances such as 'a scissors', 'this foots', 'I comed', 'nobody don't likes me', and so on (Brown, 1965; McNeill, 1970), we appreciate that his early syntax (rules for combining language elements) is far from mature.

However, one remarkable aspect of the onset of language in young children is the rapidity with which it develops. By the time the child is 4—5 years of age, he can be engaged in a reasonably interesting conversation. The amount of language now at his expressive command is considerable, not merely in terms of the range of words he knows, but also in terms of his grasp of syntax and semantics — rules related to language's structure and meaning (Chomsky, 1965; Lenneberg, 1967; McNeill, 1970). Yet despite these impressive, and impressively rapid linguistic accomplishments, children continue to experience problems in communication, certainly up to the age of 10 years (C. S. Chomsky, 1969; Palermo and Molfese, 1972; Rommetveit, 1968).

While it is relatively easy for adults to appreciate some of the communication difficulties of normal children, others are not so easy to notice. When the child makes certain kinds of mistakes, for example in pronunciation, grammar or word usage, adults may not only notice them, but attempt to assist the child by correcting him. We are no doubt familiar with hearing adults say things like: 'You don't say "I comed". You say "I came" ', or 'It's not "sellopate". It's "sellotape" ', or 'You don't say "dar". It's "car" '. And when the child's usage of a word is inappropriate — sometimes amusingly so, as in Chukovsky's (1963) example of the child who described a bald man as having a 'barefoot head' — adults may tutor the child in correct usage. (However, the way in which one tutors, if at all, some of the utterances that children produce, is not so clear. Recall another of Chukovsky's examples — of the child who said, on seeing some ponies: 'Mummy, I'm so sorry for the baby horses — they cannot pick their noses'.) An indication of the variety of problems that normal children encounter in their early language development has been presented elsewhere (Grieve and Hoogenraad, 1976).

However, while some communication problems are easily observed, other aspects of communicative difficulty in normal children are not so easy to notice, and it will be the purpose of this chapter to draw attention to them, consider their nature, and examine the ways in which they are resolved. The communication problems to be described have been studied recently, in collaboration with Alison Garton, Martin Hughes and Susan Stanley, and it is a pleasure to acknowledge their contributions. All the children studied are beyond the earliest stages of language development, and they have varying levels of semantic, syntactic and pragmatic language abilities. What is to be emphasized here is that all the children are 'normal'. Compared with other children of their age, no child is regarded as suffering from any intellectual or linguistic impairment, nor were they selected as being especially bright or linguistically advanced. They are intended to be fairly typical 3-year-olds, 4-year-olds, 5-year-olds, or whatever, and they were studied while in regular playgroups, pre-school kindergartens or primary schools. We begin by considering what happens when 3—4-year-old children encounter difficulties with word meanings. Specifically, we ask what happens when such children are presented with instructions which contain words the meaning of which they fail to understand.

Failure to Understand Word Meanings

Here we will consider how children aged 3—4 years respond to instructions containing the relational expressions 'more' and 'less'. A considerable amount of work has been conducted on this topic in recent years. Since the child's ability to undertake comparisons is a fundamental cognitive process, the way in which this process is directed by language is consequently of considerable interest. The initial work on the problem was conducted by Donaldson and Balfour (1968), who reported the somewhat surprising result that young children of this age understand the word 'less' to mean the same as the word 'more'.

In their original study, Donaldson and Balfour showed that when 3—4-year-old children were presented with 2 model apple trees, one containing say 6 apples and one 3 apples, if asked to judge which tree had more apples, children selected the more laden tree. Alternatively, if asked to judge which tree had less apples, the children also selected the more laden tree. A similar result was observed when the children had to construct, not simply judge, trees with more/less apples. For example, when presented with a pile of apples and 2 trees, one containing 4 apples and the other empty, and asked to make it so that the empty tree had more apples than the 4-apple tree, children added apples until there were more on the initially empty tree. Alternatively, if asked to make it so that the empty tree had less apples than the 4-apple tree, instead of adding 1, 2 or 3 apples to the initially empty tree, the children in fact responded as before, adding apples until there were more on the initially empty tree than on the 4-apple tree.

These results suggested that the 3—4-year-old children were assimilating the meaning of the word 'less' to that of the word 'more'. That is, at this stage of semantic development, the meanings of 'more' and 'less' are the same, rather than opposite, and the meaning that both terms have is the meaning for 'more'. Theoretical accounts of why the young child assimilates the meaning of 'less' to that of 'more' have been proposed, in terms of 'markedness' by H. H. Clark (1970), and in terms of 'semantic features' by E. V. Clark (1973). However we will not examine these theories here, for since the original finding, matters have become more complicated.

While the original finding has been confirmed in some studies (e.g. Palermo, 1973, 1974; Holland and Palermo, 1975), in other studies it has not, and several investigators have recently reported that in some contexts young children do not invariably assimilate the meaning of 'less' to that of 'more' (e.g. Kavanaugh, 1976; Townsend, 1976; Wales et al., 1976; Wannemacher and Ryan, 1978; Weiner, 1974). Particularly evident in these studies is that when children fail to understand the meaning of 'less', rather than respond to it as if it meant 'more', young children respond to 'less' in random fashion. Thus, they do not always assimilate the meaning of 'less' to that of 'more' (*see* Richards, 1979, for a recent review). Therefore instead of inquiring why young children assimilate the meaning of 'less' to that of 'more', what needs to be asked instead is why young children: (1) respond to 'less' as they do to 'more' in some contexts, and (2) respond to 'less' at random in other contexts. If we are to understand the nature of the child's difficulties with these words, both aspects of this question need to be considered.

Nevertheless, explanations proposed to account for the children's responses in such tasks have addressed only the first aspect of the question. These proposals, made by Carey (1978), and Trehub and Abramovitch (1978), try to account for the apparent assimilation of 'less' to 'more' by supposing that young children have certain *response biases*, which affect the way they respond in more/less tasks.

In Carey's study, young children were presented with a 'fussy puppet' game, in which a puppet would not drink the tea in his glass until he had just the right amount to drink. When asked to make it so that the puppet had more, or less, tea to drink, children added liquid to the puppet's glass in both cases. This response bias, to add liquid, operated despite prior exposure to a condition in which children were encouraged both to add and pour out liquid from the puppet's glass. Carey also reports that this response bias to add liquid operated when children were presented with an instruction containing an inscrutable term: to make it so that the puppet had 'tiv' tea to drink. Again, most children added liquid. This result of course raises a fundamental question about what is going on in such tasks, a question to which we will return.

In Trehub and Abramovitch's study, young children were presented with piles of objects, two piles at a time, differing in quantity, and asked to indicate the pile with more, or the pile with less. What happened was that the children selected the greater pile for both instructions, i.e. apparent assimilation of 'less' to 'more'. However, when presented with a 'neutral' instruction, to point to any pile, the children also selected the greater pile. Thus children have a response bias to select the greater of two quantities.

Interesting as these proposals are in calling attention to the importance of non-linguistic biases that may affect the child's responses in such tasks, they are directed towards accounting for only the first aspect of the relevant question: apparent assimilation of 'less' to that of 'more'. Yet still to be tackled is the equally pertinent aspect of the question: why do young children sometimes respond to 'less' at random? To put the matter another way, why do we observe a lack of apparent assimilation (random responding to 'less') in some contexts, and apparent assimilation (responding to 'less' as to 'more') in other contexts?

One way to proceed would be to suppose that in some contexts a response bias immediately operates to select the greater of two quantities. Apparent assimilation of 'less' to 'more' would then be accounted for. But in other contexts, if there is a lack of any immediate response bias to select one of two unequal quantities, then it might be expected that children would respond to 'less' at random.

As substantiation of this assumption would enable us to account for both aspects of the question at issue, we recently undertook a series of studies to identify contexts with and without response biases. Only the results of these studies need be described here (*see* Grieve and Stanley, 1980, for further details). In the tasks we set, children had to make judgements about columns of beads, threaded on vertical metal rods. What we found was that in a context consisting of 2 rods, one with 6 beads and one with 4 beads, there was no response bias – asked to select 'any' rod, the children selected at random. But in a context consisting of 3 rods, one with 2, one with 4, and one with 6 beads, there was a response bias – children regularly selected the 6-bead rod.

Thus having identified a context with a response bias (the 3-rod array of 2, 4 and 6 beads), and a context without a response bias (the 2-rod array of 4 and 6 beads), we were now in a position to examine how children responded to instructions which contained a term they might understand, namely the term 'more'. We could also examine their responses to a term whose meaning might be to them obscure, namely 'less'. In addition, since obscurity in the meaning of a term presented to the children can be guaranteed – by making it inscrutable, as in Carey's study – we also presented instructions containing the inscrutable term 'tiv', to find out what responses would be made in our two contexts to an instruction containing a term which the children could not possibly understand.

One further problem exercised us. Namely, if young children have difficulty with the word 'less', is this because of a general difficulty with the underlying concept of lesser amount, or is their difficulty restricted to this particular linguistic expression of the underlying concept? We therefore decided to examine children's responses to alternative linguistic expressions of the concept of lesser amount: specifically, the term 'less' itself, the alternative term 'fewer', and another alternative phrase that we overheard kindergarten children using to each other, 'doesn't have many'.

The results of this study were as follows. First, there was some evidence that 3–4 year-olds correctly understood the term 'more'. Secondly, there was no evidence that the children understood the term 'less'. Nor did they understand 'fewer'; nor, of course, could they understand the nonsense term 'tiv'. But, thirdly, they did understand the phrase 'doesn't have many'. Thus their difficulties with 'less' are particular to that linguistic expression of the concept of lesser amount, rather than with the underlying concept itself.

If children failed to understand the terms 'less', 'fewer' and 'tiv', how did they react to instructions containing these terms? The surprising thing is, they typically produced a response. They did not produce blank stares, queries, requests to clarify, say they didn't know the answer, or whatever. The failure-to-respond rate in this study was 3·2 per cent. This means that about 97 per cent of the time, the children responded to instructions containing words which, to them, were obscure (i.e. 'less', 'fewer'), or inscrutable ('tiv'). Thus young children seem to have a propensity to respond to instructions even if they fail to understand, or fully understand, their meaning.

If they typically responded, then how did they respond? And specifically, did they assimilate the meaning of 'less' to that of 'more'? What happened depended on whether or not the context in which the children were tested illustrated a response bias. In the 3-rod context, where there was a response bias in favour of the 6-bead rod, children responded to 'less', 'fewer' and 'tiv', according to the context's response bias, that is, they selected the 6-bead rod in response to instructions containing these terms. (It should be noted that this context requires a matching-to-sample technique to be employed; see Grieve and Stanley, 1980, for further details.) But in the 2-rod context, where there was no response bias, children responded to the obscure 'less' and 'fewer', and to the inscrutable 'tiv', at random. In other words, they made a guess.

Was there any evidence of assimilation in meaning of 'less' to 'more'? The answer has to be 'no'. If we conclude, from the fact that children responded to 'less' as they did to 'more' in the 3-rod context, that this provides evidence for assimilation in meaning of 'less' to 'more', we find that we have painted ourselves into a most uncongenial corner. Namely, following this argument, we would also have to conclude that children assimilated the meaning of 'fewer' to that of 'more', for they responded to these terms in the same way. And what is worse, we would then have to conclude that children assimilated the meaning of 'tiv' to that of 'more', for again they responded to these terms in the same way. But 'tiv' is meaningless.

If such uncongenial corners are best avoided, this argument is to be resisted. Instead, we prefer to conclude that there is no evidence for assimilations of the meanings of 'less', 'fewer' and 'tiv' to that of 'more' in the 3-rod context. This is certainly the conclusion to be drawn from the other context; in the 2-rod context, there is no evidence whatsoever of assimilations of 'less', 'fewer' or 'tiv' to the meaning of 'more'.

So rather than suppose that children assimilate the meanings of obscure or inscrutable terms ('less', 'fewer', 'tiv') to that of a term they understand ('more'), it is preferable to account for the results by observing that when children fail to understand terms in instructions with which they are presented, while they nevertheless respond, the nature of their responses varies. In a context where there is a non-linguistic response bias (the 3-rod context), their responses to obscure/inscrutable terms follow the bias. But in a context where there is no response bias to be followed (the 2-rod context), since there is no non-linguistic factor to determine the children's responses, they respond at random and make a guess.

A picture of what young children do when faced by this sort of communication problem now begins to emerge. When young children fail to understand the language of instructions that adults present, they still produce responses. Since these responses are not determined by the linguistic instruction (which is not understood), what does determine them? In the present study, we see that their responses may be determined by a non-linguistic factor, such as a response bias. Alternatively, in a context where such a non-linguistic determinant of response is absent, i.e. where there is no response bias, since there is no linguistic determinant of response (they do not understand the instruction), and no non-linguistic determinant of response (there is no response bias), they may resort to guessing. Before we consider why young children behave in these ways in face of communication difficulties, we first need to sketch in a bit more of the picture by considering some further studies.

Uncertainty about Word Reference

The studies in this section arose out of some important work completed by McGarrigle (*see* McGarrigle et al., 1978), on a well-known problem in the cognitive development of young children, namely the problem of class inclusion. The problem was first studied by Piaget and associates (e.g. Piaget, 1952; Inhelder and Piaget, 1964; Piaget and Inhelder, 1969) and, according to Piagetian theory, the problem represents the *pons asinorum* of mature classifactory ability in the child. What the child is asked to do is

Table 3. **The Class Inclusion Problem.**

Set of Horses	
Black horse ⎫ Black horse ⎬ Black horse ⎭	Included set of black horses
White horse ⎬	Included set of white horses

to compare a subclass of objects with the class to which that subclass contributes. For example, shown a set of horses, 1 white and 3 black, the child would be asked to say which is 'more': the horses (class) or the black horses (contributory subclass) (*see Table* 3). Before the age of about 7 years, children usually get this question wrong. They say that there are more black horses 'because there's only one white one', comparing subclass (black horses) with subclass (white horse), instead of subclass (black horses) with total class (all the horses). Piaget attributes this error to a characteristic of the child's thought, which precludes the simultaneous decomposition of the class to locate the required subclass (black horses), and recomposition of the subclasses to locate the required class (the horses).

The important contribution that McGarrigle made to this problem was to show that it had nothing to do with the child's ability to handle class inclusion relationships. First, he showed that 80 per cent of children aged 4 years could deal with inclusion relationships quite adequately. Then, he showed that the errors children made in comparing included sets were also made in comparing non-included sets (McGarrigle et al., 1978). For example, if the array in the task consisted not only of 1 white and 3 black horses, but also of 2 white and 2 black cows (as in *Table* 4 when the child was asked to make a non-included comparison, say between the horses and the black cows), 4-year-olds made the mistake of comparing subsets – the

Table 4. Comparison of Sets.

	Set of Horses	Set of Cows	
Set of Black Horses	Black horse Black horse Black horse	Black cow Black cow	Set of Black Cows
Set of White Horses	White horse	White cow White cow	Set of White Cows

black horses, not all the horses, would be compared with the black cows, for example.

This sort of result led McGarrigle to make a distinction between *received* and *intended* tasks. *Intended* tasks are tasks that adults present to children for completion, e.g. the comparison of a set with an included subset (Piaget's inclusion problem), or the comparison of a set with a non-included subset (McGarrigle's non-included comparisons). *Received* tasks are those tasks that children in fact complete, here the comparison of subsets. Of course received and intended tasks may coincide, as when the child completes the task as it has been presented by the adult. But with young children, received and intended tasks may often fail to coincide, and McGarrigle's point is that when this happens, we are seriously misled if we assume that this is so because of a lack of ability in the child to complete the intended task. Thus with the problem of class inclusion, the child's difficulties reside not so much in the characteristics of his mental ability, as Piaget suggests, but more in locating the intended meaning of the question that the adult has presented. Thus the child's difficulty is more communicative than cognitive.

What do children do when faced with such difficulties? Recently, we have been attempting to identify the nature of the received tasks that children complete in the context of comparisons of sets (Grieve and Garton, 1980). Using arrays similar to the one depicted in *Table 4*, we have asked 3—4 year-old children to make all the comparisons that are possible with such an array. There are in fact 15 such comparisons, but here we need only consider a sample of the possibilities in order to appreciate what occurs.

Basically, there are two types of comparison — *between-set* comparisons and *within-set* comparisons. *Between-set* comparisons involve some sort of comparison between the set (or part of the set) of horses, and the set (or part of the set) of cows. For example, we can simply ask the child to compare the horses and the cows: 'Are there more horses or more cows?' We will refer to this as a 2-term question, for only 2 terms ('horses' and 'cows') are required to specify the sets to be compared. Alternatively, we can ask the child to compare between the set of horses and the subset of black cows: 'Are there more horses or more black cows?' — a 3-term question. Or, we might ask the child to compare between the subset of black horses and the subset of white cows — a 4-term question. Notice that all of these questions call for comparisons between the two sets or their parts. All therefore involve non-included comparisons; in no case is a set to be compared with an included subset. This only occurs with some of the within-set comparisons.

Within-set questions are of two sorts. The questions invariably require the child to make a comparison within one of the sets. Sometimes the questions are 4-term: e.g. 'Are there more white horses or more black horses?', involving non-included comparisons. Otherwise, the questions are 3-term: e.g. 'Are there more horses or more black horses?', and of course it is this type of question that involves the comparison of included sets. Here the child is asked to compare the total set of horses with its included subset of black horses. These sorts of comparisons are summarized on the left of *Table 5*.

When we asked 3—4-year-old children to complete these sorts of comparisons, what we found was that some of the questions caused them no difficulty; in particular, 4-term questions, of both the within-set and between-set types, were almost invariably answered correctly. Thus here, intended and received tasks coincided. But in other cases, intended and received tasks did not coincide; specifically, 2-term between-set, and 3-term between-set and within-set questions were usually answered incorrectly. With such questions, the children appeared uncertain about the intended referents of the set names. Thus when asked whether there were 'more horses or more black cows', the children were uncertain about the intended reference of the word 'horses' — did it mean all the horses, or only some of them?; and if only some of them, which ones? In face of such uncertainties, we again observed that children typically produced a response. The failure-to-respond rate in this study was again very low, of the order of 1 per cent. Thus despite their uncertainty, the children almost invariably responded, and they did so by adapting the language of the questions, in a systematic way, into forms which they could readily process.

The nature of these adaptations is indicated on the right of *Table 5*. What happens is that with questions which specify 3 terms, if the comparison is of the between-set variety, the children take the modifier specified for one nominal to modify the other, unmodified nominal. Thus a 'horses : black cows' comparison is adapted to a 'black horses : black

Table 5. **Language Adaptations in the Child's Comparisons of Sets.**

Question presented		Example	Comparison completed	Comment
Between-set	2-term	horses : cows	black horses : black cows white horse : white cows	Language adapted
	3-term	horses : black cows	black horses : black cows	Language adapted
	4-term	black horses : white cows	black horses : white cows	Comparison completed as requested
Within-set	3-term	horses : black horses	white horse : black horses	Language adapted
	4-term	white horses : black horses	white cows : black cows	Comparison completed as requested

cows' comparison. If the 3-term comparison is of a within-set variety, the children introduce, by contrast with the modifier specified for one nominal, the alternative modifier, to modify the other, unmodified nominal. Thus a 'horses : black horses' comparison is adapted to a 'white horses : black horses' comparison. With the question that specifies 2 terms, the between-set comparison of the 'horses : cows' type, children may still adapt the question. They do so by introducing one modifier, to modify both, unmodified nominals. Thus the 'horses : cows' question may be adapted, using the modifier 'black', to a 'black horses : black cows' comparison. Or, if the other modifier is introduced, the 'horses : cows' comparison is adapted to a 'white horses : white cows' comparison. Thus what is happening is that regardless of the number of terms the question specifies — 2, 3 or 4 terms — children respond as if the questions invariably specify 4 terms, i.e. they end up comparing one subset with another subset.

Such results of course seem extraordinary. We present the child with 4 horses (3 black and 1 white) and 4 cows (2 black and 2 white), and ask whether there are more horses or more cows. And 3—4-year-olds tell us either that there are more black horses than black cows, or that there are more white cows than white horses. Or, if we ask whether there are more horses (4) or more white cows (2), the children tell us that there are more white cows because there is only 1 white horse.

Why young children should do this is something we are currently trying to unravel (Grieve and Garton, 1980; Garton and Grieve, 1980). As noted above, we suspect that in such tasks young children have considerable difficulty, not in computing the comparisons that are required (children of this age are adept in accurately comparing sets composed of small numbers of objects — see Gelman, 1978), but in arriving at the comparisons they are intended to complete. To arrive correctly at these intended comparisons, the determinant of response on which the child should closely depend is the language of the question. But how much is the child 'driven' by the language of the question?

In some respects, this is precisely what occurs, for example, in the case of 4-term within-set or between-set comparisons, which all involve subset— subset comparisons of various sorts; the child's response is driven by the language. But when the child encounters questions containing terms ('horses', 'cows') about whose intended referents he is uncertain, perhaps he assumes that this task is essentially about comparisons of subsets? Might he thereby be adapting 3-term questions into a 4-term format, which enables him to compare one subset with another? And, perhaps more surprisingly, might he also be adapting 2-term questions to a 4-term subset—subset comparison format, to accord with his assumption as to what the task is about? Now if the child supposes that the task is to compare subsets, then any questions which *fully* specify the subsets to be compared (4-term questions) are easy to deal with. But questions which 'fail' to fully specify subset—subset comparisons, that is, 3-term and 2-term questions, need to be 'adapted' to a form which does permit subset—subset comparisons. Thus the child appears to resolve his communicative difficulty here (What groups of objects is the question directing him to compare?) by adapting the language of the questions to 'fully specified' 4-term formats. As mentioned earlier, we are still trying to untangle this problem, and whether the preliminary account sketched here will prove adequate remains to be seen.

We observed above that certain aspects of the results of the present study appear extraordinary. Faced with uncertainty about the intended meanings of terms in questions, children nevertheless proceed to answer such questions, arriving at received tasks quite different from those that were intended. In the next part of this chapter, the results we will describe appear not just extraordinary, but positively bizarre. However, as we will come to see, what at first appears extraordinary if not bizarre with young children may in the end prove to be less exotic than might at first be supposed. But first, the phenomenon.

Failure to Understand Question Meanings

So far, we have been concerned with trying to discover what happens when children are given instructions or asked questions containing terms which they do not, or cannot understand, or about whose intended meanings they are uncertain. But apart from the 'tiv' questions presented in one of our studies, all our questions to children share one characteristic basic to all questions that are well formed. Namely, they are all perspicuous, or intended to be so, at least as far as adults are concerned. As we have seen, children typically respond to such questions or instructions, even when it is clear that they do not fully understand terms that our questions or instructions contain. While we will presently come to consider why this should be so, we first describe a study of the limiting case. Namely, what happens when children are asked questions which are unanswerable as they stand?

We have considered this problem by asking 5—7-year-old children two types of what we have termed 'bizarre questions' (Hughes and Grieve, 1980), but here we will illustrate the study with reference to but one type — questions which are conceptually ill-formed.

Dabblers in, or indeed afficionados of, philosophical logic will no doubt be familiar with strictures about what have been termed 'category mistakes' (Ryle, 1949). Thus, we are told, neither time nor place may be predicated of number (though we have no doubt heard both, not just predicated of, but bellowed about, number, for example at boating lakes: 'Come in Number 4, your time is up'). But before going off the Ryles, we can observe that the question 'Is red heavier than yellow?' is conceptually ill-formed. It involves a 'category mistake', predicating one category, weight, of another to which it does not literally apply, colour. Likewise, asking 'Is milk bigger than water?' mistakenly predicates stature of liquids. Such questions are not intended to be perspicuous. They demand rejection. Or, if our questioner is to be given the benefit of the doubt, they at least demand clarification or amplification: 'Say more', or 'Say what you mean'.

Yet when such questions are presented to 5—7-year-old children, their answers are ingenious and rational (Hughes and Grieve, 1980). What happens is that children tend to imaginatively construct replies, although there is a difference between the younger 5-year-olds and the older 7-year-olds in the manner in which they do so. Younger children tend to introduce elements to the context of the question in order to arrive at a reply, while older children tend instead to arrive at a reply by working from characteristics of the elements already available in the context of the question. Some examples will illustrate this difference, and at the same time give some idea of the children's ingenuity.

To the question 'Is milk bigger than water?', we found that younger children usually said 'Yes'. When asked 'Why?', they mostly told us about the origins of the liquids, e.g. water comes from taps, and milk comes from either cows or bottles. Since cows or bottles are bigger than taps, milk is bigger than water (*Q.E.D.*). By contrast, the older children tended not to introduce bovine, container or sink-appliance elements to arrive at an answer. Instead, they mostly made reference to the characteristics of the elements already in the question, telling us that milk *is* bigger than water 'because milk's got a colour', or 'because milk's more creamier', or 'because milk is heavier', or 'because milk's more thicker'.

Likewise with 'Is red heavier than yellow?' 'Yes', said a 5-year-old. 'Why?', we asked. 'Because there's much more red than yellow.' 'Why?' 'Because there's water in it.' 'There's water in what?', we asked (by this time, flummoxed). 'The paint.' The child's explanation is in fact unmysterious, as becomes clear from another child who articulates her answer more clearly. She first tells us that red is heavier than yellow, and when asked why, she says: 'Yellow is a little. Yellow's got a little plastic box and the red paint's got a big plastic box.' Get it? In school, the children use powdered paint which is mixed with water in plastic containers. So if there is more red than yellow, red *is* heavier! (Adieu, category mistakes.)

But as with the previous question, we can again see that younger children tend to introduce elements extraneous to those contained in the question, referring to containers, mixing paint with water and so on. But older children again stick more closely to the characteristics of the elements in the question, and they tell us that red is heavier than yellow 'because red's darker', or 'because red's more darker', or 'because red's a darker colour than yellow'.

The first difference, then, in the way that younger and older children tend to answer such questions, concerns the extent to which elements are introduced to the context in order to arrive at an answer. Younger children tend to do this much more than older children, who stick more closely to the characteristics of the elements given in the context.

The second difference between the way in which younger and older children answer such questions is concerned with the ways in which replies are given. What happens is that the older children tend to qualify their answers in ways that indicate their uncertainties. For example, they use phrases such as 'I think' (e.g. 'I think milk's bigger than water' or 'I think red's just as heavy as yellow'). Sometimes their answers are themselves in the form of questions: e.g. 'Milk, I think', ' "Bigger", did you say?'; or 'Red... was it "heavier"?' Most of the older children's replies exhibited some sort of qualification, but this never occurred with the younger children. It is not clear whether this indicates that older children were more attuned to the bizarre character of the questions compared with younger children, or whether younger children are not so skilled in employing verbal devices to qualify what they say ('I think'), or query what has been said to them ('Was it...?', 'Did you say...?'), compared with older children. Should the latter explanation be frequently correct, it has to be noted that it is not invariably so. Of 22 children tested in this study, only one child made no attempt to answer our bizarre questions, and he was the youngest, aged 4 years 11 months. He simply grinned, hugely, at every question, saying things like 'I don't know', 'No idea', 'Don't know', 'Never tried it before' (this last response calling to mind Brendan Behan's story (1963) about the new assistant in a Dublin bookshop who was asked if she liked Kipling. 'How could I know', she replied, 'when I never kippilled.').

In this section, we have been concerned with examining children's responses to questions using terms with which the children are wholly familiar. Here we have not been dealing with questions containing terms the meanings of which children may not know, such as 'less', 'fewer', etc., nor with terms about whose intended meanings children may be uncertain. In this study, children are completely *au fait* with the meanings of words such as 'red', 'yellow', 'milk', 'water', 'bigger', 'heavier' and so on. Here it is the conceptual nature of the questions that is ill-founded, yet even in this limiting case, where children are asked questions that are intended to be unanswerable, they respond. While there are some differences in the nature of these responses between younger and older children, the remarkable fact is that they almost invariably make a response, in ways that are rational and ingenious.

Discussion

What do the present studies show? They show that when faced with problems in communication, normal children typically respond. Thus they provide a response when the meanings of the terms in the instructions are either not understood, as with 'less' and 'fewer', or cannot be understood, as with 'tiv'. They respond to questions although the intended referents of terms in the questions are not clear to them, as with 'horses' and 'cows' in the context of comparing sets and subsets. And they typically provide responses even to questions which do not make sense and whose meanings cannot be clear to the child as the questions stand, as in the context of being asked bizarre questions.

We have seen something of the variety of resources that children bring to bear in arriving at solutions to, or at least resolutions of, such problems. If their responses are not wholly determined by the language of the questions or instructions, due to the gaps in knowledge and understanding that such questions and instructions involve, then other factors come into play. Sometimes, responses are determined by non-linguistic factors, such as a response bias. Or, failing the operation of either linguistic or non-linguistic determinants of response, the child may resort to guessing. In other contexts, where children are uncertain about the intended meanings of questions, they may adapt the language of these questions to formats they find more congenial, and proceed to answer within such language-adapted formats. And finally, when children cannot possibly know the meanings of questions, the questions being conceptually bizarre, they nevertheless continue to construct responses, either through introducing elements additional to the given context, or through paying ingenious attention to the characteristics of given contextual elements.

Why do children do this? To answer this question, we need to reflect both on the nature of communication, and the position of the child. In communication, when a speaker asks his hearer to do something, by presenting an instruction, or to say something, by presenting a question, the socially appropriate response is for the hearer to do or say something in return. Of course, he may say or do what he has been asked or requested. But if the hearer does not wish to do so (e.g. he does not wish to comply with the speaker's request), or if he is unable to do so through his lack of understanding of the speaker's question or instruction, it is still appropriate to make a response of some sort – to indicate lack of understanding, to ask for clarification, to make an excuse for non-compliance, or whatever. What is both socially inappropriate, and communicatively disruptive, is to make no response whatever, behaving as if the speaker's question or instruction had never been uttered.

Now what the child knows a lot about are social aspects of communicative interaction. The work of Bruner (1978) and Trevarthen (1974) has shown us that, from the first few weeks of life, the child is treated as a communicative partner, and long before expressive language appears in the child's repertoire of skills, he learns to communicate. Hence the heavy emphasis in some recent accounts of language development on the social functions of early language (e.g. *see* Grieve and Hoogenraad, 1979; Halliday, 1975; Ryan, 1974), and on the interactive nature of children's comprehension (e.g. Hoogenraad et al., 1978).

Thus the child knows that when he is asked to do or say something, it is appropriate to make a response, in order to fulfil the social/communicative demands of the situation. But this still leaves us with a puzzle. Namely, why does the child respond in the ways that he does – adapting the language, making use of non-linguistic biases, guessing, inventing, constructing or whatever – rather than saying that he is uncertain, that he does not know, asking for clarification, and so on?

One possibility is that the child does not have available the social skills and the verbal means of expression which enable requests for clarification of what the speaker has said. Here, presumably, the child appreciates his lack of understanding of what the speaker has said, but he is unskilled in handling the social aspects of interrogating the interrogator, and lacks the verbal devices ('Could you explain. . . ?', 'Do you mean. . . ?', 'Do you want me to. . . ?', etc.) which will achieve this end.

However, there is another possibility that deserves to be considered. Namely, what does the child construe these tasks to be? If he appreciates that before carrying out an instruction or answering a question, it is incumbent on the hearer to make sure that he knows what the speaker's instruction or question is intended to mean, then the child's lack of requests for clarification of meaning is surprising. But if the child construes the task as one in which what the speaker says is intended to be perspicuous, and to have a meaning transparent to the child, then his attempt to get on with making what sense he can of the adult's questions or instructions itself makes sense. Thus if the child construes his task to be the location, or identification, of the adult's intended meaning, a meaning moreover that the adult intends to be transparent to the child, then his lack of requests for clarification are not so surprising, and the child's making what sense he can of the situation may illustrate what, to the child, is a mundane activity.

During the course of language development, much of what is said to the child cannot, by definition, be clear to him — he is still engaged in acquiring the language. We know that while requests for clarification of meaning are occasionally appropriate in adult discourse (e.g. in philosophical discussions, academic debates, university tutorials, etc.), in normal circumstances they are not. People who make a nuisance of themselves by constantly asking for meanings to be clarified in everyday discourse are disapproved of. Trying to communicate with them is something of an ordeal, and such pedants, as we call them, are best avoided. Now just as constant requests for clarification of meaning can be highly disruptive of adult discourse, perhaps communication with children could not get off the ground if the child constantly disclaimed his lack of understanding (supposing that he could), for in the early stages the child lacks understanding of what is said to him most of the time. To this we need to add the obvious constraint that, at the time of early language development, when lack of under- standing is highly prevalent, the child simply does not have much expressive language at his command. So he has great difficulty in conveying to us his gaps in understanding, even when he wants to. Thus it may prove useful to consider one aspect of language development as consisting of a process whereby the child comes to understand, better and better, more and more of what is said to him. In the meantime, the child gets on with making what sense he can of what is said to him.

Clearly, a great deal more work needs to be done on identifying the implications of the fact that normal children typically respond in the face of communicative difficulties. However that is for the future. But before we conclude, it may be useful to offer some remarks on the possible relevance of this work with normal children, to those interested in the communication difficulties of the retarded.

Those experienced in working with the retarded will have noticed a striking difference between what normal and retarded children do when faced with communicative difficulties. As we have seen, normal children typically respond. But we know that retarded children typically do not. Having made some proposals as to why normal children behave as they do, i.e. respond, can we now briefly consider why retarded children behave as they do, i.e. fail to respond?

The difficulty with this question is that there is probably no simple answer. We know that retarded children do not understand much of what is said to them, the language at their receptive and expressive command being typically limited. Thus they are unlikely to possess the social skills and verbal devices required to turn the interrogative tables cn the speaker. However, by themselves, these factors do not account for the retarded child's typical failure to respond for, as suggested above, the normal child may also encounter such limitations. Thus it may prove useful to inquire why the retarded child fails to do what the normal child does in such circumstances. Is it that the retarded child does not bring to bear on the situation the sorts of resources that the normal child employs? For example, do retarded children employ non-linguistic biases? Are they able to adapt the language of questions? Can they construct answers by adding to the context elements additional to those already given? Do they know that when all else fails, guess? Or is it that retarded children fail to appreciate their communicative role – when asked to do or say something, it is appropriate to respond? Or is it that the fault lies as much with us as with the retarded child? If the child does appreciate what is communicatively appropriate, how often is he given a chance to respond? Just as it is often easier and quicker for caretaking personnel to feed and dress retarded individuals rather than letting them (or teaching them to) do so for themselves, so it may be easier for the retarded individual's interlocutors to plug the gaps that arise in conversational interchanges (while the retarded individual is trying to muster a response) with an excess of repetitions, 'prompts' and similar devices (see Buckhalt et al., 1978; Crystal, 1976).

Although answers to such questions are not at present available, the questions at least enjoy the merit of being empirical. And they provide an indication of what needs to be examined in a systematic consideration of why retarded children typically fail to respond when faced with communication difficulties.

References

Behan B. (1963) *Hold Your Hour and Have Another*. London, Hutchinson.

Brown R. (1965) *Social Psychology*. New York, Macmillan.

Bruner J. S. (1978) The role of dialogue in language acquisition. In: Sinclair A., Jarvella R. J. and Levelt W. J. M. (ed.) *The Child's Conception of Language*. Berlin, Springer Verlag, pp. 241–256.

Buckhalt J. A., Rutherford R. B. and Goldberg K. E. (1978) Verbal and nonverbal interaction of mothers with their Down's syndrome and nonretarded infants. *Am. J. Ment. Defic.* **82,** 337–343.

Carey S. (1978) Less never means more. In: Campbell R. N. and Smith P. T. (ed.) *Recent Advances in the Psychology of Language. Vol. 1. Language development and mother–child interaction*. London, Plenum Press, pp. 109–132.

Chomsky C. S. (1969) *The Acquisition of Syntax in Children from 5 to 10*. Cambridge, Mass., MIT Press.

Chomsky N. (1965) *Aspects of the Theory of Syntax*. Cambridge, Mass., MIT Press.

Chukovsky K. (1963) *From Two to Five*. Berkeley, Ca., University of California Press.

Clark E. V. (1973) What's in a word? On the child's acquisition of semantics in his first language. In: Moore T. E. (ed.) *Cognitive Development and the Acquisition of Language.* New York, Academic Press, pp. 65–110.

Clark H. H. (1970) The primitive nature of children's relational concepts. In: Hayes J. R. (ed.) *Cognition and the Development of Language.* New York, Wiley, pp. 269–278.

Crystal D. (1976) *Child Language, Learning and Linguistics.* London, Arnold.

Donaldson M. and Balfour G. (1968) Less is more: a study of language comprehension in children. *Br. J. Psychol.* **59,** 461–471.

Garton A. and Grieve R. (1980) On the young child's comparison of complete and incomplete sets. (Forthcoming.)

Gelman R. (1978) Cognitive development. *Ann. Rev. Psychol.* **29,** 297–332.

Greenfield P. M. (1973) Who is 'Dada'? Some aspects of the semantic and phonological development of a child's first words. *Lang. Speech* **16,** 34–43.

Grieve R. and Garton A. (1980) On the young child's comparison of sets. (Forthcoming.)

Grieve R. and Hoogenraad R. M. (1979) First words. In: Fletcher P. and Garman M. (ed.) *Language Acquisition.* London, Cambridge University Press, pp. 93–104.

Grieve R. and Hoogenraad R. M. (1976) On using language if you don't have much. In: Wales R. J. and Walker E. C. T. (ed.) *New Approaches to Language Mechanisms.* Amsterdam, North Holland, pp. 1–28.

Grieve R. and Stanley S. (1980) Less obscure? Pragmatics and 3–4 year children's semantics. (Forthcoming.)

Halliday M. A. K. (1975) *Learning How to Mean.* London, Arnold.

Holland V. M. and Palermo D. S. (1975) On learning less: language and cognitive development. *Child Dev.* **46,** 437–443.

Hoogenraad R. M., Grieve R., Baldwin P. et al. (1978) Comprehension as an interactive process. In: Campbell R. N. and Smith P. (ed.) *Recent Advances in the Psychology of Language. Vol. 1. Language development and mother–child interaction.* London, Plenum Press, pp. 163–186.

Hughes M. and Grieve R. (1980) On asking children bizarre questions. *First Language.* *(In press.)*

Inhelder B. and Piaget J. (1964) *The Early Growth of Logic in the Child: Classification and Seriation.* London, Routledge & Kegan Paul.

Kavanaugh R. D. (1976) On the synonymity of more and less: comments on a methodology. *Child Dev.* **47,** 885–887.

Lenneberg E. H. (1967) *Biological Foundations of Language.* New York, Wiley.

McGarrigle J., Grieve R. and Hughes M. (1978) Interpreting inclusion. A contribution to the study of the child's cognitive and linguistic development. *J. Exp. Child Psychol.* **26,** 528–550.

McNeill D. (1970) *The Acquisition of Language.* New York, Harper and Row.

Palermo D. S. (1973) More about less: a study in language comprehension. *J. Verb. Learn. Verb. Behav.* **12,** 211–221.

Palermo D. S. (1974) Still more about the comprehension of less. *Dev. Psychol.* **10,** 827–829.

Palermo D. and Molfese D. (1972) Language acquisition from age five onward. *Psychol. Bull.* **78,** 409–428.

Piaget J. and Inhelder B. (1969) *The Psychology of the Child.* London, Routledge & Kegan Paul.

Piaget J. and Szeminska A. (1952) *The Child's Conception of Number.* London, Routledge & Kegan Paul.

Richards M. M. (1979) Sorting out what's in a word and what's not: evaluating Clark's semantic features acquisition theory. *J. Exp. Child Psychol.* **27,** 1–47.

Rommetveit R. (1968) *Words, Meanings and Messages.* New York, Academic Press.

Ryan J. (1974) Early language development: towards a communicational analysis. In: Richards M. P. M. (ed.) *The Integration of the Child into a Social World*. London, Cambridge University Press, pp. 185–213.

Ryle G. (1949) *Concept of Mind*. London, Hutchinson.

Townsend D. J. (1976) Do children interpret marked comparative adjectives as their opposites? *J. Child Lang.* **3**, 385–396.

Trehub S. and Abramovitch R. (1978) Less is not more: further observations of non-linguistic strategies. *J. Exp. Child Psychol.* **25**, 160–167.

Trevarthen C. (1974) Conversations with a two-month old. *New Scientist* **62**, 230–235.

Wales R. J., Garman M. A. G. and Griffiths P. D. (1976) More or less the same: a markedly different view of children's comparative judgements in three cultures. In: Wales R. J. and Walker E. C. T. (ed.) *New Approaches to Language Mechanisms*. Amsterdam, North Holland, pp. 29–53.

Wannemacher J. T. and Ryan M. L. (1978) Less is not more: a study of children's comprehension of less in various task contexts. *Child Dev.* **49**, 660–668.

Weiner S. L. (1974) On the development of more and less. *J. Exp. Child Psychol.* **17**, 271–287.

Chapter Five

Clinical Presentations of Retarded Language

William Fraser

Introduction

The aim of this chapter is to show the range of communication disorders which the mentally handicapped display, and the difficulty in disentangling problems in order to recommend appropriate remedial measures. Diverse sources of evidence will be referred to, namely experimental findings, case study material and informal observations.

It is not the purpose of this chapter, or this book, to detail exhaustively every approach to the study of communication in the mentally handicapped. Several compendiums (e.g. Lenneberg and Lenneberg, 1975; Schiefelbusch and Lloyd, 1974) have done this with considerable success.

If the problem were simply slowed pace of development and simplified vocabulary, a chapter by a clinician would be unnecessary. However, emotional problems, deafness, and neurological disorders such as epilepsy are commonly superimposed. Language development is often patchy, disproportionately poor or disproportionately good compared with other aspects of intellectual development. The consequences may be bizarre: an 8-year-old epileptic child of IQ 50 with elegant syntax and an old-fashioned, extensive vocabulary, has a quaint habit of nodding his head like a sage, an exasperating tendency to punctate every discourse, irrelevantly, with the question 'Have you got a Volvo?' and, most disturbingly, a ghostly delayed echolalia – 'Miss Brodie died last night'.

The practitioner has to combine the developmental approach with cognitive and neurological approaches, and has to know where to start.

The child's speech may be (as above) misleadingly good, or misleadingly poor. There is much more to language than simply considering the child's speech or linguistic performance. We have to consider his intuitions about his language, for his competence more usually exceeds his performance. Just because a mentally retarded child does not produce good English, it does not mean necessarily that his linguistic knowledge is deficient. Competence is the set of principles a person must have to be able to communicate in a language; performance is the translation of this knowledge into action. Competence means much more than speaking. We have to differentiate between comprehending language, producing language and a total communication situation in which language is only one aspect. As Mittler (1976) has indicated, research has been largely concerned with children's expression rather than with children's understanding. Comprehension logically precedes production, and communicative competence consists of much more than speaking clearly. Mittler has also pointed out the need for more research on children's receptive abilities and, with his colleagues Wheldall (1976) and Swann (1976), has shown that many severely retarded children have not the most basic level of verbal comprehension.

How can one make the problem manageable, when we have to deal with developmental aspects, clinical and sociolinguistic aspects together; when concepts such as intelligence quotients are rendered meaningless by subjects being more than 3 standard deviations below average; when we have to consider comprehension and production and communicative competence; and have to remember that language is environmentally sensitive? The strategy of studying coding modes across several diagnostic subgroups instead of looking at one clinical group (O'Connor and Hermelin, 1974; O'Connor, 1975) goes part of the way to simplifying the problem, but there is no escape from its complexity.

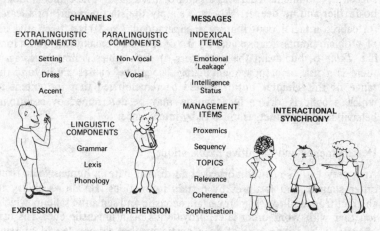

Fig. 10. Where communication can break down.

Fig. 10 shows some of the points in interaction where communication fails. The illustration (a guide list of communicative behaviours) should not mislead one into thinking that language consists of compartments and categories. It is a holistic system.

The person chooses a 'channel' e.g. verbal, and partly voluntarily, partly not, supplements it by infusion with intonation, and with non-vocal gestures. He produces various types of 'messages' for the listener; not simply the topic which the speaker wishes to communicate, but other messages about himself, or about the importance of what he is trying to say, and even aspects about himself, or the topic, which he is trying to conceal. As regards messages to help handle the interchange (interactional management), the listener must be able to understand the social ratifications surrounding the interchange, to know when to pause and when to break in; he must be able to distinguish between what is being said and what is being meant. He must be able to understand non-verbal signalling and decode the complex, grammatical structures involved in the utterances. He must be able to understand certain 'indexical' features about the speaker, such as the speaker's position, status, whether he is from a different culture or is of a different chronological or mental age. The handicapped child may not recognize the importance of some topics in relation to his own views and preferences; like a puppy out on a training exercise, he is often out for fun and, as Berry and Marshall (1978) have pointed out spends a great deal of time 'flitting about' and, so Reynell (1969) considers, can only be usefully motivated by an adult ready to facilitate, direct and listen. Problems arise at all these points in the communicative interchange for the mentally handicapped, and most strikingly perhaps in interactional management.

Mental retardation used to be 'dismissed' as a cause of slow or absent speech development. That was an end of the matter. The clinician looked no further and no deeper. Now it is simply the starting point for a search for causes, integral, contributory or superadded. *Fig.* 10 is a descriptive list of problem points. An explanatory list of causes of breakdown would look like *Table* 6, but again the usefulness of such tables is limited, as again there is a risk of compartmentalizing. 'Cognitive' causes are beyond the range of this chapter but it should be remembered that the extent to which a child is 'driven by language' may be determined by emotional behaviour and conduct, as much as by intelligence.

Developmental and Cognitive Explanations

At a very early stage the normal child discriminates a human voice from other sounds, and is upset by certain intonations. He shows ability to abstract from auditory signals certain acoustic and semantic salients which, together with word order later, provide his main linguistic cues. His first impression of language is of an acoustic medley almost devoid of regularities. He combines gross motor gestures with intonation and stress. For the mentally handicapped this mastery is constrained by physical, perceptual and environmental factors, as well as by cognitive ones.

The normal child initially makes greater progress in acoustic coding than he does in the relationship of words to meaning. Language is a complex, skilled behaviour made up of several subskills of syntax, morphology and phonology, each of which requires feedback and eventual automatization. Overlearning is necessary, and the mentally handicapped child gets little opportunity for this. He gets less opportunity to learn the grammatical forms, propositional forms and prosodic forms. He gets even fewer stabs at 'illocutionary phenomena' (statements and brief requests for actions). He gets little chance to use 'frozen forms' such as 'What's that?', 'What does that mean?', although he hears them often.

Reynell (1969) has shown that conceptual integration and language proper begin at around 18 months. The mentally handicapped should start programmes at a much younger mental age than when educationalists normally intervene. As O'Connor (1975) has conjectured, the primary signalling system comes before the secondary signalling system, and one

Table 6. Common Causes of Communication Failure.

Cognitive	Neuropathological
Attention deficit	Deafness
Discrimination deficit	Dysarthria
	Dysrhythmia
Developmental	Developmental speech disorders
	Acquired dysphasia
Inertia or	Diffuse genetic and acquired brain damage
Arrest	Autism

Environmental deficits, Social deprivation, Social status.

hemisphere has virtually developed a conceptual system before the other system of coding, the linguistic one, is consolidated. The mentally handicapped child has to be helped to catch up with his second signalling system, his language coding. The cognitive deficits described by O'Connor and Hermelin (1963) in the severely subnormal apply in kind, but to a lesser degree, in the mildly handicapped. The cognitive deficit is in acquisition due to an inability to single out the relevant features from a stimulus display. Verbal coding is not spontaneous. A child does not abandon one model of coding every time he encounters another model or another language form. The mentally handicapped child has to get sufficient experience in the displacing of things in space and the permanence of objects before he can begin language proper.

Language development correlates only moderately with intelligence. Grammar has been considered to have an 'innate' component. O'Connor and Hermelin (1963) emphasized that the failure of the severely handicapped to develop adequate speech was not so much because they were unable to understand grammar, but rather because they did not know many words. Babbling does not seem to be a 'learned' behaviour and, like walking, is less susceptible to intellectual retardation. It is only at the end of the babbling stage that Down's infants seem to fall behind in their vocalizations (Dodd, 1972). There are other explanations for this besides 'innateness'. During the first 8 months, the 'honeymoon phase'

Cunningham, 1979), the Down's infant gets a pretty normal social language experience from his mother.

Lenneberg's (1967) important conclusion in a 3-year follow-up study on non-institutionalized Down's anomalies was that the stages of language development significantly related to *chronological age* and to the periods of motor milestones, rather than to intelligence quotients. This conclusion has been the subject of much dispute. The development of grammatical structures starts with negations; children with mean utterance length of less than 2 do not understand questions, and have up to four different concepts of the negative. In the early stage 'no' means something that does not exist, in the next stage something that is false as well as something that is not existing, the next reproval or rejection as well as false and not there, and in the last stage, contrast, e.g. 'this' not 'that'. So this is a major area of concern — how much does the mentally handicapped child understand prohibitions and probations? The acquisition of transformations continues much later in childhood. Is language mainly mental age (MA) or chronological age (CA) related?

Lackner's (1968) 'slow motion perspective' shows that in such a matter as sentence length, for example, although the pattern of development is similar, normal children tend to produce longer sentences than subnormal children of matched mental age. He produced examples comparing mentally handicapped children with gifted children. Up to the age of 4 years, the mentally handicapped child of like mental age produced sentences of similar length, but beyond this age they were outstripped by the gifted children. He also made a comparison of sentence types, showing that questions first occurred at the mental age of 2 years 3 months, but that negative questions did not occur until nearly 3 years and the passive not until 3 years 3 months. Negative passives based on sentence production occurred in the mildly mentally handicapped children only at a mental age of nearly 9 years. As with normal children, sentence repetition tests showed that the subnormal, below certain mental ages, could not repeat sentences involving certain complex transformations, but uttered a structurally simpler form of such sentences.

The development of syntactic structures seems largely to follow the development of cognitive structures, i.e. mental age. The acquisition of language seems dependent on mental age, but there seems to be, as Lenneberg (1967) and Cromer (1974) suggest, crucial milestones at certain chronological ages which the adolescent person of low mental age may pass without the skill emerging. The subnormal show two main distortions of language development, which might be called 'slowing and arrest' on the one hand, and 'inertia' on the other. In the first case, the level of development of language follows that of logic, and this is both slowed and prematurely terminated in many instances. The inertia of language consists of difficulty in verbal encoding. Cromer has shown that at 6½ years some children still cannot cope with the 'easy to bite' object rule strategy, and that mentally handicapped children may 'miss the boat' for this ability because they reach the end of their chronological language development period or 'critical period'.

Swann and Mittler (1976) have demonstrated that the proportion of mentally handicapped children who have no speech does not get smaller between 6 and 16 years. Lovell and Bradbury (1967) using Berko's (1958) technique have found that the ability of mildly subnormal children to inflect, derive and analyse compound words improves little between 8 and 15 years. Furthermore, it seems that such children are less able to generalize a rule and transfer it to new words. Bradbury and Lunzer (1972) equated the groups for MA rather than CA, and reckoned that the induction of grammatical rules was 'not independent of intelligence'. Layton and Sharifi (1979) found the language of Down's children to be related to MA.

Certainly subnormal children do show specific retardation in some aspects of language, e.g. fringe vocabulary and transformations. They also show both complete and incomplete sentence forms. Normals do not (Chipman, 1980). The severely retarded child is slower to abandon incorrect sentences and to learn new forms, largely because he does not test his language against his environment, not seeing the point of doing so. Language has one noteworthy non-communicative function, a concept forming function, in which the child develops a set of habitual tendencies to notice certain details and attributes of objects, and becomes able to label things in a pragmatic, maximally useful way; a teddy is a nice textural feeling, rather than the name of a toy. This categorization will modify and expand as the child gets older. The mentally handicapped lag in the precision of their meaning systems. Words will elicit a number of associated networks in the handicapped, but the 'verbal factor', the ability of the mentally handicapped child to express ideas in terms of sounds (vocal encoding), is highly correlated with intelligence, as compared with grammar. We shall return to this link of the verbal factor with intelligence (MA/CA), and of grammar with development (MA), which has the possible complicating factor of an innate diary of 'deadlines' for the appearance of certain language behaviours (CA). Thus, as regards the innate theory of language, the clinician senses there is some substance; chronological age is important; aspects of dialogue seem inbuilt. It is noticeable that staff take account of both mental age and chronological age when they commonly address the severely mentally handicapped. They 'baby talk' mentally handicapped children (until adolescence), simplifying and injecting emotional warmth and high emphasis. With severely handicapped adults they drop the affectionate 'motherese' but keep the simplifications and the emphasis. (Yet I know that profoundly handicapped young adults love warm sounds whispered at mother distance.)

In everyday practice mental age is the overwhelming factor in retarded children's linguistic performance. Due to their retarded mental age, their linguistic failures stem right back from inattentiveness in turn-taking as an infant, and defective social learning. A mongol does not have a defective language device; given the patient direction of a Helen Keller's tutor it is not unusual for Down's children to reach the competence of S – (*see* frontispiece).

This verbal interplay of social, cognitive and maturation factors is mirrored in the non-verbal behaviour of mentally handicapped persons. The descriptive list (p. 104) could highlight many points where their non-verbal signalling is engagingly (or more commonly disengagingly) droll. Admittedly, the ability of the handicapped child to express ideas in terms of gestures is, in many mental handicap syndromes, e.g. Down's anomaly, superior to vocal encoding. Nevertheless, the mentally handicapped do signal poorly. Their problems with non-verbal communication are complicated by much non-verbal communication being 'more or less' value judgements (analogue systems) rather than yes/no (digital systems) and, moreover, gestures are only fleetingly repeated and not accompanied by the redundancy found in speech. The mentally handicapped child laughs more than the normal child. Kellett (1976) has shown that only 20 per cent of severely mentally retarded children use gesture to augment inadequate language, 18 per cent use gesture alone in order to communicate and 12 per cent prefer gesture to speech (and gesture is often crude pulling and pointing). Early childhood autistics show gaze avoidance (at least in the early years), which really means gazing extremely fleetingly at people. The mentally handicapped often fail to monitor the listener's expressions. Young normal children certainly do not, and Wheldall (1976) considers that few severely retarded children can utilize non-verbal signals. Recognition of affective facial signals develops with age; at 6–7 years children recognize pain, 7 years anger, 9–10 years fear and horror, 11 years surprise, and at 14 years contempt. Berry and Marshall (1978) have shown that the presence of an adult facilitates some verbal gestures. A mildly mentally handicapped adult often assumes positions of low status by his posture and his downward rotated head and downcast eyes. This social, environmental aspect of language is developed by Leudar in Chapter 6.

Medical 'Explanations' – Labels we can Usefully Apply

Many neuropathological classifications oversimplify the problem by regarding mental handicap as an exclusive category of speech disorder, a cause of siow speech development. An 'explanatory' classification, taking out 'mental deficiency' as a cause, still looks like *Table* 6. The mentally handicapped are a very heterogeneous group. It is difficult (apart from Down's syndrome) to get sufficient numbers together to constitute a subgroup, and generalizations about mental handicap from Down's syndrome is unwise. There are overlapping diagnoses; a mentally handicapped child may be psychiatrically ill in addition to having a neuropathological deficit. The strategy O'Connor (1975) uses is to study a single psychological process across many diagnostic groups including the deaf, the blind and the subnormal. In mental handicap, neuropathology and psychopathology do not correspond, but the study of discrete diagnostic groups will continue to shed light on mental handicap.

The mentally handicapped person might suffer simultaneously from several of the conditions in *Table* 6. Is the child deaf or retarded, autistic, dysphasic or all four? There is a high incidence of deafness in the mentally handicapped due to congenital ear anomalies, low resistance to infection and chronic catarrh causing high-frequency deafness. The profoundly deaf child simply lacks speech; he shows a poorly developed prattle, he does not show the echolalic stage, he does not use words. If he has partial hearing his speech may lack normal prosody. A deaf child uses gesture generously, even scintillatingly. A retarded child, on the other hand, will vocalize for pleasure, but will not be so effective with gesture; a child with a specific language disability is likely to produce jargon, but imitates poorly the speech of others. An autistic child does not improvize sounds, nor use sounds normally for enjoyment, and has particularly poor gesture. A mentally handicapped child who is not autistic approximates most of the normal prosodic patterns of speech. In the mentally handicapped one cannot always clearly differentiate such categories as deafness, dysphasia, auditory agnosia or autism. Inability to produce speech, but ability to write or to gesture indicate apraxia; general cross modality difficulties indicate aphasia. Ability to imitate sounds, but inability to produce sounds or names, indicate aphasia rather than agnosia.

A cooperative child should be asked to carry out movements of the lips and tongue without speech, then to produce sounds involving similar movements; if the movements can be accomplished without speech, dysarthria can be ruled out. Dysarthria means impairment of motor control, faulty innervation of speech musculature or structural abnormality of the organs of articulation. This includes effects of tongue thrust in Down's anomaly; cleft palate with nasal escape in the syndromes of the first arch (MacKenzie, 1966) (these syndromes will also foster secondary speech disorders due to hearing loss which is commonly caused by middle ear infection); palatal disproportion syndrome (Ingram, 1969), where the palate appears to be functioning normally but there is nasal escape, tongue thrust and lisping; and choanal atresia and adenitis. In such conditions there is likely to be a history of feeding difficulties.

Physiologically speaking, speech is a group of overlaid functions, so it is not surprising that multiply disabled people have multiple speech distortions. In the case of the mentally retarded, Murphy (1976) emphasizes three components of listening; most retarded children have restricted *attention span*, hence their modified *listening skills.* Upper respiratory infections result in fluctuations in hearing. Retarded children have modified *cognitive skills* and less ability to extract the salient features of signals from the environment. Darley (1974) has made the case for distinguishing dyspraxias, on the grounds that distinctly different therapy is required (viz. direct exercises in articulation), from dysphasias, where language stimulation is required. Dyspraxia is characterized by absence of paralysis of speech musculature, phonetic errors are inconsistent, poor imitation is accompanied by awareness of error, prosody is disturbed and stuttering can occur. Developmental dyspraxia is associated with X-linked mental retardation (Renpenning syndrome) (McLaughlin and Kriezsman, 1980).

Dysrhythmia (stammer, blocking, cluttering), which is due to failure of the synchronization of respiratory and articulory movements during speech, is common in many mental handicap syndromes, particularly where there is a concomitant athetoid cerebral palsy. A Down's male is more likely to stutter than a Down's female. Disorders of voicing, usually due to laryngeal disorders (dysphonia), are found characteristically in cretinism.

The developmental speech disorder syndromes (DSDS) (Ingram, 1969), which occur in children who are otherwise healthy and without demonstrable abnormalities of structure or function of speech organs, can be superimposed on mental retardation (as Case 1 demonstrates). They are commoner in males. There is often a family history of language disorder and the suggestion of brain damage. The mildly affected (articulation only) used to be called 'dyslalic', and do not prove to be a differential diagnosis for mental defect, but the moderate DSDS (developmental expressive dysphasia) and severe DSDS (developmental receptive dysphasia) may be mistaken for mental defect. Very severe DSDS (auditory agnosia, non-comprehension of sounds often called 'central deafness') can be diagnosed as deaf or mentally handicapped. They fail to recognize speech sounds until they are over 3 years. Their gestures are not nearly as sophisticated as those of the deaf child.

There are of course children who do suffer late brain damage and, thus, acquired dysphasia. These children commonly reacquire speech very rapidly, unlike dysphasic adults. This appears to be particularly rapid in the 4–7-year age group, and after 7 years acquired dysphasia seems to be permanent. Cases 2 and 3 illustrate such recovery in the 4–7 age group.

Case 1 – Male, age 17 years.
His birth was normal, his first words spoken at 2½–3 years, no sentences till 5 years. In special class from 7 years. He behaved in a disturbed and aggressive manner and spoke rapidly and incoherently, muttering much of the time. Full scale IQ 86. His main deficit seemed to be in processing, understanding and using language. On the Stanford–Binet Memory for Sentence Test (the Binet 'Fall in the Mud' story), he could not manage more than ten words. His descriptive level of expression was equal to that of a person of IQ 45–55. He was irritated when unable to find the name of words, a stammer was noted when he became anxious, and he would also clutter his speech. In reading, difficult words were either guessed or slurred over in order to rush on to the next section. With regard to his receptive ability he could recognize objects, pictures, colours and forms. He confused several words. His auditory verbal

comprehension was good for sentences, but as regards silent reading comprehension of paragraphs, he could answer only one out of three sentences correctly. Every time a question was asked, he verbally repeated it, indicating weak receptive ability. He could not repeat the alphabet through until he succeeded in reading the therapist's copy upside down. In naming he confused shoulder for elbow and knee for ankle. On oral reading he slurred words he did not know, or said he did not know. He used telegrammatic forms of words and sentences. When unable to find a word he would gesture, for example, when saying 'good-bye', touch his palm and show it to the other person as an indication he wished to shake his hand. He buffooned a great deal showing he was aware of his mild receptive dysphasia and trying to compensate for it by repeating much of what was said to him or by prompting himself with gesture. The 'clutter' was partly a minimal clonic stammer, often present in receptive asphasia.

Case 2 – K. W. age 4 years.
This little boy fell whilst holding a pencil in his mouth. Then he would not eat his dinner. His mother noticed that his speech was nasal and slurred. He woke in the night crying, and his parents found that he had a right-sided paralysis, and was mute. It was later discovered that the pencil had penetrated his palate posteriorly and possibly entered the internal carotid artery. Two days later he went to theatre where a left carotid arteriectomy and thrombectomy were performed. Postoperative recovery was good but the right hemiplegia persisted. He did not attempt to speak for 7 days after the injury although he obeyed commands. Thereafter, although he continued to have a marked right-sided hemiplegia and ignore his right hand and use his left, his speech progressed rapidly. He remained dysarthric. Tongue movement improved quickly but all consonants remained nasal. His vowels were clear and accurate. Within 3 months he was again using two- and three-word sentences but omitting articles, conjunctions and pronouns, and was able to carry out two-tier commands. Dichotic listening showed right hemisphere preference. His verbal comprehension had recovered to an age level of 4 and his expressive language to an age level of 3 years by 5 months after the incident.

Case 3 – V. J. age 7½ years.
V. was a quiet child prior to her illness, enthusiastic about her reading at school. At the age of 6 she had a left cortical vein thrombosis, probably secondary to septicaemia from pneumococcal pneumonia. This caused an obvious right-sided hemiparesis and an aphasia. She recovered single words 2 months later. At 3 months she was tested and found to have a nominal dysphasia and moderate receptive aphasia. Her expression was limited to single words, mainly nouns. After 5 months she was beginning to manage again some two-word utterances. At 6 months her Peabody Picture Vocabulary Test reception showed the level of a 3·6-year-old child and her Reynell Test 2·4 years production, 3·8 years comprehension. Her audiogram was normal. She did occasionally use jargon. Her EEG showed absence of a normal cortical activity in the damaged area. A CAT scan showed marked damage to her dominant lobe in the temporal region. One year later her picture vocabulary was at a 4·7-year-old level and on Renfrew Word Finding Vocabulary she functioned at 3·7 years. Her IQ on Stanford–Binet was 71 and on the Snijder Oomen Non-Verbal Intelligance Test 95. Though she had previously been right-handed she was now drawing with her left hand, but was drawing in the air with her right hand in a coarse manner also. She still showed a very minimal right-sided residual hemiparesis and clumsiness with poor proprioception. Dichotic listening showed a very pronounced right hemispheric preference.

Both cases 2 and 3 show that recovery of speech after extensive cortical damage is possible. Whether this is due to recovery on the damaged side or to 'switching over' is more difficult to determine. It is probably partly both. In these cases the extent of the damage, demonstrated both neurologically and electrically, makes it unlikely that much hemispheric 'language localized' area was left operating in either child on their dominant side, and dichotic listening further confirmed this. The children however have not shown full recovery, as is sometimes stated to happen in the literature, and receptive aphasia in one case was accompanied by jargon, which is said not to happen in young acquired aphasics.

Hypoxia, such as described above, in acquired dysphasic children may have serious results, but to premature infants it is catastrophic. Following hypoxia in premature infants, large structural damage, e.g. to the caudate nucleus, will usually have occurred. Hypoxia to the full-term infant may only affect the 'watershed' areas of blood supply which include language, memory and writing. Even within those who have global brain disorder there are individual and group differences and characteristic patterns. There are mentally handicapped children whose social skills are commonly far in advance of their linguistic competence, e.g. Down's, and conversely mentally handicapped children whose ignorance of certain social rules prevents them using properly their often quite adequate syntax and phonology, e.g. hydrocephalus.

There is, moreover, a close relationship between the severe social and behavioural abnormalities characteristic of childhood psychosis and 'central' dysphasic children, both lacking 'inner language' (Wing, 1975).

Three conditions — more accurately one clinical category, one clinical syndrome and one group of behaviours (Down's, hydrocephalus and the childhood psychoses) — will be given closer examination because of the insights they provide into the communication problems of the mentally handicapped.

DOWN'S ANOMALY

Down's children fail to maintain the early promise of the first year in the second and third year. At the end of the Down's babbling stage, communication falls behind (Dodd, 1972). Language development in Down's syndrome is however very variable, the appearance of the first words ranging from 12 months to 6 years. Down's syndrome children develop language functions in the same sequence as ordinary children, although with an increasing space between major developmental landmarks. Whether the comparative deterioration in Down's performance is due to limited mental potential or to neurohumoral factors (Murdoch, 1980), is as yet undetermined. Neuroendocrines may be necessary to switch on neural pathways, prime neural mechanisms and keep the developmental clock on time.

The language abilities of Down's syndrome children in some respects differ from those in other retarded groups. Kirk and Kirk (1971) claimed on the Illinois Test of Psycholinguistic Abilities that a distinctive 'Down's language profile' had been established, in which the Down's child's expression of ideas in terms of gestures (motor encoding), as compared with his verbal description of objects (vocal encoding), was superior. Evans (1977) studied 101 Down's syndrome persons from 8–31 years of age on a battery of language tests including the Illinois Test of Psycholinguistic Ability, looking particularly for age effects and a Down's language profile. A factor analysis revealed a general verbal factor (highly loaded on intelligence), a disfluent speech factor (loaded on intelligibility) and a structure of speech factor (a grammar factor which might be conjectured to have an 'innate' component). Dodd (1974) compared the phonological rules of normal and Down's syndrome children, and found that Down's syndrome children used the same twenty-three phonological rules as normal children, but did so inconsistently. Many of their errors could not be accounted for by any phonological rules, e.g. repetition of one syllable of a word 'meta meta mato' for 'tomato', or squashing of words so that only vowels were uttered, e.g. 'e e' for 'elephant', the deletion of consonant clusters. Non-Down's syndrome severely subnormals performed like age-matched children, following the rules. Down's errors cannot be explained as due to the lack of ability to form these sounds – they imitate well, or rather they make fewer errors in imitation on their second trial. Their poor performance may be due to a failure of long-term psychomotor programmes. Children with Down's syndrome have an abnormally small cerebellum, which is particularly important in motor performance and learning (Crome and Stern, 1967). Their inconsistency, perseveration and gross reduction of words may be directly due to this anatomical abnormality.

Anatomical differences also largely explain the typical weak, hoarse, low-pitched voice evident from early infancy.The Down's infant's upper articulatory aperturȩ is very tight and this gives a special fricative quality, and the narrow opening of the lips contrast with the normal wide 'bawling' shape of a normal infant when crying.

Protrusion of the tongue does not seem due to enlargement. Ardran et al. (1972) radiographically examined 8 Down's children's tongues relative to their mouth cavity. In none was the tongue enlarged, but all had enlarged adenoids and tonsils or evidence of such, and overbiting of the mandible, suggesting that the gaping mouth and protrusion of the tongue seemed to relate to the need to provide an airway, and that removal of obstruction such as adenoids, pharyngeal tonsils and the lingual tonsil would help many to close lips, favour jaw development and also improve the voice. Early detection of exudative otitis media will result in better communication (Brooks and Woolley, 1972).

Young Down's syndrome children are largely limited to the here-and-now aspects of their world. As they mature they develop some ability to perceive past and future. While maturational and intellectual factors cannot be manipulated, the environment can. Down's speech continues to improve after 12 years of age (the end of the so-called 'critical language learning' period). Young Down's syndrome adults of 16 years plus have a better overall verbal ability than Down's syndrome 8–16-year-olds (Evans, 1977). The older Down's is more likely to be in an environment of good speech models. In contrast, the mother of a Down's child may provide a less complex and more controlling type of speech than the mother of a normal child. This is more a response to Down's low expressive language level than maternal inhibition due to the knowledge that the child has Down's syndrome. It is too early to say that the speech of mothers of Down's children is, as a group, functionally inappropriate (for the controversy, *see* Marshall et al., 1973; Rondal, 1977; Gutman and Rondal, 1979). It is also rather misleading to say that Down's anomalies 'underfunction' in that their language age is lower than their mental age or IQ. A Down's anomaly of IQ 60 may have had to be jollied and patiently awaited until he passes a test item. The quality of his intellectual functioning, his spontaneity, curiosity, 'vim', is not easily measured in the artificial test situation.

Chipman (1980) has commented that Down's anomalies compared with other mentally handicapped groups are among the best or the worst, linguistically. This squares with our experience.

HYDROCEPHALUS

In childhood, hydrocephalus may lead to what has been termed a 'chatterbox personality'. Unlike many mentally handicapped children whose language output may often be low, the hydrocephalic child may be observed to speak with facility, even prolixity. This facility does not persist into adulthood. In a study comparing hydrocephalic mentally handicapped adults with a control group of mentally handicapped adults without hydrocephalus (Fraser et al., 1975), on a standardized language test (the Illinois Test of Psycholinguistic Abilities) the hydrocephalic individuals did retain a better ability compared with the control group in respect of 2 of the 9 subtests (grammatical and phonological closure). But in an informal interview, the language output of the two groups was indistinguishable.

Thus, although some superior language processing capacities are retained, the hydrocephalic adult does not continue to exhibit the hyperverbal output of the hydrocephalic in childhood. This may be due to social sensitivity, the hydrocephalic adults recognizing that hyperverbality in adult discourse is socially inappropriate and is received as prolixity. Alternatively, it may be that hyperverbality is rewarded in childhood, with caretakers encouraging language output, even if it is 'chattering', in mentally handicapped children, such encouragement being gradually withdrawn as the child grows older, lest the socially acceptable chattering child become the socially unacceptable long-winded adult.

Thus again we must pay heed to the fact that language and its use typically feature for the handicapped in social situations, and that aspects of that society not only have effects, but that these effects may differ at different times in the individual's life. The possibility, that language behaviour typical of childhood subsequently changes, evolves and adapts as the child matures, must therefore be borne in mind.

THE CHILDHOOD PSYCHOSES

Autism is commonly defined as a disorder evident before 30 months of age, in which there is a profound and general failure to develop normal social relationships, together with delayed and deviant language development and the presence of ritualistic or compulsive phenomena (Rutter, 1977). Many autistic children are moderately or severely intellectually retarded. These will tend to show more resistance to change, and compulsive attachment to objects, than the smaller numbers who are of normal non-verbal intelligence. Those of normal intelligence tend to show a greater variety of rituals. Almost all show retarded language development, more so the mentally retarded ones. Very occasionally a child may have immaculate grammar and prosody, like the hydrocephalic phenomenon described above, and yet have all the other features of autism — a quaint old-fashioned child. In such cases temporal cortex seems to have been spared. There seems to be a defect of inner language (Wing, 1975), causing a marked impairment of imaginative play. Echolalia is a pronounced feature, as is pronominal inversion using 'you' for 'I' in particular. Autistic children tend to be very sensitive to noise, and although musical ability seems to be preserved, the prosody of their language output is affected. The islets of intellect, and the deficits, reflect the functions of the hemispheres; intact functions such as pure tones and visual short-term memory, memory for faces, and topography being located in the non-dominant hemisphere, whilst impaired functions such as auditory attention, auditory verbal memory and verbal reasoning are usually located in the dominant temporal hemisphere, with the left frontal region governing verbal fluency and regulating behaviour. Some 98 per cent of right-handed people have left hemisphere dominance for speech, but only about 60 per cent of left-handed people. O'Connor and Hermelin (1967) demonstrated that autistic children benefited from meaning in visual recall, but not from meaning in verbal recall. Aurnhammer-Frith (1969) further showed that although they did not benefit from sense in verbal recall, autistics benefited just as much as normals from emphasis in recall. This suggested a satisfactory superficial memory store responsible for phonological shaping of an utterance, i.e. an echo-box memory. An explanation for the autistic's deficits, based on damage to cortical areas which have a meagre or easily compromised watershed area of blood supply, does not seem sufficient for pure childhood autism where a hereditary predisposition may also apply.

Childhood psychotics are not a homogeneous group. Three obvious divisions can be made (Kolvin et al., 1971): (1) *idiopathic* – infantile psychosis (IP), early childhood autistics, born so or who become autistic soon after birth, generally apathetic towards sounds and social contact from birth; (2) *secondary* or complicated autism, in which, after a normal early childhood development, there occurs a dramatic, or insidious deterioration or arrest of abilities often associated with encephalitis and hypsarrhythmia; (3) *a late onset psychosis* which seems to be the onset of an adult-type schizophrenia (a *dementia praecocissima*) in the early or mid-school years, associated with a family history of mental illness. In such an illness language development has been normal until school age and is therefore fully developed, and the features of communication disorder are those of schizophrenia.

Schizophrenic language is quite different from autistic language. In schizophrenia language will often show intrusion of irrelevant or extraneous linguistic association. These include topic drift, and particularly semantic disturbances, semantic dispersion and semantic dissolution. Schizophrenic language is, in general, less redundant, less predictable and therefore less intelligible. There is a high frequency of the pronoun 'I'. There is a lower 'different word' count and type token ratio and the adverb–verb quotient is lower for schizophrenics than for normals. In the absence of treatment, as the disorder progresses, prosodic abnormalities appear, e.g. abnormal strangled voice and unusual pitch. Phonetic hash is not a feature and grammar only breaks down in the most deteriorated schizophrenics. At that stage, word salads, private language and neologisms are a feature, and the terminal communicative stage is that of great poverty of speech, mutism and social withdrawal.

A series of particularly illuminating studies of the language of 'nuclear', early childhood autism has been carried out by Baltaxe and Simmonds (1975), who investigated the linguistic competence of an 8-year-old autistic child by means of her bedtime soliloquies. Bedtime soliloquies were chosen because autistic children lack spontaneous daytime verbalizations, and the examples were free from situational and linguistic context intrusions, which confound echolalic autistic verbalizations during the day.

The soliloquies of the autistic subject showed no evidence of a dialogue with an interlocutor. No altercation took place (not surprisingly). Weir (1962) found that normal soliloquies were governed by a 'leitmotiv'. This was also true of the autistic child's soliloquies. The autistic subject did relate sequences phonologically, syntactically and systematically, using also processes of expansion, substitution and deletion. What was absent was attention to the internal structure of the resultant sequences; the absence of the necessary context sensitivity. The language appeared to show only surface structure operations without attention to deep structure – a mapping problem.

Baltaxe and Simmonds (1977) have shown that severely and moderately autistic children break not only grammatical rules but also situational rules, most commonly seen as a switching from an informal to a formal code. Baltaxe's classic example is worth quoting here: Q. 'Do you have a girlfriend?' Autistic adolescent: 'No, I have not met such a nice lovely young lady as yet. Where in heck is that Goddam blonde?'

When autistic children of normal or near normal intelligence acquire adult speech, deficits are still noticeable. In addition to breaking situational constraints their prosody (i.e. their stress, rhythm and intonation) still remains quaint. Baltaxe (1980) has recently commented that their speech is improperly modulated, produced with over-precision. They seem to string words together as if they were in isolation, and she hypothesizes that they continue to have difficulties in the perception of rhythm and pitch modulation.

Such abnormalities have been clearly described since 1964 by Wolff and Chess, and by Cunningham (1966), but it is only since 1975 that such a specific clustering unique to pure infantile autism has been surmised.

Four examples illustrate pure infantile autism in a severely retarded person (Case 4), in a young person of normal intelligence (Case 5), complicated infantile autism (Case 6) and late onset psychosis (Case 7).

Case 4 – Age 10 years.
Even as a baby, A.C. was not responsive to physical handling, nor cuddly or warm but inert. Normal separation anxiety did not seem to be marked. Her speech development was slow and, indeed, she has never learned to use the word 'I' and remains at the level of occasional telegram phrases. It was clear that by the time she reached play-school, she was retarded. As she grew older there was evidence of a much wider vocabulary. She would frequently repeat snatches of nursery rhymes or fairy tales, often connecting up two different stories out of context. She repeated a good deal of overheard adult conversation in a singsong fashion. Echolalia became more evident as she became more verbal. Only on one occasion did she call anyone by name. On a couple of occasions towards the end of T.'s sessions, she extended her hand and said good-bye, and one day greeted T. with 'How are you yesterday?' As her quantity of speech increased it was also noticeable that often there was a mimicry of baby talk, she enjoyed baby sounds. She would frequently crawl into the doll's crib in which she would sit all hunched up. She showed no neurological signs. Her IQ was 65.

Autistic children of normal intelligence are often grossly disabled by obsessional or phobic behaviour.

Case 5 – Age 17 years.
S.P. showed normal development until 3 years when it was noticed that his speech was not advancing. A diagnosis of autism was made and appropriate education arrangements made. His intelligence was in the normal range when assessed at ages 7 and 10 years; his verbal functioning was described as exhibiting the autistic child's typical 'literal concrete' approach to verbal situations. He was working academically when 10 years, at 3 years below his chronological level. In adolescence he became increasingly obsessional and particularly concerned about food. He wanted to eat more green vegetables than his younger sister, and would become upset when mistakes were made about food quantities or food was spilled. When upset he would

repeat himself over and over again. Admission to hospital was necessary when he started to wake his parents at night to tell them things he had forgotten to do at work, and particularly items of food he had not talked about. He felt he had missed one word in the sentence and had to go back repeating the sentence. His speech was described as 'hesitant', studied, with effort, concerned to clarify everything, over-precise and robot-like, and the content irritatingly repetitive, like this sample from a letter in hospital:

'Could the day nurses allow me to always have seconds of meat and seconds of protein when there is any left. Could they please tell the waitresses to allow me to have seconds of meat and of protein when there is any left because I love a lot meat and a lot of fish. I am very unhappy about tea because other patients when offered seconds. I wanted to have seconds of chicken casserole, but the waitress put the maining chicken casserole down the sink. I am very worried because I want my Mum to bring in my three whole slices of cheese which is my favourite food every day when I go to. . . which I am starting on Monday instead of sandwiches provided by the hospital. I am very homesick in the hospital and I am very misarable since I came into hospital. In this case I can not sleep at night and I feel very tired during the day. When Mum comes to visit tommorrow evening I must tell her once my facts and feelings about food at home. I want her to comfort my facts and feelings about food and if she does I promise I won't talk to her about food on any other days she comes in.

Case 6 – Age 12 years.
M.L.'s development was normal up until the age of 1¼ years, after which her ten meaningful words were reduced to 'mum' and 'dad' and remained so for 5 years. The child had measles at 6 months and was overactive thereafter. At 5 years two-word utterances appeared and the child could sing 'Abide with me' perfectly. She had intermittent seizures from the age of 2. She has a high-pitched singsong echolalia, but no useful speech beyond the level of a 1½ -year-old. She is severely mentally handicapped.

Case 7 – Age 12 years.
A.T.'s development was normal until the age of 7 when she became increasingly weepy, timid, overdependent and out of touch emotionally; she had frequent obsessional ideas about Dr Who being mixed up with her thoughts. Psychological testing showed her abilities to be between 50 and 60 on the WISC. Her father had a paranoid psychotic illness. She now spends much of the time looking out of the window or doing weird drawings of insects. One gets the uncanny feeling of there being someone else in the room, even when she is not talking to herself. Her intelligence is normal. She now requires neuroleptic drugs. Her speech is as follows: 'I feel so fine. Yes, I was in London on holiday. . . in Dunedin, down in English. . . away far down, near Aberfeldy. . . to see God. . . to get some new girls for you. . . for Johnny Cash. . . Jesus superstar'.

Doing Something Useful

It is clear that large portions of a handicapped person's communicative competence are subject to environmental influence. Although neurological deficits and developmental milestones may be immutable, even in those discrete clinical categories such as Down's anomaly, the range of competence is large. The scope for improvement is also large.

Precise intervention entails knowing where the child is getting his word processing or mapping wrong (*see* Grieve's Chapter 4), knowing when to provide help, and how intensively (when maladaptive behaviours continue untreated they may become almost irreversible, *see* Chapter 7); and knowing how to train semi-skilled staff and parents to observe and to influence their children's language (*see* Chapter 8 by Wirz).

Precise intervention also means objective measurement, and the creation of profiles and base-lines. Communication interventions involving pre-test and post-test components, such as McConkey and his colleagues (1980) apply, are in the minority. Measurement scales abound, many standardized, many locally devised. There is no uniformity between schools, centres and therapy departments on measures. Some professionals like to use a scale nobody else has used! The more isolated an establishment, the more likely a professional will be found devising a scale of his own. There is a case, particularly with the severely and profoundly handicapped, for tests to be as function-based as possible. It is the communication people use, not the skills they show in tests, which needs measuring. Such is the variety of scales that there is a need for a 'Low Technology Information' bank, such as exists in medical education, so that we might know at least what is going on and where.

The next best thing, in the space available, is to say a little about a range of measures which are either common in assessment centres or available in University departments.

Sheila Wirz (*see* Chapter 8) emphasizes that assessment and remediation are a multiprofessional effort, and describes the speech therapist's role. The paediatrician, child psychologist or school doctor is likely to delegate programme leadership, but cannot delegate his responsibility, for example to exclude deafness.

There is no apology for returning to the subject of deafness. Impaired hearing is too common in mentally handicapped and socially deprived populations to dismiss it with the earlier mentions. In order to assess a child's hearing abilities under the mental age of 2 years, identification audiometry is employed, using either distraction responses (for example, crinkling of tissue paper) or tests of sound localization in which the child turns his head or eyes towards a sound coming from any of several loud-speakers; but, as Murphy (1976) has pointed out, the localization of sounds can occur in the absence of any processing cortex! A decorticate child can hardly be said to be hearing, and the reliability of distraction techniques is affected if the child is hungry, curious or otherwise pre-occupied. Murphy points out that if the child is visually involved under the age of 6 months he will not respond to a sound. Children of 2–5 years can often be tested with pure tones in the form of play audiometry. For children who cannot cooperate, use can be made of galvanic skin response audiometry, evoked potential audiometry and tangible reinforcement operant conditioning audiometry.

Screening of children's hearing, as distinct from testing, is normally carried out in the UK now by Sheridan (Stycar) testing (1958), which involves identification of pictures from an array. School health doctors use this test. In the near future electronic cradles to detect deafness in new-born babies will become standard screening equipment in maternity hospitals.

Lloyd (1977) has developed tangible reinforcement operant conditioning audiometry in order to test the profoundly retarded. A cafeteria procedure is used to see what the child prefers from a wide range of edibles. The child, having indicated his preferences, is tested to see if he works for that item, and then he is conditioned to make an effort to get it when he hears a sound.

Audiologists depended in the past on spondees (i.e. phonetically balanced word lists), but these are not very useful with retarded subjects, and tests have been developed of speech reception thresholds and speech discrimination using the limited lexicons of children. For some basic auditory abilities, such as sound sensitivity, an easily specified stimulus such as a pure tone or white noise is used, but for high-level abilities, e.g. speech processing, stimuli such as phrases and everyday conversation are necessary.

As regards measures of speech and language, starting with the common ones, speech therapists and psychologists are qualified to administer the Reynell Test (1969), which measures encoding and decoding development in children. The Illinois Test of Psycholinguistic Ability (Kirk and Kirk, 1971) measures decoding and encoding, automatic sequential (the quality which allows us to speak without a moment's hesitation) and grammatical closure. The Carrow Test (1977) involves expression and imitation tests. Conventional tests such as the Terman–Merrill (1960) simply provide a global estimate of overall intellectual ability, and the Wechsler (1955) range of tests, although they discriminate verbal from performance abilities, do not distinguish between competence and performance. Standardized tests are available to test comprehension for single words, the most commonly used being the Peabody Picture Vocabulary Test (Dunn, 1959), but this does not test communicative competence. There are problems also of coaxing the child to attend to the visual array.

Methods used in analysis of free speech generally correlate fairly highly with psychological tests. The best measures for predicting the degree of language development are the mean of the 5 longest responses, the number of one-word responses, the number of different words and the structural complexity score. Of these, Shriner and Sherman (1967) have shown that the best single predictive measure was the mean length of response. Speech clinicians occasionally use more sophisticated techniques such as the 50-response speech sample from which one calculates the mean length of response (Templin, 1957). Sophisticated linguistic procedures are now available to measure the level of linguistic complexity, such as the Development Sentence Score (DSS), which is an analysis of a child's spontaneous speech samples, weighting different scores for parts of speech and specific grammatical constructions (Lee and Canter, (1971). The Indiana Scale of Clausal Development (ISCD) (Deaver and Balman, 1971) is based on a 'slot-filler' grammar, and classifies the spontaneous utterances of children whose chronological age is 1½–3 years. The Linguistic Analysis of Speech Samples (LASS) (Engler, et al., 1973) uses contrastive analysis, the central idea of which is that the child's speech is contrasted with that of other children of his own age and development. These tests generally, of course, are for children with concatenative speech. A grammatical analysis which encompasses the one-element utterance is the LARSP (Language Assessment and Remediation Profile) (Crystal et al., 1976), which is convenient in that it samples free speech which can later be transcribed and analysed. This, however, can take several hours. Language ability is likely to be a much better predictor of future cognitive development in the first year than motor ability. Too many developmental tests are saturated with motor items and methods need to be developed to assess 'proto-language', comprehension and communicative competence in everyday settings. There is moreover no readily available way to assess non-verbal communication, or to indicate that a handicapped person is under stress, but Leudar is shedding light on this topic (*see* Chapter 6). Wirz (*see* Chapter 8) reviews programmes; a theme of this chapter is to highlight problems and gaps in our knowledge in practice.

Structured training programmes often suffer from their thoroughness, which turns in practice into inflexibility. The child's existing knowledge can be ignored, and the programmes assume that the child's preferences and behaviour can be overridden. As Kiernan et al. (1980) emphasize, one has to start from 'where the child is'. Gillham's programme (1979), for instance, is sensitive to what the child knows. He has shown that the first 50 words of Down's and normal children do not differ, and has written a 'bench manual' for psychologists, teachers and parents, to provide a 'first word language programme', by short daily sessions, using a step-by-step comprehension approach to speech development and a goal vocabulary which the parents choose from developmental word lists of 'first' words. Three levels of teaching are employed: 'showing', 'choosing' and 'using'.

There are operating principles for structured language programmes but, before their implementation, the child needs to have something to say and what he says needs to have effects. He requires experience of concepts and relationships and a way to say them – syntax. Words, however, are not enough. On many series of studies of mentally handicapped children on single-word vocabulary, such children are equal to normal children both in recognition and in naming. This is true only of nouns, not prepositions (Lyle, 1960; Grieve and Fraser, 1977). It is speculated that as the mentally handicapped child spends a longer time at the one-word stage, he accumulates more items at that stage, or it is much easier to learn single words than to combine them. It is also likely to be partly due to the way that we talk to handicapped children resulting in 'word shooting', that is, names fired back. Chipman (1980) found mentally handicapped children used proportionately more subject—verb and verb—object constructions. Layton and Sharifi (1979), like Leonard et al. (1976), found more action verb types in 3—5-year-old retarded children than in normals of that age, rather confirming that Down's syndrome and other MH groups 'live in the present'. Language, of course, is not simply a matter of labelling, but also consists of reference to events and things unseen, in the past and future. The mentally handicapped person may get less experience of the form 'Do you remember when we last saw a butterfly, train, etc.?' When we are planning the first words that we hope a profoundly handicapped or very young child will use, we generally make up our list from the following types: words referring to objects which can be seen or touched; words which are frequently used and most useful ('car' rather than 'Ford', but 'cabbage' rather than 'vegetable'); relational words involving non-existence or disappearance such as 'all gone'; identifying words such as 'this', 'that'; recurrence, e.g. 'more'; cessation, e.g. 'stop'; rejection, e.g. 'no'; actions-on-objects, such as 'give', 'eat', 'get', 'put', 'down', 'sit', 'go'; attributes of objects, e.g. 'dirty', 'nice', 'good', 'big'; and persons' names.

Structured language training programmes often consist of distinct linguistic conditions, such as training in verbs, subject—verb and subject—verb—object constructions. For instance, initially a start may be made with say 10 action verbs, 'sit' 'and' and 'look'. The child is first required to imitate the tutor's body action, 'do this', 'stand', and then required to match to identical objects when the tutor says 'match'. He is required to manipulate the object when the tutor says 'show me girl', then 'what is "blank" doing?' Under subject—verb training the child is required to make non-verbal responses by pointing to a picture, 'point to boy sitting'. In addition to the structured programme, the children receive language training during token exchange and free play, and practice the subject—verb—object construction: 'I go to the bathroom', 'I want candy', and non-existence such as 'all gone sweetie'. Locatives are difficult because they are abstract and temporary. The use of dolls will help.

There are several programmes based on behavioural principles for helping children who are at an early stage of linguistic development. These include helping children to reach the one-word labelling stage by programmes of imitation training using systematic rewards and shaping techniques (e.g. Bricker and Bricker, 1970), and helping them to acquire two-word utterances (Jeffree et al., 1973). Tierney evaluates these methods in Chapter 7.

It is important not to focus only on programme content. The parent's style is important. In work with a parents' workshop, we have been surprised at the extent to which parental caretakers fail to maintain face-to-face contact with their retarded children during attempts to communicate. This became apparent when we video-recorded child—parent dyads using a 'split-screen' technique, where one camera was trained on the child and recorded on one side of the video display, and where the second camera was trained on the parent and recorded on the opposite side of the display. With this technique, it became immediately apparent from the split-screen recording when parent and child failed to maintain face-to-face contact. Secondly, the fact that the interaction was recorded made it possible to show the parents what they typically did when interacting linguistically with their children. In our workshop studies, we found that parents were often as surprised as we were at how little face-to-face contact was maintained – they were simply not aware of what they were doing when talking to their children.

Of course the importance of face-to-face contact in the adult–child dyad may not only reside in the fact that it provides the child with information from facial expression. It also permits the adult to monitor the child's attention, and to adjust aspects of his communication should the child's attention begin to wander. In other informal studies, we found that those experienced in working with the handicapped practised this constantly, while inexperienced caretakers did not. Thus when we video-recorded sessions where retarded children were shown pictures by (1) an experienced teacher of the handicapped and (2) inexperienced nursing staff, differences were immediately apparent. The inexperienced caretakers exhibited what might be described as 'good quality transmission' of information, concentrating on careful pronounciation of instructions directed to the child, and careful indication of the pictorial array to which the instructions referred. In contrast, the experienced caretaker spent a great deal of time monitoring the child's attention, and adjusting aspects of her production to capture and maintain that attention, e.g. through exaggerated, sometimes flamboyant gestures with her hands; through exaggerating her intonation, making it more rhythmic; through increasing the intensity of crucial aspects of the instruction; and so on. Thus, though both inexperienced and experienced caretakers were reckoning with mental age, the experienced were utilizing some of the principles of 'motherese'. For optimal communication with the retarded, adults should ideally (automatically) ensure the following: each utterance is addressed to the child or handicapped person individually, and it should be linked to the child's name to cue him. Clear, or even exaggerated, facial gestures should accompany the speech, and the child should be looking; if he is not looking he is not listening. The topics should concern things which are interesting and enjoyable to the handicapped person, and the speaker should check that the listener is able to decode the message, particularly its grammatical aspects, since severely mentally handicapped people may not recognize the negative or passive voice in a sentence. Consistent labels are necessary. The interlocutor should encourage verbs and prepositions rather than nouns and 'yes' and 'no' in replies. Time to reply must be adequate. How is this set of principles accomplished without making the adult more self-conscious? Not by destructive criticism of each professional's style, but by showing examples of professionals on video who incorporate these principles.

Workshops and programmes for parents run into trouble when the child is unresponsive, the improvement possible is only marginal, or the axioms are badly presented and cramp the caretaker's style. They are not rules for mothers. Problems which recurred in our workshops included parents' repeated requests to have more individual programmes and help for their offspring; parents spending too much time with the child (more than 15 minutes tuition per day), tiring, fatiguing him rather than utilizing the time effectively; parents trying to reach targets with too little patience too quickly; uncertainty as to what level of expertise the parents should be trained to; parents who requested programmes for children who were decorticate (there are some children who do not make progress and cannot be placed in such programmes); and what to do after the end of the course. It is interesting that the manuals which were part of the course were not generally well received by the parents, as not giving any specific help to their child, but were well received by the staff. The work of Heifetz (1977) and Baker (1977) has shown that manuals alone can be as effective as manuals plus workshop training (at least as measured by post-training questionnaires and test of parental expertise and self-help skills). However, the effects of workshop training are likely to be more pervading and prolonged than those of manuals alone. The main obstacle which almost every parent reported was limited time. Heifetz and Baker have said it is hypocritical for an agency to train parents on programmes which the agency itself is not carrying out. The double standards of inside and outside the institution are very apparent in the UK today. Work in the community is fashionable, in the institution less so.

Later On

A chapter cataloguing difficulties and focusing on the complexity of language can still end on a note of optimism. Although 'effortless' language acquisition diminishes after mid-childhood, even after the age of 16 years, improvement in language functioning can occur because of the handicapped person's improved motivation and access to experiences and concepts (Gilbert and Hemming, 1979). His vocabulary will continue to expand although his grammar may have 'missed the deadline'. This has been noted in Down's syndrome (Evans, 1977). The most important interventions that we can make after the end of the 'sensitive' learning period is to provide experience in the use of language; speaking with effect, giving the mentally handicapped opportunities to 'manage inter-actions' and talking about a wide range of topics. The informal dialogue of most articulate, mildly mentally handicapped adults consists of the local football team's activities and 'She said to me, so I said to her, so she. . .'! The mentally handicapped often speak with facility about such issues, and one should not be beguiled into believing that their language will be as effective on less familiar topics, The mentally handicapped person has a language mediational deficit. Language does not 'commit' him to action (O'Connor, 1975). There is no necessary direct connection between the statement (after advice) 'I understand and I am going to work hard now' and any outcome in terms of hard work. The statement 'I have learned from my mistake and I am going to be tidier' is not necessarily going to be followed by any change in behaviour. This is not dishonesty; the individual is keen to please.

This chapter has largely been concerned with organic causes, but the clinician is only too aware that as the handicapped person grows older the influence of bad environments can engulf every effort to help. Environmental deprivation affects in particular the semantic elements of language. The grammatical structure of language is less affected. Bhagat and Fraser (1970) found that environmental influences had affected the meaning of sex, and attitudes towards sex, in the mildly and border-line mentally handicapped adolescent, sometimes in a dangerous unreflective direction. The more severely handicapped person's use of words such as 'good' seems to be modified and to be more 'child-like', meaning 'safe' and 'clean' rather than 'honest' 'kind' and 'beautiful'. The effect of institutionalized living is particularly perfidious with often abrupt loss of friendship ties, and staff turnover of 100 per cent per annum. Hospital predilection for conformity, for remaining silent and for following institutional social rules of behaviour is particularly damaging to language. (It is worth mentioning here that the National Health Service was never designed to provide residential care!)

The clinician is also only too aware of how little he understands of the world the retarded person lives in. How does the handicapped person perceive himself as a retarded person? A study of the meaning of death to the retarded is also long overdue. Construct theory may answer such questions. Most retarded adults achieve equanimity in a modified version of our world, but some find it too confusing. Maladaptive behaviour such as mannerisms, head banging and withdrawal may be an attempt to make meaning in a world otherwise without consequences for actions. States of excitement can also follow inability to process, and make sense of, too complex information. The perplexed, psychotic, mentally handicapped person often seems, by his communications, to be simply 'overloaded' with topics which he cannot process.

The exciting difference for clinical practice from a decade ago is that we now have more relevant and adequate linguistic frameworks, enabling more precise and utilitarian formulations to be made.

Acknowledgement

The studies involving the author were funded by the Scottish Home and Health Department, the Mental Health Foundation and the Royal College of Physicians of Edinburgh. They were made possible through the cooperation of Fife Health Board, Fife Regional Council and of many colleagues.

References

Ardran G. M., Harker P. and Kemp P. (1972) Tongue size in Down's syndrome. *J. Ment. Defic. Res.* **16**, 167.

Aurnhammer-Frith L. L. (1969) Emphasis and meaning in recall in normal and autistic children. *Lang. Speech* **12**, 29.

Baker B. L. (1977) Support Systems for the Parents as Therapist. In: Mittler P. (ed.) *Research to Practice.* Proceedings of the IVth IASSMD Conference. Baltimore, University Park Press.

Baltaxe C. and Simmonds J. Q. (1975) Language and childhood psychosis. *J. Speech Hear. Disord.* **40**, 439.

Baltaxe C. and Simmonds J. Q. (1977) Language Patterns of Adolescent Autistics. In: Mittler P. (ed.) *Research to Practice.* Proceedings of the IVth IASSMD Conference. Baltimore, University Park Press.

Baltaxe C. (1980) Prosodic Abnormalities in Autism. In: Mittler P. (ed.) *Frontiers of Research.* Proceedings of the Vth IASSMD Conference. Baltimore, University Park Press.

Berko J. (1958) The Child's Learning of English Morphology. *Word.* **14**, 150.

Berry P. and Marshall B. (1978) Social interactions and communication patterns in mentally retarded children. *Am. J. Ment. Defic.* **83**, 44.

Bhagat M. and Fraser W. (1970) The meaning of concepts to the retarded offender. *Am. J. Ment. Defic.* **75**, 26.

Bradbury B. and Lunzer E. A. (1972) The learning of grammatical influence in normal and subnormal children. *J. Child Psychol. Psychiatry* **13**, 239.

Bricker W. A. and Bricker D. D. (1970) Development of receptive vocabulary in severely retarded children. *Am. J. Ment. Defic.* **4**, 599.

Brooks D. N. and Woolley H. (1972) Hearing loss and middle ear disorders of patients with Down's syndrome. *Am. J. Ment. Defic.* **16**, 21.

Carrow E. (1977) Test of Auditory Comprehension of Language. *Learning Concepts,* Lamar, Texas.

Chipman H. (1980) Language acquisition by Mentally Retarded Subjects. In: Mittler P. (ed.) *Frontiers of Research.* Proceedings of the Vth IASSMD Conference. Baltimore, University Park Press.

Crome L. C. and Stern J. (1967) *The Pathology of Mental Retardation.* London, Churchill.

Cromer R. F. (1974) Receptive language in the mentally retarded: processes and diagnostic distinctions. In: Schiefelbusch R. L. and Lloyd L. (ed.) *Language Perspectives, Acquisition, Retardation and Intervention.* London, Macmillan.

Crystal D., Fletcher D. and Garman G. (1976) *The Grammatical Analysis of Language Disability.* London, Arnold.

Cunningham C. (1979) The Down's Baby. Paper delivered at National Conference of APMH, Edinburgh.

Cunningham M. A. (1966) Studies of Autism. Association of Professions for the Mentally Handicapped. *J. Child Psychol. Psychiatry* **7**, 143.

Darley F. L. (1974) *The Diagnosis and Appraisal of Communication Disorders.* Englewood Cliffs, N.J., Prentice-Hall.

Deaver R. and Balman P. (1971) Cited by Longhurst T. M. and Schmidt T. A. M. (1972) In: Linguistic Analysis of Childrens' Speech. A Comparison of Four Procedures. *J. Speech Hear. Disord.* **36**, 240.

Dodd B. (1972) Comparison of babbling patterns in normal and Down's syndrome infants. *J. Ment. Defic. Res.* **16**, 35.

Dodd B. (1974) Cited by Cromer R. In: *Language Perspectives, Acquisition, Retardation and Intervention*. London, Macmillan.

Dunn L. (1959) *The Peabody Picture Vocabulary Test*. Minneapolis American Guidance Service.

Engler I. F., Hannah E. P. and Longhurst J. M. (1973) Linguistic analysis in speech samples: A practical guide for clinicians. *J. Speech Hear. Disord*. 38, 192.

Evans D. (1977) The development of language in mongols: a correlative study. *J. Ment. Defic. Res*. 21, 103.

Fraser W., Agnew J. and Grieve R. (1975) The linguistic behaviour of the hydrocephalic mentally handicapped adult. *Br. J. Ment. Subnormality* 27, 42.

Gilbert K. A. and Hemming H. (1979) Environmental change in psycholinguistic ability of mentally retarded adults. *Am. J. Ment. Defic*. 83, 453.

Gillham R. (1979) *The First Words Language Programme*. London, Allen and Unwin.

Grieve R. and Fraser W. (1977) Integration of linguistic and extra linguistic information in the mentally retarded research to practise in mental retardation. In: Mittler P. (ed.) *Research to Practice*. Proceedings of the IVth IASSMD Conference. Baltimore, University Park Press.

Gutman A. J. and Rondal J. A. (1979) Verbal operants in mothers' speech to nonretarded and Down's syndrome children matched for linguistic level. *Am. J. Ment. Defic*. 83, 446.

Heifetz L. J. (1977) Professional Preciousness and the Evolution of Parent Training Strategies. In: Mittler P. (ed.) *Research to Practice*. Proceedings of the IVth IASSMD Conference. Baltimore, University Park Press.

Ingram T. T. S. (1969) Disorders of speech in childhood. *Br. J. Hosp. Med*. 2, 1607.

Jeffree D., Wheldall K. and Mittler P. (1973) Facilitating two word utterances in two Down's syndrome boys. *Am. J. Ment. Defic*. 2, 177.

Kellett B. (1976) An initial survey of the language of ESN (S) children in Manchester: the results of a teachers' workshop. In: Berry P. (ed.) *Language and Communication in the Mentally Handicapped*. London, Arnold.

Kiernan C., Read C. and Jones B. (1980) Behaviour modification in the development of communication skills. In: Mittler P. (ed.) *Frontiers of Research*. Proceedings of the Vth IASSMD Conference. Baltimore, University Park Press.

Kirk S. A. and Kirk W. D. (1971) *Psycholinguistic Learning Disabilities: Diagnosis and Remediation*. University of Illinois Press.

Kolvin I., Ounsted C. and Roth M. (1971) Cerebral dysfunction and childhood psychosis. *Br. J. Psychiatry* 118, 467.

Lackner J. R. (1968) A developmental study of language behaviour in retarded children. *Neuropsychologia* 6, 301.

Layton T. L. and Sharifi H. (1979) Meaning and structure of Down's syndrome and non-retarded children's spontaneous speech. *Am. J. Ment. Defic*. 83, 439.

Lee L. and Canter S. (1971) Developmental sentence scoring: a clinical procedure for estimating syntactic development in children's spontaneous speech. *J. Speech Hear. Disord*. 36, 315.

Lenneberg E. H. (1967) *Biological Foundations of Language*. New York, Wiley.

Lenneberg E. and Lenneberg E. (ed.) (1975) *Foundations of Language Development – A multidisciplinary approach*. New York, Academic Press.

Leonard L. B., Bolders J. G. and Miller J. (1976) An examination of the semantic relations in the language usage of normal and language disturbed children. *J. Speech Hear. Res*. 19, 371.

Lloyd L. (1977) The Assessment of Auditory Abilities. In: Mittler P. (ed.) *Research to Practice*. Proceedings of the IVth IASSMD Conference. Baltimore, University Park Press.

Lovell K. and Bradbury M. (1967) The learning of English morphology in ESN children. *Am. J. Ment. Defic*. 71, 603.

Lyle J. G. (1960) The effect of an institution environment upon the verbal development of imbecile children. *J. Ment. Defic. Res.* **4**, 1.

MacKenzie J. (1966) The 1st arch syndrome. *Dev. Med. Child Neurol.* **8**, 55.

Marshall N. R., Hegrenes J. R. and Goldstein S. (1973) Verbal interactions: mothers and their retarded children vs mothers and their non-retarded children. *Am. J. Ment. Defic.* **77**, 415.

McConkey R. (1980) Spreading the Word. In: Mittler P. (ed.) *Frontiers of Research.* Proceedings of the Vth IASSMD Conference. Baltimore, University Park Press.

McLaughlin J. and Kriezsman E. (1980) Developmental dyspraxia in a family with X-linked retardation. *Dev. Med. Child Neurol.* **22**, 84.

Mittler P. (1976) The teaching of language skills. In: *Language and the Mentally Handicapped.* Proceedings of the IMS Conference. IMS Publications, pp. 16–43.

Murdoch J. C. (1980) Hypothalamic-pituitary target organ functioning in adults with Down's syndrome. In: Mittler P. (ed.) *Frontiers of Research.* Proceedings of the Vth IASSMD Conference. Baltimore, University Park Press.

Murphy K. (1976) Hearing and Language. In: *Language and the Mentally Handicapped.* Proceedings of the IMS Conference. IMS Publications, pp. 11–16.

O'Connor N. and Hermelin B. (1963) *Speech and Thought in Severe Subnormality.* London, Pergamon.

O'Connor N. and Hermelin B. (1967) Auditory and visual memory in autistic and normal children. *J. Ment. Defic. Res.* **11**, 126.

O'Connor N. and Hermelin B. (1974) Specific deficits and coding strategies. In: Clarke A. M. and Clark A. D. *Mental Deficiency.* London, Methuen.

O'Connor N. (ed.) (1975) *Language, Cognitive Deficits and Retardation.* London, Butterworths/IRMMH.

Reynell J. A. (1969) A developmental approach to language. *Br. J. Commun. Disord.* **4**, 33.

Rondal J. A. (1977) Maternal speech in normal and Down's syndrome children. In: Mittler P. (ed.) Proceedings of the IVth IASSMD Conference. Baltimore, University Park Press.

Rutter M. (1977) Infantile autism and other child psychoses. In: Rutter M. and Hersov L. (ed.) *Child Psychiatry, Modern Approaches.* London, Blackwell.

Schiefelbusch R. and Lloyd L. (ed.) (1974) *Language Perspectives, Acquisition, Retardation and Intervention.* London, Macmillan.

Sheridan M. (1958) *The Stycar Hearing Tests.* Slough, NFER.

Shriner T. H. and Sherman D. (1967) An equation for assessing language development. *J. Speech Hear. Res.* **10**, 41.

Swann W. and Mittler P. (1976) Language abilities of ESN(S) children. *Spec. Educ.* **3**, 24.

Templin C. (1957) *Certain Language Skills in Children.* Institute of Child Welfare, Monograph Series 26.

Terman–Merrill Test (1960) Slough, NFER (revision.)

Wechsler D. (1955) *Adult Intelligence Scale.* Slough, NFER.

Weir R. (1962) *Language in the Crib.* The Hague, Mouton.

Wheldall K. (1976) Receptive language development in the mentally handicapped. In: Berry P. (ed.) *Language and Communication in the Mentally Handicapped.* London, Arnold.

Wing L. (1975) A study of language impairments in severely retarded children. In: O'Connor N. *Language, Cognitive Deficits and Retardation.* London, Butterworths/IRMMH.

Wolff S. and Chess S. (1965) An analysis of the language of fourteen schizophrenic children. *J. Child Psychol. Psychiatry* **6**, 29.

Non-verbal Communication

Chapter Six

Strategic Communication in Mental Retardation

Ivan Leudar

Introduction

Until about a decade ago, the topics that interested psycholinguists implied an assumption that the focal aspect of communicative competence is an individual's knowledge of language (linguistic competence). Of course, the ability to produce grammatically well-formed sentences (and to understand them) is crucial in everyday communication. It ensures that we can say what we mean and that our audiences can infer what we mean from what we say. A command of one's language is especially important when the topic of a dialogue is an event which is hypothetical or which occurred in the past. However, studies of our knowledge of language neglected the way we use it. In order to account for what we do when we speak, psycholinguists turned their attention from linguistic to pragmatic competence and to the structure of intersubjectivity (*see*, for example, Watzlawick, et al., 1967; Halliday, 1973; Rommetveit, 1974). This led to the current interest in the preverbal communication in children (e.g. Waterson and Snow, 1978), non-verbal communication in adults (e.g. Argyle, 1969; Birdwhistell, 1970) and, finally, in attention being paid to the social organization of communication. This shift in research interest was marked in the studies of the communication of average subjects. But with some exceptions (Bedrosian and Prutting, 1978; Marshall et al., 1973; Naor and Balthazar, 1975; Price-Williams and Sabsay, 1979), this shift is overdue in the field of mental retardation. Consequently I cannot present a detailed summary of the research on communication (and non-verbal communication in particular) as I had intended. If I did so, this chapter would be short indeed. I shall attempt to develop a framework for the study of communication in mental retardation, basing it on recent developments in semiotics, philosophy of language, and on the theory of universal pragmatic competence developed by Habermas (1970a, 1970b). I shall argue that the communicative environment of the mentally retarded is systematically distorted; it does not allow them to engage in certain overt speech acts and forces them to communicate covertly.

Deficit and Subject Orientated Speech

But first let me consider some methodological issues. The salient aspect of most of the research in the psycholinguistics of mental retardation is that it looks for deficits. Researchers are interested in which syntactic rules a retarded person uses or does not use, how his articulation departs from conventions and which meanings fall beyond his cognitive capacity. One determines this by comparing the performance of retarded and matched non-retarded groups. At first sight this may seem a reasonable research strategy. After all, we are dealing with mental retardation and deficits. These are by definition deviations from norms and conventions set by the behaviour of average individuals. So it may follow that the goal of the psycholinguistics of mental retardation is a systematic and objective description of the shortcomings of retarded persons' linguistic and communicative competence, supplemented by explanations of the origins of these short-comings and if possible by ways of remedying them. In fact, the situation is not as simple. The first problem is that the above research strategy (which I shall call 'deficit oriented') implies, but does not specify, how particular deficits will affect communicative performance and the quality of life of the mentally retarded. We are left guessing about what will be the relative contributions to communicative failure of, for example, articulatory deficits, producing ungrammatical sentences, or the inability to make one's utterances relevant to the topic of conversation. Further, it is not known how average subjects react to specific communicative impairments. There is a certain amount of information about how 'normals' react to the handicap itself (Gibbons et al., 1979; Severance and Gasstrom, 1977; Farina et al. 1976), but no knowledge of how average audiences react, for example, to articulatory impairment in mental retardation. These are empirical questions, answers to which may be valuable in planning remedial programmes. This objection is not too serious. It simply calls for additional research on how semantic, phonological and syntactic deficits affect every-day communicative performance of the mentally retarded. There is a second problem with the deficit orientated research which is more serious. It is that it characterizes the communication of the retarded by default, by what it should be like, but is not. It does not tell us about the rules and strategies intrinsic to the communication behaviour of the retarded. These may be unconventional in comparison to the communicative behaviour of average speakers from necessity. Possible reasons are cognitive and linguistic handicaps on the one hand, and the social position of the retarded on the other. I am going to deal with social determinants of the communicative strategies which the retarded adopt in everyday encounters. But it should be noted that an inadequate command of conventional means of com-munication does not imply that the functions which such means serve in everyday communication cannot be satisfied by other means. The retarded use gesture to describe objects, whose name they do not know or cannot express clearly. Instead of orientating an audience's attention to that object by naming it they may combine pointing, eye contact, and a non-verbal cry to reach the same goal (i.e. to direct the audience's attention to a certain event). In other words the function that certain means of communication customarily serve may be extended (for example, gesture may cease to be a speech accompaniment and become the focal means of expression) and elaborated to satisfy the individual's expressive needs. Some Down's syndrome subjects develop complex gestures for contents they cannot express clearly in speech. An example is a gesture that a 7-year-old mongol G. M. developed for the radio-microphone that he was obliged to wear regularly, the name of which he could not remember or pronounce clearly. The gesture consisted of repeatedly touching his index fingers together in the middle of his chest, where the microphone was usually placed. He used this gesture repeatedly and it was also adopted by some other mongols in the group. A second example is a gesture which expresses annoyance and rejection, simultaneously, which was consistently used by a 6-year-old mongol S. D. The gesture consisted of an up-and-down movement of his right hand, followed by pointing the same hand towards the rejected person. The number of up-and-down movements was related to how annoyed he was, and the pointing gesture was sharper the more definite the rejection was. Such adaptive strategies are not likely to be discovered by deficiency orientated research. On the contrary, they are likely to be labelled 'deviant'. The rationale is simple. We should look at what the retarded actually do in everyday encounters.

In the present chapter I shall focus on the social situation of the mentally retarded and its effects on their communicative strategies. I shall attempt to develop a framework for the study of communication which is suitable for this purpose.

A Framework for the Study of Communication in Mental Retardation

Since strict a priori definitions may make one insensitive to the variety of phenomena under study, initially I shall define communication only vaguely: as a process in which one individual (the agent) controls (or attempts to control) the actions, beliefs and feelings of people around him (who are subjects of his control). I shall argue that there are various strategies for affecting others in communication. I shall argue further that the choice of a particular communicative strategy is not arbitrary, but reflects the social relationship of the participants in a communicative encounter.

According to Chomsky (1980), an individual can be viewed as a system composed of several subsystems (competences). The ones usually mentioned are linguistic, pragmatic and cognitive competences. Linguistic competence is usually defined as the individual's knowledge of language: 'a grammar of a language purports to be a description of the ideal speaker's intrinsic (linguistic) competence. . . (it) must assign to each of an infinite range of sentences a structural description indicating how this sentence is understood by the ideal speaker—hearer' (Chomsky, 1965). Cognitive competence could be defined as the individual's ability to identify new phenomena as instances of an already existing concept (*see* Harrison, 1973) or, alternatively, the stage of the cognitive development they have reached (Piaget, 1950). Pragmatic competence is the individual's mastery of the rules that govern social interaction: 'his mastery of dialogue constitutive universals' (Habermas, 1970a, 1970b, *see* the discussion later in this chapter). The individual's performance in a communicative encounter reflects not only his communicative competence (which reflects the interaction of linguistic, pragmatic and cognitive competence) but also the aspects of the social and physical context in which the encounter occurs. Neither the concept of competence itself, nor the distinction between linguistic, pragmatic and cognitive competences are uncontroversial. But, since they seem useful rhetorical devices, I shall use them.

The linguistic and cognitive competences of the mentally retarded are referred to in other chapters of this book, and will not be dealt with in this chapter. There is some evidence that pragmatic competence predates linguistic competence in children (Bruner, 1975), and that in mental retardation, linguistic handicap does not necessarily imply pragmatic incompetence (Price-Williams and Sabsay, 1979).

Communication and Intention

The origins of the study of pragmatic competence can be traced to the work of Austin (1962), who introduced the term 'act of speech'. He distinguished acts of saying something (locutionary acts) from acts of doing something by saying something (performatives). According to Austin, there are several types of speech acts. Illocutionary acts are 'Acts such as informing, ordering, warning, undertaking, etc., i.e. utterances which have a certain conventional force'. Perlocutionary acts, on the other hand, are '. . . what we bring about or achieve by saying something such as convincing, persuading, deterring and even, say, surprising or misleading' (Austin, 1962). In recent psycholinguistic publications, the terms 'speech act' and 'illocutionary act' are used interchangeably (*see*, for example, Clark and Clark, 1977).

Illocutionary acts are therefore acts in which we attempt to influence our communicative partners, though not all the actions through which we attempt to influence others are illocutionary (speech) acts.

In everyday life we affect people around us in a variety of ways. We discuss, insinuate, gesture, remain silent when we are expected to speak, grunt, engage in aggression and in deceit. Some of these are open and explicit, others are covert and may involve manipulation. Speech act theory focuses on the 'unaetiolated', overt and explicit uses of language. These involve making one's intentions plain, that is, making overt the intentions about how we would like to affect our audience. The actual decision on whether the illocutionary force of a speech act will be taken up (for example, whether a warning will be heeded), is the audience's. This is clear in the work of Grice (1957, 1975). Grice attempted to define meaning in terms of the intentions that a speaker must have when, say, issuing an utterance. According to Grice (1957), if a speaker is to mean something by an utterance x he must:

1. Intend to produce, by uttering x a certain response r in his audience A (intention I1).
2. He must also intend that his intention to evoke r by issuing the utterance x will be recognized by A (intention I2).
3. Finally, he must intend that the audience's recognition of his intention I2 shall be the reason for the response r (intention I3).

Grice sums up his definition by stating that: 'To mean something by an utterance one must intend to induce a belief by it by means of the recognition of this intention.' As Strawson (1964) pointed out, 'An essential feature of the intentions that make up the illocutionary complex is their overtness.'

The above definition introduces constraints on communicative actions to isolate those by which we affect our communicative partners overtly. One problem is that this strategy can lead to an infinite regress. Strawson, for example, suggested that even the intention I2 should be made plain intentionally by the speaker. In other words, a speaker should attempt to make it plain to his audience that he is making his intentions plain. And the listener should realize this. He should be aware that the speaker suggests how he should behave, what he should believe and feel, but does no more than suggest. (Below, I shall combine Grice's intentions I2 and I3 and call them the 'intention to communicate overtly' (Io). I shall refer to the intention I1 as the 'intention to control others' (Ic).)

Grice's definition concerns the speaker. Now which of his intentions must be fulfilled if the listener is to understand him correctly? According to Strawson (1964), the listener should realize that the speaker intended to affect him in a certain way by his utterance. And further, the listener should be aware that the speaker intended to induce this effect through having his intention to induce it recognized.

The above definitions simplify actual communication. We rarely express one message in one utterance. Halliday (1973) pointed out that (grammatical) language allows us to convey more than one message in one sentence. In one utterance we may express an idea, our feelings about it and our attitude to the listener. (Consider, for example, the sentence 'John cheated us again, as I told you he would', pronounced in an upset voice.) Do we have to intend to induce each of these effects and have each of these intentions recognized 'to mean' openly?

In other cases we may intend to induce one effect, through having our intention to evoke it recognized, but also produce some further effect(s) contingent solely on the first effect. As when 'informing' someone, in order to frighten and/or warn them. The 'further effects' are presumably not intentionally produced.

We are often uncertain about what we intend by our words. Our intentions often become clear to us only as a result of our audience's reactions. In other words in a conversation, a speaker's intentions may be, at least in part, a function of what intentions his audience attributes to him.

So, Grice's definition excludes several modes of interaction (as it was meant to). In particular, it excludes those in which meaning is not mediated through reciprocal recognition of intentions. However, in the present context, I do not wish to exclude any manner in which people can affect each other. Rather, I want to relate different possible uses of language (and of other communicative means) systematically. This can be done by relaxing the requirements of intentionality in Grice's definition.

Grice specified two constraints that an action must satisfy if it is to count as an instance of open communication. To communicate openly the speaker must intend to affect his audience. And he must intend to do so by making this intention plain. If a speaker satisfies both these constraints, I will call his communicative action 'overt'. (Examples of overt communicative behaviour are explicit speech acts, such as warning somebody by saying 'I warn you!' or implicit ones such as performed in saying 'Careful!'.)

It is possible to relax the second contraint (Io), without relaxing the first one (Ic). A speaker may intend to affect his audience but without behaving so as to make his intention to do so overt. I will call this manner of communicating 'covert'. There are two closely related ways of communicating covertly. First the agent does not intend the subject to be aware that or how he was affected. (A good example of a covert communication is the behaviour of psychologists in a majority of social psychology experiments, especially those that use a conditioning paradigm. *See*, for example, Beattie and Bradbury, 1979.) A real life example might be making one's audience uneasy by, for example, deliberately altering the frequency of eye contact, smiling, etc. Secondly, the agent may make his behaviour informative to the subject intentionally, but in such a way that the subject will consider that behaviour informative rather than intentionally communicative. Covert communication is closely akin to manipulation, since in both cases the agent attempts to affect the subject without his knowledge. But the two are not identical, since in manipulation the agent intends that his intention to affect his audience will not be recognized. Consider, for example, insinuation. Obviously, the first constraint cannot be relaxed, without also relaxing the second one. If the agent behaves in a certain way (say he sighs) and such a behaviour is not directed at the subject, he cannot have intended this action to be interpreted as an intentional expression. (Of course, the agent's unintentional sigh may have affected the subject, it is informative.) So, the agent may communicate overtly, covertly, or he may just behave without intending to affect anybody.

It was suggested above that in order for the subject to understand the agent correctly, he must recognize that the agent intends to affect him in a certain way, and also that the agent intends to do so by having his intention to do so recognized. In other words, the listener must perceive the speaker's action as intentional and intentionally overt. Since recognition of an intention by a listener may be erroneous, it will be simpler to talk about attribution of intention. In an actual communicative event, the listener can interpret the speaker's behaviour in the following ways.

First, he may not perceive it as an intentional action. So neither Ic nor Io is attributed to the speaker's action. For example, a cough may be interpreted as a physical symptom (rather than an intentional comment).

Secondly, the subject may decide that the agent intends to affect him in a certain way but without attributing to him the intention that he wants to do so overtly. In other words the subject surmises that the speaker wishes to affect him covertly or manipulate him. So the subject attributes to the agent the intention Ic but not the intention Io. For example, someone may try to make a space for himself on a crowded seat by moving closer to me (rather than by saying 'Move up!'). To which, if I realize his intention, I may reply 'Are you trying to push me out?'

Finally, the audience may attribute to the speaker both intentions; to affect them in a certain way (Ic) and to do so overtly (Io). (If I am told 'Move up', I know that the speaker is attempting to get me to move and is making it plain intentionally.) Therefore, the audience may interpret the speaker's behaviour in three ways. Either no intentions are attributed, or only the intention Ic is attributed, or both Ic and Io are.

The three possible ways an agent may behave (in our scheme), and the three ways the subject may interpret his behaviour combine into nine possible (ideal) communicative events. This is shown in *Table* 7 below.

The communicating events 1, 2, 5 and 9 are interesting, since only in these were either the agent or the subject or both successful.

In the event 1, the agent did not intend anything by his action, at least nothing concerning the subject. And the subject did not attribute to him any intentions for acting the way he did. Of course, the agent's action may have still affected the subject. It may have done so by being informative and consequently being a potential minor premise for an inference. (An example is inferring that someone is not well if he keeps sneezing.) Or alternatively, it may have affected the listener without his awareness of it by having a mechanical signal value for him. (Examples might be walking in a crowd and avoiding passers-by without being aware of it, or 'response matching' in which case behaviours and the speech of interactants become similar with prolonged and repeated interactions, without the participants being aware of it. *See* Argyle, 1969; Lennard and Bernstein, 1960; Welkowitz and Feldstein, 1969.)

Table 7. The Communicative Events.

Subject's Intentionality Attributions to Agent's Actions

Agent's Intentions	No intentions attributed	Only the intention Ic attributed	Both intentions (Ic and Io) attributed
None	Event 1 (a) Behavioural inertness (b) Co-action	Event 4 Non-communicative action Interpreted as an attempt at covert communication	Event 7 Non-communicative action interpreted as an attempt at overt communication
Ic	Event 2 Covert communication	Event 5 'Transparent' covert communication	Event 8 Attempt at covert communication interpreted as overt communication
Ic and Io	Event 3 Attempt at overt communication perceived as non-communicative action	Event 6 Attempt at overt communication perceived as an attempt at covert communication	Event 9 Overt communication

In the communicative event 2, the speaker intended to induce a belief or evoke a reaction in his audience by behaving in a certain way. He succeeded in that his intention Ic was not recognized by his audience (and he never had the intention Io). Whether he actually induced the effect that he intended to is a different question. If I tap my fingers on a table to 'express' impatience without feeling impatient, just to make my 'partner' uneasy I may succeed or I may fail, irrespective of whether the audience realized that I was 'acting' with the intention to affect him. In the communicative event 5, the attempt at covert communication failed; the subject realized that the agent was 'acting'. However, when communicating covertly, the agent may deny the intentionality of his actions if challenged.

In the communicative event 9, the agent intended to affect the subject in a certain way, by having his intention to do so recognized and the subject attributed to him both intentions. (When I say 'I beg you not to go', my audience will probably conclude that I intend to induce them to stay and that I am making this intentionally plain.)

The remaining events can be classified into those in which intentionality is incorrectly ascribed to actions of the agent (events 4, 7 and 8), and those in which the intentionality of the speaker's actions was not recognized by the listener (events 3 and 6). Consideration of each of these may be useful for understanding breakdowns of communication, with which we are not dealing.

It should be noted that presently we are not concerned with the speaker's particular intentions or with the particular intentions the listener attributes to the speaker for behaving the way he does. We are dealing with whether the speaker's actions are intentional and overtly so, and whether the speaker judges them to be so.

To summarize our analysis of interaction so far, we have isolated three kinds of communicative events:

1. *Coaction.* The interactants' behaviours are mutually contingent without their so realizing, and without their intending to affect each other.

2. *Covert communication.* The agent affects his subject through his actions intentionally, but without making his intentions plain (covert communication proper), or he intends that his intention Ic will not be recognized by the subject (i.e. manipulation).

3. *Overt communication.* Interaction of the agent and the subject is mediated through reciprocal recognition of intentions.

Semiotic Analysis of Communicative Behaviours

What kinds of communicative behaviours might we expect to find in the above communicative events? If they are to be of any use in analysing the communication of the mentally retarded, we must determine what kinds of communicative behaviours are 'appropriate' for each of them. To do so I shall have to digress to semiotics. To begin, I shall define some of its basic terms (and will have to simplify them in the process). Peirce (1932) defined a sign as '. . . something which stands to somebody for something in some respect and capacity'. (As, for example, smoke may stand for fire to somebody who knows that there is a causal relationship between the two.) Signs are then said to consist of 'signifiers' (e.g. sound of a spoken word) and 'signifieds' (e.g. the meaning of that word). So the signifier stands for the signified, but not to everybody. For example, to understand facial expressions, one must understand social conventions of how particular emotions are and are not expressed. So the 'standing for relationship' (i.e. the relationship between signifier and signified) is mediated by the interpreter's knowledge of the world. In semiotic terms signs are said to have interpretants. According to Morris (1946), the interpretant of a sign is a 'disposition to respond, because of the sign, by a response of some behaviour family'. Since not all signs are interpreted behaviourally, Peirce (1932) defined 'interpretant' as 'another sign, translating and explaining the first sign'. Signs are usually classified according to the nature of the relationship between their two aspects – signifier and signified. Such relationships can be natural as the relationship between smoke (the signifier) and fire that causes it (the signified). Or such relationships can be abstract and perhaps conventional, as, for example, is the relationship between the phonological form of a word on the one hand, and its semantic meaning and possible referents, on the other. On this basis, Peirce (1932) distinguished indexes, icons and symbols. Indexes are signs for which there is temporary contiguity between the signifier and the signified; the two are linked naturally and non-arbitrarily. A behavioural example of an index could be feeling grief and spontaneously bursting into tears. In indexes, the signifier '. . . is contiguous with its signified or is a sample of it' (Sebeok, 1975). A symbol on the other hand is a sign 'without either similarity or contiguity, but only with a conventional link between its signifier and its denotata, and with an intentional class for its designatum' (Sebeok, 1975). Finally, an icon is a sign 'with topological (or temporary) similarity between a signifier and its denotata (i.e. its signified)' (Sebeok, 1975). Icons, then, lie somewhere in between the indexes and the symbols. There is a physical resemblance between the signifier and the signified, but the temporary contiguity between the two is not necessary. In other words icons can be produced intentionally. (It is also the case that judgements of resemblance are to a large degree a matter of conventions.)

The classification of signs in terms of the nature of the relationship of signifiers and signifieds is not uncontroversial. In the case of indexes, where the relationship is to be natural, it is still the case that (at least where social behaviours are concerned) the form of signifiers is conventional. For example, a certain facial expression may be an index of grief in that it is contiguous with that feeling and is not produced intentionally. However, the manner in which grief is expressed is itself socially shaped. So, at least for human behaviours, the signifier aspect of natural signs (i. e.

indexes) is conventional in form. The way we express emotion is a form of life (*see* Wittgenstein, 1958). On the other hand, the arbitrariness of the relationship between the signifier and signified in the case of symbols is only relative. Such relationship is specified by the code which the communicants share.

Each of the sign types may hold a signal value for its interpreter, that is it may act as a signal. Sebeok (1975) defined signals as 'sign tokens which mechanically or conventionally trigger some reaction on the part of an observer'. There is a difference between the kind of signal value that indexes and symbols have. Indexes occur naturally while symbols are produced intentionally. So while indexes signal some state of their source to the interpreter, symbols signal the speaker's communicative intentions. Indexes may affect their subject either by acting as stimuli, or they may be used as minor premises for conscious inferences. If we go back to the three communicative events, we can see that indexes are appropriate vehicles of social influence for co-action (but symbols are not), and symbols are appropriate for overt communication (but indexes are not). For covert communication the matter is more complex. The agent's task is to produce (intentionally) a behaviour which will either affect the subject who remains unaware of it, or will be interpreted by him as a natural index. (Consider the difference between 'He makes me feel uneasy', 'He looks depressed' and 'He said "I am depressed"'.) So, if an agent wishes to affect his audience covertly, he must produce a sign which will resemble (i.e. will be an icon of) the signifier of an indexical sign which, if produced naturally, might induce the required effect.

Therefore we can characterize the three kinds of communicative events further by stating which behaviours are appropriate to each of them.

In *co-action* the interactants affect each other through producing natural indexes which have 'mechanical signal values' for both of them.

To *communicate covertly,* the agent should produce a behaviour similar in appearance to one that would be a natural expression of a certain state, and that would affect the subject in a certain way (even though that 'certain state' is not necessarily actual). If the agent succeeds, the subject considers the behaviour he perceives to be an index, or he is affected by it without being aware of it.

Finally, in *overt communication,* the speaker produces symbols which the subject interprets as symbols.

Social Context of Communication

How are the communicative events that I have isolated relevant to the study of communication in mental retardation? Why should any person, and a retarded one in particular, resort to covert communication when they have the ability to communicate overtly? Some of the reasons are to be found in the social context of the interaction of the mentally retarded.

In each act of communication an individual can function as an agent of influence or as its subject. Ordinarily such roles are reversible, that is, as interaction develops reversal of roles will occur. The agent may become the subject and vice versa. Such reversibility is crucial if one or both of the interactants decide to renegotiate their social roles, or when they disagree about what they talk about and attempt to reach a consensus. I will argue that in many interactions of the mentally retarded, the reversibility of communicative roles is suspended by the rigid institutional structures in which they find themselves. (For example, the roles of therapist—patient, trainer—trainee and retarded—normal are not reversible, and at the same time they partly determine who is to be the agent and who is to be the subject of social influence.) I shall argue that covert communication is one of the strategies that the mentally retarded may use to satisfy their expressive needs in socially distorted communicative situations. Relevant to this discussion is the theory of 'communicative competence' proposed by Habermas (1970a, 1970b). Habermas was concerned with '. . . systematic investigation of general structures which appear in every possible speech situation' (McCarthy, 1973). According to him: 'Producing a situation of potential ordinary language communication is itself a part of the general competence of the ideal speaker. . . . In order to participate in normal discourse, the speaker must have at his disposal . . . basic qualifications of speech and symbolic interaction (role behaviour) which we may call communicative competence' (Habermas, 1970b). The communicative competence itself consists of the mastery of dialogue constitutive universals. These allow an individual to produce an 'ideal speech situation' (at least in principle), in the light of which actual communicative events may be interpreted. The dialogue constitutive universals that he proposes are the following:

1. personal pronouns and their derivatives;
2. forms of address and speech introduction;
3. deictic expressions;
4. non-performative verbs and some modal verbs;
5. performative verbs.

The last category is interesting from our point of view. Since every speech act contains, at least implicitly, a performative, Habermas's classification of performatives is also a classification of speech acts. Habermas classifies performatives into:

a. communicatives – these are exemplified by verbs such as express, speak, mention;
b. constantives – these are performatives, such as to state, to assert, to explain;
c. representatives, which relate to emotional and attitudinal self-representation of the speaker before the hearer;
d. and finally, regulatives (e.g. command, forbid, allow, warn, etc.).

According to Habermas, in a smoothly functioning language game there is a consensus formed from the mutual recognition of the four validity claims: the utterance is understandable, its propositional content is true, the claims that the speaker makes are sincere and, finally, the speaker has the right to perform the speech act that he performs. Of course, situations arise in which interactants disagree; their disagreement may concern their respective social roles, or they may disagree with respect to the truthfulness of a proposition. When such disagreements occur, and if the interaction is to continue, a new consensus needs to be reached in metacommunication. Metacommunication requires (according to Habermas) the virtual suspension of communicative constraints. Each of the participants must be able to challenge the validity claims of his partner. The interactants must be able to and allowed to justify their beliefs and norms discursively. The result of a discussion must be solely a function of the better argument. For this to be possible, there must be no external constraints which would systematically weight the power distribution between the communicative partners in favour of one party. According to Habermas, the communicative structure is free from such constraint only when both participants have an equal chance to select and employ speech acts. This is not the case for the mentally retarded who, with some exceptions (interacting with each other, with their families and friends), find themselves in interactions which are systematically institutionally constrained. In such a situation the parties do not have equal opportunities to:

1. initiate and perpetuate discourse;
2. put forward and question statements, explanations or justifications;
3. express their attitudes and feelings freely;
4. regulate behaviour by commanding them, giving permissions, or opposing commands that have been given.

I suggest that, especially in institutional settings (such as subnormality hospitals), the retarded find themselves consistently in subordinate roles without the power of control; trainees are not to command their trainers, patients are not to advise their doctors and the retarded are not to question the conceptual interpretations of the world by the non-retarded subjects. In other words, they may be excluded from certain overt speech acts by virtue of their social role. It is possible that at least some of the retarded adapt to such a social context and satisfy their expressive needs by engaging in strategic communication. I have described above one kind of strategic communication — covert communication.

Some Empirical Evidence

Is there any empirical evidence that the communication of the mentally retarded is distorted, that the cause of such a distortion is the social context characterized by non-negotiable social roles, and that the mentally retarded use covert communication as an adaptive communicative strategy? So far, I have established that covert communication is logically possible.

It remains to be seen whether the retarded communicate covertly. What empirical evidence could there be? Firstly, the evidence that the verbal communication of the mentally retarded is distorted. I suggested that at least in certain circumstances, the mentally retarded often do not have equal opportunity to initiate and perpetuate discourse. If this is the case, their use of language should not be spontaneous. I further suggested that the retarded do not have the opportunity to regulate the behaviour of their partners by commanding them, giving permissions, etc. Consequently they should not use commands, permission, warnings, with audiences of higher status. Both of these predictions were confirmed in a recent study (Leudar, 1979). It was found that the spontaneity of speech of the mentally retarded was much lower than that of their communicative partners. They volunteered few verbal comments. Secondly, they made few demands on their partners, they asked few questions and issued virtually no commands (such as 'Give me that jigsaw piece' etc.). They asked many fewer questions than their audiences did. I also suggested that the mentally retarded have less opportunity to express their attitudes and feelings, overtly. On this point the evidence is only anecdotical. It has been observed that the mentally retarded have problems in describing their feelings, or perhaps are unwilling to do so. (W. I. Fraser, personal communication).

So there is some evidence that the communicative performance of the mentally retarded is distorted. Now is it the case that the cause of such a distortion is the social context? The mentally retarded are not expected to communicate covertly with everybody, only with partners who are in a position of non-negotiable authority. The more frequent such encounters, the more established the covert communicative strategy ought to be. So the mentally retarded who are institutionalized are prime candidates for covert communicators, and their verbal performance should be distorted to a higher degree. There are no directly relevant empirical studies, but there is some tangential evidence. Covert communication does not only mean that a person intentionally affects others without them being aware of it. It also means that he uses the overt means of expression less, and is perhaps less skilled at using them.

The comparisons of the linguistic skills of the institutionalized and the home-reared mentally retarded show that the institutionalized subjects are indeed less linguistically skilled. (See, for example, Centerwall and Centerwall, 1960; Lyle, 1960; Sievers and Essa, 1961.) However, this evidence is not easy to interpret, since the speech samples these studies use usually confine the speech to peers and to those in the position of authority. There is some anecdotical evidence that the mentally retarded use language less with audiences with institutional, non-negotiable power. An example could be T.H., a 17-year-old male mongol, who rarely talks to the staff at the training centre where he is employed. One could assume that he is linguistically incompetent. However, it has been accidently established that when in the sole company of his peers, he is verbally skilled. However, since he is

not institutionalized, the case does not bear directly on the above prediction. There is a need for systematic observations of communicative
behaviour of the mentally retarded in and outside of the institutions. So
the evidence that the distortion of the communicative performance of the
mentally retarded is socially caused is, so far, only tangential.

The difference between the institutionalized and non-institutionalized
subjects is only a matter of degree. In both cases, they have a non-
negotiable social role – being mentally retarded. I have looked at the
communicative behaviour of a non-institutionalized group of Down's syndrome subjects (Leudar, 1979). They were observed with their peers, with
the non-retarded members of the staff at a training centre, and with non-
retarded strangers. The retarded were not spontaneous speakers and they
tended to place few demands on their audiences. This was so irrespective of
the social distance from their audience. The verbal communicative patterns
of the mentally retarded did not reflect the social distance from their audiences. The two groups of non-retarded subjects, on the other hand, behaved
differently towards the retarded, according to whether they were familiar
with them or not. The trainers attempted to increase the speech rate of the
retarded by asking them many questions, which the retarded readily
answered. However, such a strategy did not influence the spontaneity of the
speech of the mentally retarded. The strangers did not adopt this strategy.
They tended to comment on joint activities, not expecting replies.

I also looked at the body posture and body mobility of the partners
during the interactions. It has been found that the body posture and body
mobility reflected the mongols' social relation to their audiences. With the
strangers, they moved less, and especially so during the initial stages of
interactions. When they moved in the presence of strangers, their movements were more circumscribed. With strangers, they kept more distant,
they oriented their bodies either neutrally or away from them but not
towards them. They often closed their posture by placing one or both
arms over their chest. In other words, mongols' posture and the manner in
which they moved their bodies was a function of the social distance from
their audience. This was not the case for the two groups of non-retarded
subjects. The trainers and the 'strangers' adopted similar postures and
moved their bodies in a similar manner. So the social distance was expressed
in different modalities by the retarded and by the non-retarded subjects.
The retarded did so in the non-verbal medium, the non-retarded in speech.
Of course, we cannot be certain that the retarded used posture intentionally,
in order to communicate covertly. We are currently analysing films of the
interactions in detail to decide on this point.

Conclusion

I have attempted to analyse the communication of the mentally retarded
bearing in mind their social position. I have argued that the subordinate

roles in which they are placed systematically distort their communicative performance. There is some evidence that their social environment does distort their communicative performance. I have argued that at least some of the mentally retarded adapt to the distorted communicative situations and communicate covertly. It is clear that such adaptations are unlikely to be uncovered by the deficit oriented research strategy. I have focused on non-verbal strategic communication, since the retarded seem to be more at home with gesture than with speech.

Acknowledgements

I am grateful to Terry Bloomfield, John McShane and Bill Fraser for their help with the style and the content of this chapter. They are not responsible for the views which I express.

References

Argyle M. (1969) *Social Interactions.* London, Methuen.

Austin J. L. (1962) *How to Do Things with Words.* London, Oxford University Press.

Beattie G. W. and Bradbury R. J. (1979) An experimental investigation of the modifiability of the temporal structure of spontaneous speech. *J. Psycholinguist. Res.* 8, (3), 225–248.

Bedrosian J. L. and Prutting C. A. (1978) Communicative performance of mentally retarded adults in four conversational settings. *J. Speech Hear. Res.* 21, 79–95.

Birdwhistell R. L. (1970) *Kinesics and Context.* Philadelphia, University of Pennsylvania Press.

Bruner J. S. (1975) The ontogenesis of speech acts. *J. Child Lang.* 2, 1–19.

Centerwall S. A. and Centerwall W. R. (1960) A study of children with mongolism reared in the home compared to those reared away from home. *Pediatrics* 25, 678–685.

Chomsky N. (1965) *Aspects of the Theory of Syntax.* Cambridge, Mass., Massachusetts Institute of Technology (MIT) Press.

Chomsky N. (1980) Rules and representations. In: *The Behaviour and Brain Science.* (Forthcoming.)

Clark H. H. and Clark E. V. (1977) *Psychology and Language.* New York, Harcourt Brace Jovanovich.

Farina A., Thaw J., Felner R. D. et al. (1976) Some interpersonal consequences of being mentally ill or mentally retarded. *Am. J. Ment. Defic.* 80, 414–422.

Gibbons F. X., Sawin L. G. and Gibbons B. N. (1979) Evaluation of mentally retarded persons: 'sympathy' or 'atronization'. *Am. J. Ment. Defic.* 84 (2), 124–131.

Grice P. (1957) Meaning. *Philos. Rev.* 66(3), 377–388.

Grice P. (1975) Logic and conversation. In: Cole P. and Morgan J. L. (ed.) *Syntax and Semantics,* vol. 3: *Speech Acts.* New York, Academic.

Habermas J. (1970a) On systematically distorted communication. *Inquiry* 13, 205–218.

Habermas J. (1970b) Towards a theory of communicative competence. *Inquiry* 13, 360–375.

Halliday M. A. K. (1973) *Explorations in the Functions of Language.* London, Arnold.

Harrison B. (1973) *Form and Content.* Oxford, Blackwell.

Lennard H. L. and Bernstein A. (1960) Interdependence of therapist and patient verbal behaviour. In: Fishamn J. A. (ed.) *Readings in the Sociology of Language*. The Hague, Mouton.

Leudar I. (1979) Some aspects of communication in Down's syndrome. Paper presented at the International Conference on Social Psychology and Language, Bristol, 1979.

Lyle J. (1960) Some factors affecting the speech development of imbecile children reared in an institution. *J. Child Psychol. Psychiatry* 2, 121–129.

Marshall N. R., Hegrenes J. R. and Goldstein S. (1973) Verbal interactions: mothers and their retarded children vs mothers and their nonretarded children. *Am. J. Ment. Defic.* 77, 415–419.

McCarthy T. A. (1973) A theory of communicative competence. *Phil. Soc. Sci.* 3, 135–156.

Morris C. (1946) *Signs, Language and Behaviour*. New York, George Braziller.

Naor E. M. and Balthazar E. E. (1975) Provision of a language index for severely and profoundly retarded individuals. *Am. J. Men. Defic.* 79, 717–725.

Peirce S. (1932) *Collected Papers*. Hartshorne C. and Weiss P. (ed.). Cambridge, Mass., Harvard University Press.

Piaget J. (1950) *Psychology of Intelligence*. London, Routledge and Kegan Paul.

Price-Williams D. and Sabsay S. (1979) Communicative competence among severely retarded persons. *Semiotics* 26, 35–63.

Rommetveit R. (1974) *On Message Structure*. London, J. Wiley.

Sebeok T. A. (1975) Six species of signs: some propositions and strictures. *Semiotics* 13, 233–260.

Severance L. and Gasstrom L. (1977) Effect of the label 'mentally retarded' on causal attribution for success and failure outcomes. *Am. J. Ment. Defic.* 81, 547–555.

Sievers D. J. and Essa S. H. (1961) Language development in institutionalised and community mentally retarded children. *Am. J. Ment. Defic.* 66, 413–420.

Strawson P. F. (1964) Intention and convention in speech acts. *Philos. Rev.* 73(4), 439–460.

Waterson N. and Snow C. (1978) *The Development of Communication*. New York, Wiley.

Watzlawick P., Boavin J. H., Helmick A. B. et a. (1967) *Pragmatics of Human Communication: A Study of Interactional Patterns, Pathologies, and Paradoxes*. New York, W. W. Norlan.

Welkowitz J. and Feldstein S. (1969) Dyadic interaction and induced similarity. In: *Proceedings of the 77th Annual Convention of the American Psychological Association*.

Wittgenstein L. (1958) *Philosophical Investigations*, 2nd edition. Oxford, Blackwell.

Intervention

Chapter Seven

Behaviour Modification in Communication Deficit

Ian Tierney

Introduction

There is now abundant evidence that behavioural techniques, especially those derived from operant conditioning, are effective modifiers of human behaviour. Yet in developing the one skill which most clearly distinguishes man from other animals — the ability to convey complex instructions, descriptions and reflections — progress using behavioural techniques has been slow. In populations deficient in communication skills, most notably those suffering from mental handicap and autism, while the establishment and maintenance of self-help skills for daily living skills (such as eating, drinking, dressing and toileting) are now commonly taught using applied operant conditioning or behaviour modification techniques, the use of behavioural techniques to teach even rudimentary levels of useful communication to these populations has proved relatively unrewarding. (Useful communication in this context refers to spontaneous, self-initiated and discursive communication rather than labelling or question answering behaviour which communicates little socially useful information.) This state of affairs suggests either that communication is not 'behaviour' in the sense that motor acts appear to be, or that the analysis of the factors necessary for communication is incomplete.

To date, evidence reviewed by Garcia and de Haven (1974), Yule et al. (1975), Yule and Berger (1975) and Harris (1975) supports the view that the radical behaviourism of the early users of behaviour modification in communication deficit led to an underestimation of the role of cognitive development in the acquisition of communication skills. In particular there has been an underemphasis on semantics, possibly as a result of the influence of the theories of linguistic structuralism and transformational grammar. More recently the views of theorists such as Macnamara (1972) have suggested that, in normal development, infants use meaning as a clue to language rather than language as a clue to meaning. Consequently the emphasis in behaviour modification of severe communication deficit has shifted from the development of labelling or question-and-answer responses, to increasing response generalization (using a word appropriately in more than one context), identifying the cognitive development necessary for specific areas of linguistic growth and, in particular, examining ways of developing semantic structure and intent in communication.

Unfortunately, although these new areas of research have been clearly delineated (Yule et al., 1975; Yule and Berger, 1975), as yet there have been few studies which offer encouragement to the therapist wishing to use behavioural techniques in cases of communication deficit.

It is not the aim of the present discussion to review in detail the many studies of behavioural intervention in this area; that, as mentioned earlier, has been ably done by others. Rather it is the intention to discuss features which these studies have in common, and to look in more detail at three aspects of early cognitive development which the literature suggests are prerequisites for early language development in normal children. These are sustained attention, the logic of inference and the matching-to-sample skills necessary for inference. It may be that behaviour modification has much to offer in the development of these basic cognitive skills with individuals who have severe communication deficit.

Before dealing in detail with these aspects of cognitive development, brief overviews will be given of the contribution made to date by behaviour modification, and of the techniques employed.

Severity of Communication Deficit

Behaviour modification has arguably had greatest impact in the development of self-help skills in the severely and profoundly mentally handicapped populations. Haywood (1979) has demonstrated that there has been a significant annual increase in the proportion of papers, published in the *American Journal of Mental Deficiency* between 1969 and 1978, dealing with aspects of severe/profound retardation compared to papers describing aspects of mild/moderate retardation. One of the reasons for this change has been the cost-effectiveness of behaviour modification techniques, which establish new adaptive behaviours in populations where such behaviours were previously absent. This tendency, to concentrate behavioural research in the most severely disadvantaged groups, has also been evident in communication training. In individuals without any form of communication, the demonstration of increased vocalization, then word shaping, then extensive labelling vocabulary, is particularly encouraging for the therapist. In their reviews of behaviour modification in speech therapy, Weiner (1969) and Yule and Berger (1972) illustrate this tendency for behaviour therapists to concentrate on the establishment of very basic speech behaviour.

This is not to say that behavioural research into the improvement of verbal skills in mildly or moderately retarded individuals has not taken place. Indeed, between 1968 and 1976 many behavioural journals, most notably the *Journal of Applied Behavior Analysis,* contained numerous reports documenting the successful improvement of syntax in this population. Expressive and receptive response classes which have been developed include generative verb usage (Schumaker and Sherman, 1970), question asking (Twardosz and Baer, 1973; Bondy and Erickson, 1976), generative use of plural endings (Guess et al., 1968; Sailor, 1971), adjectival inflection (Baer and Guess, 1971), and prepositional usage (Sailor and Taman, 1971). Other studies show increases in utilization of known language skills (Beveridge and Tatham, 1976), verbal regulation and behaviour (Burland, 1971), verbal social behaviour (McClure, 1968) and the production of compound sentences (Odom et al., 1969). Nevertheless, it could be argued that the moderately retarded individual whose communication deficit, although not gross, is still disabling, requires more attention from behaviour therapists. This is particularly so as this population is being encouraged to move from the institution into the community, where communication skills are at a premium.

Behaviour Modification Techniques in Communication Deficit

The basic elements of behaviour modification vary little, irrespective of the nature of the desired behaviour. First a detailed observation of existing behaviour is made. Those environmental events, pleasant and unpleasant, which cause changes in the individual's behaviour are noted. Then the desired behaviour is examined in detail, and if necessary reduced to smaller units of behaviour. Finally, by making pleasant events (rewards or reinforcers) contingent on the production of the desired behaviour, or sub-units of that behaviour, the desired behaviour is formed and its production increased in frequency.

BASE-LINE OBSERVATIONS

It is important to know the extent of an individual's existing behavioural repertoire in the particular area of behaviour that is being studied. In communication deficit it is important to know exactly what vocalizations, verbalizations and gestural communication the individual already possesses, and how often these are used. Detailed questioning of parents and caregivers, plus several days of structured observation should provide the necessary base-line measures. By the same method, rewards or reinforcers which prove really effective for that individual should be identified.

TARGET BEHAVIOURS

Before starting any behaviour modification, the description of the target behaviour should be clearly established. In the case of establishing speech, the aim should be one or two key words, the significance of which can be taught to the individual in a planned way. In the Lovaas (1966) study discussed below, these 'words' were 'ba-ba' (baby) and 'ma-ma' (mummy).

SHAPING

By reinforcing successive approximations to the desired response, a response or behaviour which is at first far removed from the desired behaviour may be 'shaped' into the desired behaviour. Lovaas (1966) used a shaping procedure to develop labelling speech in a mute autistic child. Having first established that the child preferred tangible food rewards to the more social rewards of hugging and praise, the child was reinforced for attending and having eye contact with the therapist. Rewards were contingent, that is, given immediately the desired response was produced. At first any vocalization was rewarded, then only sounds which approximated to one specific consonant. Once established, this consonant was rewarded only occasionally, and a new contrasting consonant was developed. In this way, the child learnt to produce the 'ba-ba' and 'ma-ma' sounds.

STIMULUS CONTROL

Having established the sounds in a non-discriminate way, the child was then reinforced only when he repeated 'ba-ba' in imitation of the therapist saying 'ba-ba', or later only when he was shown a doll. Initially, stimulus control was facilitated by prompting the child with the therapist giving the correct response at the appearance of the doll, then by prompting with the initial consonant only, and finally fading out the prompts completely. In children who are echolalic or who already imitate, modelling or imitation learning is a short cut to developing the correct response, which does away with the need for shaping the response.

MAINTENANCE OF BEHAVIOUR

If behaviour is reinforced intermittently and in an irregular manner, then the behaviour is less likely to disappear (or extinguish) when reinforcement is finally removed altogether. Hopefully, by the time the tangible reinforcement is removed, the increased interaction and social reinforcement engendered by the new behaviour will maintain this behaviour.

RESPONSE GENERALIZATION

Lovaas (1966) has commented that: 'As in the case of all language training it is crucial that training be extended beyond the concrete training sessions into a more informal training within the child's day-to-day environment'. It is interesting to note that in their excellent reviews, Garcia and de Haven

(1974), Harris (1975) and Yule and Berger (1975) still report very limited evidence that improved speech usage generalizes outside the therapeutic setting. They point out that for this to occur, other therapists need to work with the children in other settings.

It is in the discussion of response generalization that the weakness of the radical behaviour approach to language first appears. Until Garcia and de Haven (1974) first introduced the concept of 'generative response class', there was no adequate way that those constrained by operant conditioning terminology could discuss the generative use of plural endings and verb and adjectival inflections in individuals trained in the use of only a few responses of each type (Guess et al., 1968; Baer and Guess, 1971; Baer et al., 1972). As Yule and Berger (1975) have pointed out, behaviours which form a generative response class are similar to verbal behaviours which psycholinguists might say show 'rule usage'. What is learnt is a rule which allows a response to be produced in contexts other than the specific context in which it was learnt, rather than having to learn that response in each of the other contexts. Although some therapists, most notably Baer and his colleagues, have been successful in developing limited generative responding, the necessary requirements for teaching such responding have yet to be clearly stated in the literature. Harris (1975) concludes that it is relatively easy to establish generalized responding within a given class, be it gross motor imitation, verbal imitation or a given grammatical construct. What is lacking is the means to develop the next step: the use of such generalized responses with semantic intent in other stimulus contexts.

There is some evidence that severely retarded individuals will generalize speech with semantic intent if training has involved a number of therapists in several settings (Garcia, 1974). In this study, each subject was taught the same short 'conversational' speech form by more than one therapist. Probe enquiries within the speech form elicited generalizations which had meaning. Similarly, Lovaas (Lovaas et al., 1973) demonstrated a measure of successful verbal generalization with autistic children, and also documented the regression which took place once the maintaining reinforcement contingencies were withdrawn. What is not clear in these successful studies is the function of the therapists. Does exposure to several therapists simply reduce the salience of particular therapists as discriminative stimuli for particular behaviours; or does contact with several people, all of whom are behaving in a structured, predictable manner, develop behaviours unconnected with the target behaviours which allow generalized responding with semantic intent to take place?

One recent use of a generalized response which has little semantic intent but functions to make the individual more acceptable socially, is the elimination of echolalic responding to questions by severely autistic children. This was achieved by introducing the generalized verbal response 'I don't know' (Schreibman and Carr, 1978). Any training which increases the likelihood of constructive interaction in this population has value

(Rutter and Sussenwein, 1971). Furthermore, this study illustrates that the autistic individual can discriminate syntactic variables and respond appropriately.

Finally, there has been considerable recent interest in the teaching of gestural communication (sign or symbol) to the non-communicating mentally retarded (Kiernan, 1977; Van Biervliet, 1977; Carr et al., 1978). These systems clearly have a useful role in teaching communication to non-communicating mildly or moderately mentally retarded individuals. However, as Murphy et al. (1977) have commented, there is little to be gained in teaching sophisticated responses if the individual lacks the basic cognitive skills necessary to generalize these responses to contexts where they can be used to convey meaning and intention.

COGNITIVE PREREQUISITES FOR COMMUNICATION

As mentioned earlier, in the last decade there has been a marked change in ideas about the development of language and cognition in normal children. In what is perhaps the most influential statement of these new ideas Donaldson (1978) states, 'in 1972 John Macnamara wrote a paper which stands Chomsky's argument about the language acquisition device upon its head. In place of the claim that children have an 'acquisition device' whose content is highly specific to language, with the result that language acquisition shoots ahead of the other skills of the mind, Macnamara proposed that children are able to learn language precisely because they possess certain other skills — and specifically because they have a relatively well-developed capacity for making sense of certain types of situation involving direct and immediate human interaction.'

When considering the mentally retarded individual, and particularly the autistic or more severely retarded individual, who has been brought up in institutions, it is reasonable to suppose that (1) the amount and variety of human interaction in which they participate may be suboptimal, and (2) that due to neurological immaturity or damage, the prerequisite cognitive skills are slow to develop. As the individual matures physically, and still remains a non-communicator, the prerequisite cognitive skills are less and less likely to develop.

Many writers, most notably Bloom (1974), Slobin (1973), Cromer (1974) and Donaldson (1978), have emphasized the role of cognitive development in normal language acquisition and have highlighted the need for information on the cognitive prerequisites for early language development. What are these prerequisite cognitive skills likely to be, and how can they be assessed and then developed in the mentally retarded?

In a recent study, Rogers (1977) attempted to document the cognitive development of profoundly retarded children. Sensori-motor skill stage attainments were found to follow Piaget's hypothesized invariant sequence in general. However the parallel stage performance across various domains was not apparent. This evidence was taken to support Piaget and Inhelder's (1969) contention that the cognitive development of the profoundly retarded individual differs from the normal individual, primarily in rate of development. If this is the case, then the recent evidence that specific cognitive skills like matching and equivalence judgements precede and predict semantic integration in normal children (Daehler et al., 1979; Johnson and Scholnick, 1979) must have relevance to training communication skills. Furthermore infant antecedents of cognitive functioning like attentiveness have recently been reported as reliable predictors of reading ability at age 10 years in the normal population (Kagan et al., 1978). The recent work of Webb and Koller (1979), which found that sensori-motor training significantly improves awareness and intellectual skills, suggests that behavioural methods of sensori-motor pretraining may have an important contribution to make.

INFERENCE AND MATCHING SKILLS

In her book, *Children's Minds,* Margaret Donaldson (1978) analyses in detail the development of logical inference by very young children. She maintains that deductive inference is an essential element of early language, and that the notion of compatibility — where the existence of one state of affairs may sometimes rule out the existence of another (p. 41) — is fundamental to deductive inference. She continues: 'As soon as a child identifies an object as a dog by saying "That bow-wow", his statement is incompatible with an infinite number of others that could be made.' Implicit in this example is the skill of matching-to-sample, identifying two stimuli as being the same in some sense. This cognitive skill is so basic that with the mentally retarded its existence is assumed, even in the case of severely mentally retarded individuals. However, in a recent study the present author was able to demonstrate its existence in the cognitive repertoire of only one out of fourteen severely and profoundly mentally retarded individuals (Tierney, forthcoming). There are other reasons why teaching matching-to-sample skills to mentally retarded individuals may be very important.

As previously mentioned, imitation training is frequently used in communication training with the severe and profoundly handicapped (Petersen, 1968). Much has been written about the imitation process and the necessary preconditions for success (Bandura, 1968; Gewirtz and Stingle, 1968; Baer and Sherman, 1964). The two principal interpretations vary in the emphasis which is put on matching-to-sample skills as a prerequisite for imitation. Gewirtz and Stingle (1968) suggested that generalized imitation is a functionally related class of behaviours (similar in many ways to the later 'generative response class' of Garcia and de Haven, 1974), acquired through extensive reinforcement, and maintained by differential reinforcement. This explanation was an extension of

Skinner's (1953) description of imitation learning as multiple matching-to-sample discriminations. The fact that Baer and Sherman (1964) had demonstrated imitation of responses which had never been reinforced, following reinforcement for other imitative behaviour, does not rule out the possibility that matching-to-sample behaviour involves simple cognitive skills necessary for successful imitation learning. The ability to match the stimulus properties of alike stimuli (to choose from a range of stimuli a match for a presented stimulus), does seem to be closely allied to the imitation process (Porton, 1976). However, unlike imitation, which usually involves matching complex stimuli, matching-to-sample is a skill which can be taught using very simple stimuli with one, or at the most, two stimulus properties, an advantage when it is remembered that rate of learning is inversely related to the number of dimensions in a stimulus (Etaugh and Van Sickle, 1971). Simple skills like colour discrimination have been taught very successfully to mentally retarded individuals using 'errorless discrimination' learning (Davis et al., 1975). This technique develops discriminations, or matching behaviour, in individuals in such a way that they do not make mistaken discriminations. It has been shown that these mistaken discriminations, common in trial-and-error learning, are not necessary for efficient learning as was once thought (Terrace, 1966).

Initially, Davis et al. presented only 2 stimulus cards to the subject. One was a very bright red, the other a very pale green. The subject was told that the red card was red and was asked to point to the red card. On doing so the subject was rewarded with praise and a small piece of his favourite candy. The subject was repeatedly asked to point to the red card and was always correct, thus gaining rewards. After 20 such trials the pale green card was replaced with a slightly brighter green, and the subject was again asked to point to the red card. In this way the subject was finally able to make 20 correct responses when the 2 cards, red and green, were equally bright. Using the same method in the next session the colour green was the target. In later sessions more and more colours were introduced until, after 2 months, he was able to discriminate between red, green, blue, yellow, orange, black, white, brown, purple and pink. Other perceptual skills like discrimination of size, weight and shape have been successfully taught using similar techniques (Sidman and Stoddart, 1967; Davis et al., 1975; Walsh and Lamberts, 1979).

It can be argued that by establishing a skill like colour matching, one is in fact engaged in very basic cognitive training, encouraging and expanding whatever discrimination 'rules' the individual already possesses. Likewise it can be conjectured that for individuals whose behaviour is characterized by relatively random and functionless events, the use of systematic contingent rewards or other consequences introduces such individuals to concepts of causality which, together with discrimination learning, are almost certainly prerequisites for communication (Slobin, 1973).

Foxx R. M. (1977) Attention training: the use of overcorrectional avoidance to increase eye contact of autistic and retarded children. *J. Appl. Behav. Anal.* 10, 489–499.

Garcia E. (1974) The training and generalisation of a conversational speech form in non-verbal retardates. *J. Appl. Behav. Anal.* 7, 134–149.

Garcia E. and de Haven E. D. (1974) Use of operant techniques in the establishment and generalisation of language: a review and analysis. *Am. J. Ment. Defic.* 79, 169–178.

Gewirtz J. L. and Stingle K. G. (1968) The learning of generalised imitation as the basis for identification. *Psychol. Rev.* 75, 374–397.

Guess D., Sailor W., Rutherford G. et al. (1968) An experimental analysis of linguistic development. *J. Appl. Behav. Anal.* 1, 297–306.

Harris S. L. (1975) Teaching language to non-verbal children with emphasis on problems of generalisation. *Psychol. Bull.* 82, 565–580.

Haywood H. C. (1979) What happened to mild and moderate retardation? *Am. J. Ment. Defic.* 83, 429–431.

Hermelin B. and O'Connor N. (1963) The response and self-generated behaviour of severely disturbed children and severely subnormal controls. *Br. J. Soc. Clin. Psychol.* 2, 37–43.

Hermelin B. and O'Connor N. (1964) Effects of sensory input and sensory dominance on severely disturbed children and on subnormal controls. *Br. J. Psychol.* 55, 201–206.

Howlin P., Marchant R., Rutter M. et al. (1973) A home based approach for the treatment of autistic children. *J. Autism Child. Schizo.* 2, 308–336.

Johnson J. W. and Scholnick E. K. (1979) Does cognitive development predict semantic integration? *Child Dev.* 50, 73–78.

Kagan J., Lapidus D. R. and Moore M. (1978) Infant antecedents of cognitive functioning: a longitudinal study. *Child Dev.* 49, 1005–1023.

Kiernan C. (1977) Alternatives to speech: a review of research on manual and other forms of communication with the mentally handicapped and other non-communicating populations. *Br. J. Ment. Subnormality* 23, 6–28.

Koegel R. L. and Covert A. (1972) The relationship of self-stimulation to learning in autistic children. *J. Appl. Behav. Anal.* 5, 381–387.

Lovaas O. I. (1966) A programme for the establishment of speech in psychotic children. In: Wing J. K. (ed.) *Early Childhood Autism: Clinical, Educational and Social Aspects.* Oxford, Pergamon.

Lovaas O. I., Koegel R. L., Simmonds J. Q. et al. (1973) Some generalisation and follow-up measures in autistic children in behaviour therapy. *J. Appl. Behav. Anal.* 6, 131–166.

Macnamara J. (1972) Cognitive basis of language learning in infants. *Psychol. Rev.* 79, 1–13.

McClure R. (1968) Reinforcement of verbal social behavior in moderately retarded children. *Psychol. Rep.* 23, 371–376.

Murphy G. H., Steele K., Yeow J. et al. (1977) Teaching a picture language to a non-speaking retarded boy. *Behav. Res. Ther.* 15, 198–201.

Ney P. G. (1973) Effects of contingent and non-contingent reinforcement on the behavior of an autistic child. *J. Autism Child. Schizo.* 3, 115–127.

O'Connor N. (1970) Speech and thought in the retarded. In: Primrose D. A. A. (ed.) *Proceedings of the Second Congress of the International Association for the Scientific Study of Mental Deficiency.* Amsterdam, Swets & Zeitlinger.

Odom R. D., Liebert R. M. and Fernandez L. (1969) Effects of symbolic modeling on the syntactical production of retardates. *Psychonomic Sci.* 17, 104–105.

Petersen R. F. (1968) Some experiments on the organization of a class of imitative behaviors. *J. Appl. Behav. Anal.* 1, 225–235.

Attention Deficits

As mentioned earlier, Kagan et al. (1978) have recently identified 'attentiveness' in normal infancy as a reliable predictor of IQ and reading ability at age 10 years. Both the latter variables were also positively correlated with social class, which suggests that attentiveness in infancy may be an environmentally controlled variable.

Before teaching any behaviour, it is necessary for the teacher to command the attention of the individual being taught. There are conditions, most notably autism and minimal brain damage/hyperactivity, where distractibility, stereotyped mannerisms, or obsessive attention to apparently irrelevant stimuli, are diagnostic of the condition. Language deficit, severe in the case of autism, is a frequent concomitant of these conditions. Lovaas (1966), Zeaman and House (1963) and Koegel and Covert (1972) have all stressed the importance of maximizing attention training.

There has been considerable behavioural research into ways of increasing attending behaviour, particularly in cases of severe autism (Walker and Buckley, 1968; Brooks et al., 1968; Foxx, 1977). Some of these studies deal with differential positive reinforcement, others an avoidance procedure, where attending avoided unpleasant consequences (Foxx's functional movement training avoidance). Recently, however, it has been suggested that under certain conditions, particular stereotyped behaviours may result in 'inattention' when they are used by an individual to control autonomic arousal, even in retarded populations other than those formally diagnosed as autistic (Baumeister and Forehand, 1973; Tierney et al., 1978). By engaging in stereotypy, attention is diverted from stimuli which may cause uncomfortable levels of arousal in environments from which there is no other escape. Prior to teaching, it is necessary to reduce or remove stereotypy and to increase vigilance or attending behaviour. Tierney et al. (1979) have discussed a behaviour modification procedure which reduced a common stereotypy, body rocking, in a group of profoundly retarded adults in ward environments. Instead of employing the more usual procedure of contingent rewards, non-contingent or randomly distributed rewards were used. On average, each individual who was body-rocking in the ward received a reward every 10 minutes. The actual intervals varied from 1 to 19 minutes. The procedure for delivering the rewards is believed to be an important variable. The nurse would deliver the candy directly into the individual's mouth, not talking or interacting with the individual at all, even to the point of avoiding eye contact. In this way receiving these rewards was as neutral an experience as possible, and there were few signals from the nurse that could be misconstrued or wrongly interpreted. While at an objectively measured level there was a decrease in body-rocking from base-line levels, it was also our impression that the individual body-rockers became more alert, and their gaze changed from aimless staring to searching for information about the likelihood of another reward. It is unclear what the therapeutic mechanism is in this non-aversive procedure, but one suggestion is that the random, unthreatening rein-forcers increase vigilance and attention without causing an increase in fear or anxiety, which would cause an uncomfortable level of arousal leading to more stereotypy. Additional support for this view is given by Ney (1973), who reported that the eye contact behaviour of an autistic child increased during non-contingent reinforcement as compared to the base-line amount of eye contact.

In addition to attention deficits characterized by stereotyped behaviours, there are attention and short-term memory difficulties which are not obvious, the assessment of which is made difficult because of the limited behavioural repertoire of many severely or profoundly retarded individuals. Procedures for assessing such conditions have been described by O'Connor (1970). In studies of responsiveness, Hermelin and O'Connor (1963) showed differences between autistic and mentally retarded individuals on such measures as amounts of self-generated behaviour and stimulus-orientated behaviour. Again, Hermelin and O'Connor (1964) have shown differences between these two groups in measures of 'resistance to change' or 'insistence on sameness', both concepts being closely related to attentional 'effort'. Several attempts have been made to remedy such states. In a study of preschool autistic children, Rutter and Sussenwein (1971), using a developmental and behavioural approach, demonstrated changes in attention as a result of intruding into the child's withdrawn state. Recently emphasis has been placed on the parental role in the treatment of autistic children, using such behaviour modification techniques at home (Howlin et al., 1973; Lovaas et al., 1973; Schopler and Reichler, 1971). In the light of the recent evidence reported by Tierney et al. (1978, 1979), it would appear that such methods might usefully be used in the non-autistic, non-verbal mentally retarded, prior to communication training.

Conclusion

The cognitive prerequisites for verbal communication in normal children have only recently become the subject of detailed study. It is likely that these prerequisites are in part the result of an infant's early interaction with his/her environment. The basic skills of selective attention, discrimin-ation of similarity or difference, the use of inference, and awareness of causation are all believed to be forming during the sensori-motor stage, preceding the use of functional verbal expression. To date behavioural techniques have not been very successful in developing functional language (verbal or gestural) in previously non-communicating individuals. Rather these techniques appear in the main to develop rote learning of phrases which have little semantic intent and which are highly context-specific. Generalization of the phrases to contexts other than those in which they were learnt is rare. It may be that prior to teaching the non-communicating

mentally retarded, behavioural techniques should be used to establish and/or develop the cognitive skills now being identified as prerequisites for language in normal children.

Acknowledgement

The author is very grateful to Dr R. Grieve for his comments on the draft form of this chapter.

References

Baer D. M. and Guess D. (1971) Receptive training of adjectival inflection in mental retardates. *J. Appl. Behav. Anal.* **4**, 129–139.

Baer D. M., Guess D. and Sherman J. A. (1972) Adventures in simplistic grammer. In: Schiefelbush R. L. (ed.) *Language of the Mentally Retarded.* Baltimore, University Park Press.

Baer D. M. and Sherman J. A. (1964) Reinforcement control of generalised imitation in young children. *J. Exp. Child Psychol.* **1**, 37–49.

Bandura A. (1968) A social learning interpretation of psychological dysfunctions. In: London P. and Rosenham D. (ed.) *Foundations of Abnormal Psychology.* New York, Holt, Rinehart and Winston.

Baumeister A. A. and Forehand R. (1973) Stereotyped acts. In: Ellis N. R. (ed.) *International Review of Research in Mental Retardation,* Vol. 6. New York, Academic Press, pp. 55–96.

Beveridge M. C. and Tatham A. (1976) Communication in retarded adolescents: utilization of known language skills. *Am. J. Ment. Defic.* **81**, 96–99.

Bloom L. (1974) Talking, understanding and thinking. In: Schiefelbusch R. L. and Lloyd L. L. (ed.) *Language Perspectives — Acquisition, Retardation and Inter-vention.* New York, Macmillan.

Bondy A. S. and Erickson M. T. (1976) Comparison of modeling and reinforcement procedures in increasing question-asking of mildly retarded children. *J. Appl. Behav. Anal.* **9**, 108.

Brooks B. D., Morrow J. E. and Gray W. F. (1968) Reduction of autistic gaze aversion of reinforcement of visual attention responses. *J. Spec. Educ.* **2**, 307–309.

Brown R. (1970) The first sentences of child and chimpanzee. In: Brown R. (ed.) *Psycholinguistics: Selected Papers.* Illinois, Free Press.

Burland M. (1971) The implication for speech therapy of a study of the verbal regulation of behaviour in multiply handicapped children. *Br. J. Disord. Commun.* **6**, 120–124.

Carr E. G., Binkoff J. A., Kologinsky E. et al. (1978) Acquisition of sign language by autistic children. I: expressive labelling. *J. Appl. Behav. Anal.* **11**, 489–501.

Cromer R. F. (1974) The development of language and cognition: the cognitio hypothesis. In: Foss B. (ed.) *New Perspectives in Child Development.* Penguin, Harmondsworth.

Daehler M. W., Lonardo R. and Bukatko D. (1979) Matching and equivalence judg ments in very young children. *Child Dev.* **50**, 170–179.

Davis J., Robinson F. M. and Cullen C. (1975) Learning colours. Part I: *Apex* **2**, 1 15; Part II: *Apex* **3**, 14–15.

Donaldson M. (1978) *Children's Minds.* London, Fontana.

Etaugh C. F. and Van Sickle D. (1971) Discrimination of stereometric objects photographs of objects by children. *Child Dev.* **42**, 1580–1582.

Piaget J. and Inhelder B. (1969) *The Psychology of the Child.* London, Routledge and Kegan Paul.

Porton D. A. (1976) Learning to imitate in infancy. *Child Dev.* 47, 14–31.

Rogers S. J. (1977) Characteristics of the cognitive development of profoundly retarded children. *Child Dev.* 48, 837–843.

Rutter M. and Sussenwein F. (1971) A developmental and behavioral approach to the treatment of pre-school autistic children. *J. Autism Child. Schizo.* 1, 376–397.

Sailor W. (1971) Reinforcement and generalization of productive plural allomorphs in two retarded children. *J. Appl. Behav. Anal.* 4, 305–310.

Sailor W. and Taman T. (1971) Stimulus factors in the prepositional usage in three autistic children. *J. Appl. Behav. Anal.* 5, 183–190.

Schopler E. and Reichler R. J. (1971) Developmental therapy by parents with their own autistic child. In: Rutter M. (ed.) *Infantile Autism: Concepts, Characteristics and Treatment.* London, Churchill Livingstone.

Schreibman L. and Carr (1978) Elimination of echolalic responding through the training of a generalized verbal response. *J. Appl. Behav. Anal.* 11, 453–463.

Schumaker J. and Sherman J. A. (1970) Training generative verb usage by imitation and reinforcement procedures. *J. Appl. Behav. Anal.* 3, 273–287.

Sidman M. and Stoddart L. T. (1967) The effectiveness of fading in programming a simultaneous form of discrimination for retarded children. *J. Exp. Anal. Behav.* 10, 3–15.

Skinner B. F. (1953) *Science and Human Behavior.* New York, Macmillan.

Slobin D. I. (1973) Cognitive prerequisites for the development of grammar. In: Ferguson C. A. and Slobin D. I. (ed.) *Studies of Child Language Development.* New York, Holt, Rinehart and Winston.

Terrace H. S. (1966) Stimulus control. In: Honig W. K. (ed.) *Operant Behaviour: Areas of Research and Application.* New York, Appleton-Century-Crofts.

Tierney I. R., McGuire R. J. and Walton H. J. (1978) Distributions of body-rocking manifested by severely mentally deficient adults in ward environments. *J. Ment. Defic. Res.* 22, 243–254.

Tierney I. R., McGuire R. J. and Walton H. J. (1979) Reduction of stereotyped body-rocking using variable time reinforcement: practical and theoretical implications. *J. Ment. Defic. Res.* 23, 175–185.

Twardosz S. and Baer D. M. (1973) Training two severely retarded adolescents to ask questions. *J. Appl. Behav. Anal.* 6, 655–661.

Van Biervliet A. (1977) Establishing words and objects as functionally equivalent through manual sign training. *Am. J. Ment. Defic.* 82, 178–186.

Walker H. M. and Buckley N. K. (1968) The use of positive reinforcement in conditioning attending behaviour. *J. Appl. Behav. Anal.* 1, 245–252.

Walsh B. F. and Lamberts F. (1979) Errorless discrimination and picture fading as techniques for teaching sight words to TMR students. *Am. J. Ment. Defic.* 83, 473–479.

Webb R. C. and Koller J. R. (1979) Effects of sensori-motor training on intellectual and adaptive skills of profoundly retarded adults. *Am. J. Ment. Defic.* 83, 490–496.

Weiner A. E. (1969) Speech therapy and behavior modification: a conspectus. *J. Spec. Educ.* 3, 285–292.

Yule W. and Berger M. (1972) Behavior modification principles and speech delay. In: Rutter M. and Martin J. A. M. (ed.) *The Child with Delayed Speech.* Clinics in Developmental Medicine, No. 43. London, Spastics International Medical Publications: Heinemann.

Yule W., Berger M. and Howlin P. (1975) Language deficit and behaviour modification. In: O'Connor N. (ed.) *Language, Cognitive Deficits and Retardation.* London, Butterworths.

Yule W. and Berger M. (1975) Communication, language and behaviour modification. In: Kiernan C. C. and Woodford F. P. (ed.) *Behaviour Modification with the Severely Retarded*. Amsterdam, Scientific Publication Associates.

Zeaman D. and House B. J. (1963) The role of attention in retardate discrimination learning. In: Ellis N. R. (ed.) *Handbook of Mental Deficiency*. New York, McGraw-Hill.

Chapter 8

The Pragmatics of Language and the Mentally Handicapped

The Speech Therapist's Role

Sheila Wirz

Introduction

A basic theme of this book is that the communication skills of the mentally handicapped population differ from, and are usually less well developed than, similar skills in the rest of the population. This chapter will make some proposals about the ways in which these communication deficits can be remedied, concentrating on the practical management of language facilitation techniques.

The translation into English of the work of Luria (1961) and Vygotsky (1962) coincided in the UK with the work of Bernstein (1959, 1960) and Lawton (1968), and contributed to a reappraisal of the role of language in the educational process. Russian psychology described the directive and regulative functions of early language and stressed the role which language played in the development of 'higher mental functions of the child'. In contrast Piaget (1959) argued that in early childhood, experiences are necessary before a child can meaningfully acquire language skills to describe these experiences.

These contrasting views together ensured an increasing awareness of the role of language in British pedagogical practice between the mid-1960s and mid-1970s, as illustrated by the variety of government reports: Plowden (1967), Bullock (1975), Scottish Primary Memorandum (1965). In special education too there was an increasing awareness of the importance of language in developing a child's educational potential, as illustrated by the work of Mittler (1974), Mittler et al. (1974), and by other reports from the Department of Education and Science such as the report *Educating Mentally Handicapped Children* (DES, 1975), and the Melville Report *Training of Staff for Centres for the Mentally Handicapped* (DES, 1973).

Recognizing the relationship between developing language skills and cognitive skills was one important factor which increased interest in language facilitation with the mentally handicapped. Equally important was the view that all individuals, however handicapped, should be encouraged to use some form of communication. No longer was it accurate or appropriate to consider spoken/written language as 'real' communication, with other media being 'poor shadows'. Work with American sign language (Stokoe, 1972; Bellugi, 1972) in the USA has demonstrated that sign language is an autonomous language. McNaughton (1975) and Vanderheim (1975) have shown that Blissymbolics (which employs visually presented symbols) can be used as a communication system by individuals who are too physically and/or mentally handicapped to use spoken or written language. No longer are speech therapists concerned only with spoken language (if indeed they were ever so exclusive), but with the whole range of communication activities.

With this increasing interest in the need to develop language skills in the mentally handicapped, speech therapists become an important if not a key member of the language facilitation team. If this is the case, then a number of questions immediately arise. Are there enough speech therapists working with the mentally handicapped to undertake sole responsibility for language development? Is it appropriate that the speech therapist should be forced to make a choice as to which section of the mentally handicapped population can receive speech therapy? Should the 'lucky' group be less handicapped educationally subnormal mild (ESN(M)) children in special schools, or more handicapped educationally subnormal severe (ESN(S)) children in schools and units, or profoundly handicapped children in day care centres, or mentally handicapped adults in subnormality hospitals and other institutions?

In the UK, the Quirk Report (1972) provides the most recent official figures of the need for language therapy with handicapped children, compared with the distribution of speech therapy resources. This report suggested that '20 per cent of mentally handicapped children . . .' and '. . . 50 per cent of severely subnormal children required speech therapy'. At that time the suggested establishment of speech therapists was one for every 10 000 schoolchildren in the total population. Despite increases in the numbers of speech therapists since the Quirk Report, there are still insufficient numbers for them to assume responsibility for the implementation of all language facilitation work with handicapped children, let alone with institutionalized mentally handicapped adults.

Speech therapists have a vital role to play in language facilitation work with the mentally handicapped, but in order to ensure that all handicapped children and adults benefit from intervention programmes, it seems crucial that speech therapists dismiss the aura of mystique surrounding some of their work, and instead encourage a multidisciplinary team approach to language facilitation. It is the speech therapist, among the multidisciplinary team (medical doctor, psychologist, nursing staff, social worker, paramedical staff and parents), who, through her training, brings to the problem of language facilitation skills from speech pathology, psychology, phonetics and linguistics, and neurology – a truly holistic overview. It may be necessary in some institutions to explore and discuss professional dynamics of medical, psychology and therapy staff. The author has been encouraged in visits to speech and hearing centres, and day care centres in the USA to see how professional status does not always affect team leadership in specific areas of care. There are potential problems, if it is assumed in case discussions or therapy planning meetings that the medical doctor will always be chairman!

The recent report in the UK by the Department of Education and Science and Scottish Education Department's committee of enquiry into the education of handicapped children (Warnock, 1978) makes reference to this need for an interdisciplinary approach to the education of young handicapped children. Recommendation 4/28 suggests that local education authorities who are responsible for providing education for all handicapped children should be given the means to provide multidisciplinary assessments. Following such proposals on multidisciplinary assessment, the Warnock Report goes on to explore the possibility of multidisciplinary therapy/teaching. Recommendation 16/21 suggests that there should be some dual qualifying courses for therapist–teachers, to ensure that the division between therapy and teaching does not become too sharply defined with handicapped children.

A Multidisciplinary Team Approach

In a recent paper (Wirz, 1978), attention has been drawn to the multidisciplinary team concerned with the development of communication skills of the mentally handicapped. There it is suggested that this 'team' is in fact every adult who is in contact with the client. Rather than follow traditional professional boundaries in the description of this team, it seems more useful to draw a distinction between those adults who are in daily contact with the child, compared with those who are in frequent (i.e. less than daily) contact with the child.

Those in daily contact with the child will be concerned with the actual implementation and daily review of the child's language progress. They will be the *implementers* of the language programme. Those adults who see the child less frequently will be the *monitors*, observing changes in the child's communication skills over periods of time.

The implementers will include parents, residential or nursing staff, teachers or nursery teachers, classroom aides, and domestic/servicing staff, who are in daily contact with the child or mentally handicapped adult.

As the speech therapist is rarely in daily contact with the handicapped individual she must head the monitoring group. Other members of this monitoring group will include family and school doctors, social worker, psychologist, health visitor and, possibly, other therapists, medical and dental personnel.

Leading the multidisciplinary team requires the organization of in-service courses and review meetings among the professionals concerned with each group of clients. Experience in running in-service courses for a range of professionals concerned with mentally handicapped individuals (nurses, teachers, instructresses, social workers, etc.) over several years suggests that short courses should not aim to train quasi speech therapists, but they can increase interest and develop skills in the area of communication among professionals involved in day-to-day contact with the handicapped child or adult.

Observation of Communication Skills

An important component of any in-service course designed to heighten professionals' awareness of language with the mentally handicapped is to help these professionals to observe their clients' communication skills in a structured and objective manner. The following observation schedule (*see* Appendix I) was developed by the author at Moray House College of Education in Edinburgh, and has been modified over the years in response to comments of teachers in schools for the mentally handicapped, instructresses in junior occupation centres (or, more recently, ESN(S) schools), nurses in hospitals for the mentally handicapped and by speech therapists.

The model of communication used in compiling this checklist is similar to that suggested by Laver and Hutcheson (1972). This model suggests that there are three principal components to communication: linguistic aspects, paralinguistic aspects and interaction management. Linguistic aspects of communication include the understanding and expression of language structure, the understanding and use of vocabulary, and the phonological development of the child. Paralinguistic aspects of communication include vocal aspects such as voice quality and prosody, and non-vocal aspects such as eye contact, gesture and facial expression.

Finally, interaction management refers to the ability of the child to interact with peers, with familiars or with adults in dyadic, small-group or large-group situations, and with the child's or adult's ability to use proxemics and sequencing skills in these varying situations.

Using this model of communication, it is possible to take a holistic view of children's communication skills, rather than the more traditional emphasis on spoken language skills (which in this model form only one-third of the communication process). This model is illustrated in *Fig.* 11. In the model, attention is not drawn to the different media of communication which can be used to express the linguistic components, instead it is assumed that for most of this population, the spoken medium will be employed.

The checklist is divided into six main areas of observation:

1. Expression — refers to 'linguistic output'.

2. Listening/comprehension – refers to 'linguistic input'.
3. Language usage – refers broadly to observations of interaction management.
4. Articulation – comments on the articulation abilities and intelligibility of a speaker.
5. Paralinguistic observations – refers to paralinguistic or non-verbal aspects of communication.
6. Imitation – refers to the speaker's ability to imitate spoken and unspoken stimuli.

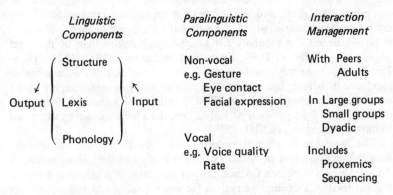

Fig. 11. Model of communication.

While this checklist is of course a very crude tool, it is reported to be a useful way of focusing nurses' or teachers' attention on the communication behaviour of their patients or pupils. A glance at the checklist shows that while it follows the stages of language acquisition, it is not strictly developmental, especially in the later stages of each section. The advantage of having a checklist which follows developmental stages is that it will quickly identify the child whose language development is slow but following usual patterns of acquisition (e.g. most Down's syndrome), compared with a child whose language development shows a bizarre pattern of acquisition (e.g. a brain damaged child with autistic features).

There is some evidence of the utility of this checklist in a study of 33 ESN(S) children with chronological ages of 12–15 years and mental ages of 2·0 up to 5·10 years (Wirz and Miller, 1976). In this study it was found that there was a close relationship between the observations noted for each child on this checklist by instructresses in a junior occupation centre (now an ESN(S) school) and the scores of the Reynell Language Development Scales (Reynell, 1976).

In using the checklist it should of course be borne in mind by all adults in contact with the child/adult that his language skills are at best going to be commensurate with his mental age rather than his chronological age.

Communication Breakdown

The observation of functional communication can probably be done by any informed adult who is in regular contact with the client, using a checklist such as the one suggested above. However, the assessment of communication breakdown is rightly the province of the speech therapist, and it is she who has the skills to attempt such assessment and prescribe appropriate remedial help. It will be the speech therapist who recognizes the difference between slow maturation and bizarre development of communication skills, and who carries out appropriate remediation. There are a variety of studies which show that the incidence of speech disorders is higher among the mentally handicapped population than in the total population (Williams, 1969; Evans and Hampson, 1968; RNID, 1978; Lloyd, 1976). Surveys such as these also show that there is a higher incidence of hearing loss among the handicapped. In a recent survey of the incidence of hearing loss among ESN(S) and ESN(M) children, 9 per cent of ESN(M) and 11 per cent of ESN(S) children were known or suspected to have a hearing loss (RNID, 1978).

The incidence of voice disorder is high too; 20 per cent of mentally handicapped speakers in William's (1969) study had disordered voices. A 3-year Medical Research Council project currently in progress is attempting to develop a descriptive system for voice quality and voice dynamics among a range of pathological speakers, including mentally handicapped groups (Laver and Wirz, MRC Grant No. G 978–11–92/N). Using an existing theoretical model for the phonotic description of voice quality (Laver, 1979), it is hoped to be able to typify the vocal characteristics of certain groups of mentally handicapped speakers. The vocal characteristics being investigated include laryngeal and supralaryngeal components of voice quality and dynamic features of spoken output. Vocal profiles can then be built up typifying various groups of speakers. It is hoped to be able to specify acoustic and physiological correlates for these characteristic vocal profiles.

The incidence of stammering is also higher among mentally handicapped speakers; 7·5 per cent in the Williams (1969) study, and in the Newcastle study of stammering 9 per cent of ESN(M) school population stammered, compared with 1 per cent of the normal school population (Andrews and Harris, 1964).

Parental Involvement

The role of parents as implementers of language facilitation programmes is vital if there is regular parent–child contact. It is obviously a very efficient use of resources if the speech therapist can utilize the enormous commitment of time and emotion which parents can bring to helping their child. Work at the Hester Adrian Unit, and elsewhere, has demonstrated the efficacy of parents in developing the language skills of their children (Cunningham and Jeffree, 1971; Jeffree and Cashdon, 1971; Jeffree and McConkey, 1974; Johnson and Katz, 1973; Cooper et al., 1974). Regular workshops are an important component of language programmes involving parents, with time for demonstration, discussion and advice, in order to maintain parental motivation and objectivity. Some speech therapists may choose to use parental guidance programmes which are specifically designed for each individual child, while others may use one of the commercially available programmes. Portage (Shearer and Shearer, 1972) and the Language Acquisition Programme (Kent, 1974) are among the commercial schemes which are widely used. The developmental charts developed at the Hester Adrian Research Centre (Jeffree and McConkey, 1978), although not an actual 'programme', are a very useful commercially available observation scheme which can be used to supplement specifically designed developmental programmes.

Strategies for Language Development

A COMMUNICATION ENVIRONMENT

There is a wide choice of language intervention programmes available for the mentally handicapped. These range from the structured behaviour modification approaches of Sloane and McAulay (1968), Bereiter and Engelmann (1966) and Kent (1974), to the cognitive approaches of Furth (1974) and Cooper et al. (1978), or the sociodramatic play approaches of Smilansky (1968). Lloyd (1976) and Cooper et al. (1978) review the literature concerning the range of language facilitation techniques which can be used with the mentally handicapped.

Whatever rationale the therapist chooses in her planning of an intervention programme, it is essential that the stimulation provided for the mentally handicapped child or adult is structured. Fenn (1976) draws the analogy from maths learning: '... if a child gets all his sums wrong should he be given more and more sums until he gets them right?' Obviously such handling of maths learning problems would be absurd. But is it not similarly absurd to suggest that a child with an intact hearing mechanism who has failed to develop language skills as well as his peers of similar mental age, should simply be provided with generalized language stimulation? This mere provision of more and more language is as doomed to failure as the extra practice with sums. Unless he is shown how to utilize language, this rich, stimulating environment can leave him unscathed. He needs to be given such richness in diluted doses, through a structured remedial programme. It will fall to the speech therapist to ensure that the structure of the programme is understood, and adhered to, by the implementers of the language programme.

It may be that for some older mentally handicapped adults, who have been housed for many years in large institutions, lack of language stimulation has been and remains a major contributory factor to their poor communication skills. Lyle (1960) showed the deleterious effects which lack of stimulation in large institutions can have on a patient's language skills.

However, one must be cautious and not assume that enriching the language environment of an institutionalized mentally handicapped individual solves the problem, for in institutions there is often a reduction in the patient's need to communicate. Understandably, nursing staff in large institutions wish to complete basic chores such as washing, laying out clothes, dressing, giving food, etc., quickly and efficiently. But how often are these caring activities carried out without any need for the patient to interact with the nurse? In schools for ESN(M) and ESN(S) children there is a growing awareness of the need to involve pupils in interaction, rather than relegating them to be the silent recipients of care. With improved staffing levels in long-stay institutions, and/or the use of volunteers as implementers of language programmes, it is to be hoped that this awareness of the need for patients to interact could become more central to the regime of long-stay hospital wards.

In general terms, then, pragmatic considerations will include first the choice of a language stimulation programme, which both suits the need of the mentally handicapped individual, and which is practical within his environment of home, school or institution. Secondly, it is necessary to ensure that the caring regime allows time and opportunity for the individual to use his communication skills in order to satisfy his own needs.

REMEDIAL LANGUAGE PROGRAMMES

Planning a remedial language programme involves consideration of 4 main areas (Wirz and Francis, 1978):
1. attention and awareness;
2. listening;
3. understanding;
4. expression.

The aim of such training is to develop a child's listening and understanding skills, then speaking skills, and finally his self-monitoring skills. This later stage may not be achieved by the more profoundly handicapped.

Attention and awareness training involves, at a very simple level, encouraging the child to tolerate closeness, or to interact with the teacher/ therapist, for example in play, in looking together at books. At a slightly higher level it might involve encouraging imitative responses of gross movement, of fine movement, of sounds. Throughout such training it would be necessary to take account of the actual time a child could attend to a given task, and gradually increase this attention span. Later awareness training would include activities such as a recognition of the constancy of objects, classification and grouping activities, etc.

Listening skills can be trained at a very elementary level by helping the child to become aware of the differences between sound and lack of sound. Later, localization of sound, or sound discrimination might be the task. *Learning to Listen* (LDA, 1976) provides activities at these levels. As sound awareness and listening skills improve, the child may be helped to develop his understanding skills.

Understanding. At a very simple level this involves word to object matching, and later word to picture and phrase to picture matching. Later understanding exercises involve increased length of commands, understanding prepositions, tenses or modifiers, etc. More advanced stages in training understanding would be to help the child understand simple stories, or explanations, first with accompanying actions and later without.

Expression. At a basic level, training a child's expressive language skills will involve object naming with single words, and later with modifier and noun or short phrases. During the child's single word stage, attention should be paid not only to the use of single nouns, but also to verbs and modifiers. Later, sequenced stories, role-play activities, and retelling events are among the activities which a therapist teacher can use to help the child to use more mature language structures such as questions, auxiliary verbs, tense, etc. This type of remedial language programme will help the mentally handicapped child to develop language skills, the nuts and bolts of his communication.

NON-VERBAL COMMUNICATION

It has been assumed above that the development of a young child's or adult's language skills is the focus of attention, and that these language skills would predominantly involve the spoken medium. But what of the mentally handicapped adult who has failed to develop spoken language? In recent years there has been a growth of interest in developing non-verbal communication skills among such clients. With increased knowledge in this field it has become possible to predict at an earlier stage which children are likely to need non-verbal communication as either an alternative or supplementary form of communication. Various communication boards and mime systems have been used for many years by speech therapists (e.g. Levett, 1971), but recently attention has been directed to the use of systematic symbol systems for communication. It is important here to draw a distinction between visual or mime systems, which can be used to signal an individual's needs (such signal systems are usually very restricted), and systems which involve visual or spatial symbols. By using symbol systems rather than signalling schemes, much wider communication possibilities emerge. Systematic symbol systems divide broadly into those which employ the written medium and those employing the spatial medium.

Using the spatial medium as a means of communication with the mentally handicapped is, of course, not a new idea. Natural gestures for approval, disapproval, affection, distaste, etc., and iconic gestures for food, drink, sleep, hot, cold, toilet, etc., can be used and understood by most people including the mildly and moderately handicapped. However, a gesture system does not have to become very large before iconocy alone is insufficient, and a degree of arbitrariness must be introduced. Some systems have introduced these arbitrary items from theoretical rationale, for example the Paget Gorman sign system which is based upon a classificatory system. Paget Gorman sign language, despite the apparent disadvantage of requiring quite fine motor movements, has been used satisfactorily with mentally handicapped and physically handicapped children (Fenn and Rowe, 1975).

Another sign system, Makaton, has taken iconic and arbitrary signs from British sign language (the language of the congenitally deaf subculture in the UK), and developed a simple sign language suitable for mentally handicapped clients (Cornforth et al., 1974). Makaton is probably the commonest sign system used by speech therapists in the UK, with the mentally handicapped. This system can be used both as a medium for language facilitation, developing a client's understanding, lexical and expressive abilities, and as a basic medium of communication for those clients who have a very restricted communication potential. The main disadvantage of sign systems such as Paget Gorman or Makaton, is that the system must be learned by all individuals in contact with the handicapped individual if communication is to be readily achieved.

The commonest symbol system using the written medium is Blissymbolics. Developed by McNaughton (1975) in the Ontario Crippled Children's Centre, Toronto, this sytem of symbol communication has proved to be useful at various levels of communication (McNaughton, 1975; Vanderheim, 1975). Initially, Blissymbolics was used to provide a system of expression for those children who were too physically handicapped to have developed spoken or written language, but whose comprehension of spoken language had developed relatively normally. Such children without any form of expressive communication, unless spotted by an alert parent, psychologist or medical officer, had often been relegated to institutions for the mentally handicapped. Many speech therapists working with Blissymbolics in hospitals for the mentally handicapped have found some adult in-patients who, given this system of communication, learn quickly to express themselves, often for the first time, casting doubt on the assessment of their abilities which led to their hospitalization. A second and equally important use of Blissymbolics is as a means of developing the language skills of the mentally handicapped clients, or those whose auditory perception (rather than acuity) is so greatly impaired that they can make no sense of incoming auditorily presented language. In such cases, Blissymbolics is used both by the teacher/therapist and by the client. A third use of Blissymbolics is to display a limited number of symbols on a communicator board for more handicapped individuals, enabling them to indicate their basic needs. The overriding advantage of Blissymbolics over sign language systems is that it does not have to be learned by the person in contact with the mentally handicapped Blissymbolic user. Any literate person can communicate with a Bliss user.

Social Skills Training

The medium of communication will then be chosen to match the child's or adult's needs, and it may be written, spoken or signed. The language acquisition programme designed for the pupil or patient will ensure that he develops the linguistic skills needed for his chosen medium of communication. Such skills are the 'nuts and bolts' of communication referred to above. Ensuring that the pupil's or patient's environment provides opportunity for him to use his skills will make certain that these 'nuts and bolts' do not become rusty through disuse. But there is a third important area of consideration which is often overlooked, that of social skills training, which enables the child or adult to become more aware of interaction, and to understand how effective communication depends not only on his language skills (in whatever medium), but also on how these skills are used.

Social skills training is an area of developing interest among speech therapists working with the mentally handicapped. While such training has been considered to be of great relevance to the mentally ill for some time (Trower et al., 1978), it is a comparatively recent phenomenon for this work to be applied to the mentally handicapped. Francis (1979) is a speech therapist who has developed such training with ESN(M) children and adolescents. This work is reported to have favourable results both by teachers and by the pupils themselves.

Assessment of Progress

In any language programme which involves the use of structured remedial materials or the introduction of a non-verbal communication system, or any form of speech therapy, it is important to be able to assess the efficacy of the intervention.

Assessments of efficacy at a quantitative level are relatively straight-forward. One can measure changes in vocal pitch, e.g. by laryngographic measurement (Wirz and Anthony, 1979), or changes in vocal tension by spectrographic measurement (Spector et al., 1979). Similarly, by phonetic analysis it is possible to quantify changes in the articulatory skills of a speaker or, by language test scores, show improvements in language skills. However, such quantitative assessments describe skills which a speaker has achieved, and they do not necessarily take account of how a speaker uses these skills in social settings. Assessment of usage is most important among mentally handicapped speakers, and it inevitably involves qualitative judgements as to how much, and how effectively, he uses his skills. This assessment of functional communication is of equal importance to any quantitative measures.

At the beginning of this chapter I implied that it was advisable to try to facilitate language development among mentally handicapped children and adults. A reasonable response to such a suggestion would be to ask 'Why bother?' There are, I suggest, two main reasons for bothering. First because of the intimate relationship between language development and cognitive development; as Gurney (1976) suggests, 'educational failure is primarily linguistic failure'. Many would consider that Gurney's remark was an overstatement but few would challenge its basic theme. Secondly, every individual, however handicapped, is a member of a social unit, and to ensure that he interacts as well as possible with his peers is beneficial not only to the handicapped individual himself, but also to all those in contact with him.

These, I suggest, are the two principal reasons why we must ensure the maximum development of communicative potential among all mentally handicapped individuals.

Appendix 1. Suggested Checklist for Observation of Communication Skills

	Date	Consistently	Occasionally	Never
Expression				
1. Crying (undifferentiated)				
2. Crying (differentiated, to indicate different states, e.g. hunger, discomfort, etc.)				
3. Mouthing				
4. Produces vowel sounds				

	Date	Consistently	Occasionally	Never
5. Produces consonant sounds				
6. Produces bizarre sounds (dissimilar to the consonants and vowels of the mother tongue)				
7. Produces a range of consonants				
8. Produces single syllable sounds using bizarre sounds				
9. Produces single syllable sounds using the consonants of mother tongue most of the time				
10. Produces double syllable sounds				
11. Produces expressive jargon (including changes of intonation and rate)				
12. Produces meaningful noises (consistently)				
13. Produces one meaningful word				
14. Produces 3/4 meaningful words				
15. Produces 2-word combinations (not imitated combinations)				
16. Produces 3-word combinations				
17. Uses only labels (nouns)				
18. Uses action words (verbs)				
19. Refers to self by name				
20. Uses 'me'				
21. Uses 'I'				
22. Uses negative				
23. Uses plurals				
24. Uses past tense				
25. Uses future tense				
26. Uses simple modifiers (to describe objects or actions)				
27. Uses adjectives appropriately				
28. Uses a wide range of adjectives				
29. Uses adverbs				
30. Uses a wide range of adverbs				
31. 'Invents' his own adjectives/adverbs if needed				
32. Labels familiar objects				
33. Has an especially good vocabulary/nouns (give a few examples)				
34. Asks questions (with rising intonation)				
35. Asks questions with question word				
36. Uses prepositions to show position (e.g. in, on, under)				
37. Uses articles, definite and indefinite (the, a)				

	Date	Consistently	Occasionally	Never

Listening/Comprehension

1. Cries in response to crying child
2. Quietened by familiar voice
3. Looks for sound
4. Listens to music
5. Differentiates between pleased and displeased voice
6. Responds to own name
7. Responds to 'No'. Responds to 'All done' or other well-known phrases
8. Gives objects on request
9. Names pictures on request
10. Names parts of the body
11. Responds to simple one-grade commands if accompanied by gesture (involves only one component to the task)
12. Responds to one-grade commands without accompanying gesture
13. Listens to simple stories
14. Understands content of stories (object and action)
15. Understands sequence of stories, can repeat beginning and end of story
16. Understands sequence of stories, can describe main characters
17. Understands sequence of stories, can give a resumé of story
18. Responds to two-grade commands (involving 2 distinct components to the task)
19. Responds to three-grade commands (involving 3 distinct components)
20. Understands a fable — the events of the fable (literal understanding)
21. Understands a fable — the meaning of the fable (opinion)
22. Understands commands using prepositions (e.g. in, on, behind)
23. Follows instructions of a *task* without needing an accompanying demonstration

	Date	Consistently	Occasionally	Never
Language Usage				
1. Will speak if spoken to				
2. Will imitate conversation, by asking or commenting				
3. Will talk to strangers				
4. Talks to other children				
5. Sings to himself				
6. Talks to himself				
7. Asks for things he wants with accompanying gesture				
8. Asks for things he wants without accompanying gesture				
9. Spontaneously tries to express *ideas* to other people (disregarding poor language structure)				
10. His conversation is bound to the concrete, i.e. events rather than ideas				
11. He is easy to understand				
12. He is difficult to understand				
13. He uses questions – a little				
14. He uses questions – a lot. Give examples				
15. Willingness to use verbal communication				
a. to teacher				
b. with peers				
c; with strangers				
16. In what situations does he use language?				
17. Is it relevant language?				
18. Is gesture a predominant feature?				
19. Is there a non-verbal means of communication?				
20. Do his intonation patterns help intelligibility?				
21. Are there repetitive phrases?				
22. Does he form sentences rather than speak in single syllables?				
23. Is there any frustration regarding language?				
24. Is he willing to repeat?				
25. Is his language appropriate to language of home environment?				
Articulation				
1. Any disordered articulation				
2. Intelligibility (Is his speech easy to understand?)				

	Date	Consistently	Occasionally	Never

Paralinguistic Observations

1. Willingness to cooperate; attends to another person
2. Attends to visual stimuli
3. Attends to auditory stimuli
4. Glances at speaker
5. Glances at material presented
6. Gazes at speaker
7. Gazes at material presented
8. Ability to imitate actions related to self
   with physical prompt
   without physical prompt
9. Ability to imitate actions unrelated to self
   with physical prompt
   without physical prompt
10. Ability to indicate by simple directional gesture
11. Uses gesture instead of oral communication
12. Uses gesture to supplement oral communication
13. Indicates by posture/gesture a response to speech
14. Uses facial expressions appropriately
15. Uses facial expressions inappropriately
16. Uses physical communication instead of oral (e.g. patting, hugging)
17. Uses physical communication to supplement oral
18. Uses physical communication excessively

Imitation

1. Copies sounds
2. Copies simple rhythm tapping
3. Copies complex rhythm tapping
4. Copies spoken rhythms
5. Copies spoken babble patterns
6. Copies word patterns
7. Can learn simple rhymes/jingles/songs
8. Learns new songs, poems readily
9. Repeat rhymes, etc., with rhythm
10. Repeats rhymes, etc, without rhythm (more as word strings)

	Date	Consistently	Occasionally	Never
11. There are some imitated utterances in his 'conversation'				
12. There are many imitated utterances in his 'conversation'				

References

Andrews G. and Harris M. (1964) *The Syndrome of Stuttering*. London, Heinemann.

Bellugi U. (1972) Studies in Sign Language. In: O'Rouke T. (ed.) *Psycholinguistics and Total Communication*. Washington D.C., *Am. Ann. Deaf.*

Bereiter C. and Engelmann S. (1966) An academically orientated pre-school programme for culturally deprived children. In: Hechinger F. M. (ed.) *Pre-School Education Today*. New York, Doubleday.

Bernstein B. (1959) Public language: some sociological implications of a linguistic form. *Br. J. Sociol.* **10**, 311–326.

Bernstein B. (1960) Language and social class. *Br. J. Sociol.* **11**, 271–276.

Bullock Sir A. (1975) *A Language for Life*. London, H.M.S.O.

Cooper J., Moodley M. and Reynell J. (1974) Intervention programmes for preschool children with delayed language development. *Br. J. Disord. Commun.* **9** (1), 81–92.

Cooper J., Moodley M. and Reynell J. (1978) *Helping Language Development*. London, Arnold.

Cornforth A., Johnson K. and Walker M. (1974) Teaching sign language to deaf MH adults. *Apex*, **21**, 23–24.

Cunningham C. and Jeffree D. (1971) *Working with Parents*. Manchester, NSMHC and Hester Adrian Research Centre.

Department of Education and Science (1975) *Educating Mentally Handicapped Children*. Education Pamphlet No. 69. London, HMSO.

Evans D. and Hampson M. (1968) Language of mongols. *Br. J. Disord. Commun.* **3** (2), 170–182.

Fenn G. (1976) Against verbal enrichment. In: Berry P. (ed.) *Language and Communication in the Mentally Handicapped*. London, Arnold.

Fenn G. and Rowe J. (1975) An experiment in manual communication. *Br. J. Disord. Commun.* **10**(1), 3–17.

Francis E. (1979) Social skills training. *Education in the North*. **16**, 14–22.

Furth H. (1974) *Thinking Goes to School*. New York, OUP.

Gurney R. (1976) *Language Learning and Remedial Teaching*. London, Arnold.

Jeffree D. and Cashdon A. (1971) SSN children and their parents: an experiment in language improvement. *Br. J. Educ. Psychol.* **41**, 189–194.

Jeffree D. and McConkey R. (1974) Extending language through play. *Spec. Educ.* **1**, 13–16.

Jeffree D. and McConkey R. (1978) *P.I.P. Development Charts*. London, Hodder & Stoughton.

Johnson M. and Katz C. (1973) Using parents as change agents for their children. *J. Child Psychiatry* **14**, 181–201.

Kent L. (1974) *Language Acquisition Programme for the Severely Retarded*. Champaign, Ill., Research Press.

Laver J. and Hutcheson S. (1972) *Communication and Face to Face Interaction.* Harmondsworth, Penguin.

Laver J. (1979) The description of voice quality in general phonetic theory. *Work in Progress.* Department of Linguistics, University of Edinburgh.

Laver J. and Wirz S. (1979) Vocal profiles of speech disorders. Medical Research Council Grant No. G978/11/92/N.

Lawton D. (1968) *Social Class, Language and Education.* London, Routledge & Kegan Paul.

Learning Development Aids (1976) *Learning to Listen.* Wisbech, Cambs., Learning Development Aids.

Levett L. (1971) A method of communication for non speaking SSN children. *Br. J. Disord. Commun.* 2, 64–7.

Lloyd L. (1976) *Communication Assessment and Intervention Strategies.* Baltimore, University Press.

Luria A. R. (1961) *The Role of Speech in the Regulation of Normal and Abnormal Behaviour.* Oxford, Pergamon.

Lyle J. G. (1960) Some factors affecting speech development of imbecile children in an institution. *J. Child Psychol. Psychiatry* 2, 121–130.

McNaughton S. (1975) *Teaching Guildlines – Blissymbolics Communication.* Fareham, Mass., Farleys.

Melville C. (1973) *The Training of Staff for Centres for the MH.* London, HMSO.

Mittler P. (1974) Language and communication. In: Clarke A. M. and Clarke A. D. B. (ed.) *Mental Deficiency: The Changing Outlook.* London, Methuen.

Mittler P. et al. (1974) Assessment and remediation of language comprehension and production in SSN children. Final report to SSRC. Hester Adrian Research Centre.

Piaget J. (1959) *Language and Thought of the Child.* London, Routledge & Kegan Paul.

Plowden J. (1967) *Children and Their Primary Schools.* London, HMSO.

Quirk R. (1972) *Speech Therapy Services.* London, HMSO.

Reynell J. (1976) *Language Development Scales.* Windsor, National Foundation for Educational Research.

RNID (1978) *Results of Survey of Hearing Loss in ESN(S) and ESN(M) Children.* London, Royal National Institute for the Deaf.

Scottish Education Department (1965) *Primary Education in Scotland.* London, HMSO.

Shearer M. and Shearer D. (1972) *The Portage Programme: A Model for Early Childhood Education.* Reston, Virginia, Council for Exceptional Children.

Sloane S. and McAulay C. (1968) *Operant Procedures in Remedial Speech and Language Training.* Boston, Mass., Houghton Mifflin.

Smilansky S. (1968) *The Effects of Sociodramatic Play on Disadvantaged Pre-school Children.* New York, Wiley.

Spector P., Subtelny J., Whitehead R. et al. (1979) Programme to reduce vocal tension in hearing impaired speakers. *Volta Rev.* 81, 81–90.

Stokoe W. (1972) Classification and description of sign languages. In: *Current Trends in Linguistics,* Vol. 12. The Hague, Mouton.

Trower W., Bryant P. and Argyle M. (1978) *Social Skills and Mental Health.* London, Methuen.

Vanderheim D., Brown W., McKenzie P. et al. (1975) Symbol communication for the mentally handicapped. *Ment. Retard.* 13(1), 34–37.

Vygotsky L. S. (1962) *Thought and Language.* Trans. Haufmann and Vakar. Cambridge, Mass., MIT.

Warnock M. (1978) *Report of the Committee of Enquiry into Education of Handicapped Children and Young Adults.* London, HMSO.

Williams R. (1969) *Speech Disorders and Hearing Loss in a Hospitalized Subnormal Population.* London, Royal National Institute for the Deaf.

Wirz S. L. (1978) Language facilitation with the mentally handicapped: preparation of the multidisciplinary team. In: Fink O. (ed.) *Future Special Education*. Reston, Virginia, Council for Exceptional Children.

Wirz S. L. and Anthony J. (1979) The use of the voiscope in improving the speech of deaf children. *Br. J. Disord. Commun.* **14**(2), 137–153.

Wirz S. L. and Francis E. (1978) *Strategies for language development in mentally handicapped children*. Edinburgh, Moray House College of Education.

Wirz S. L. and Miller P. (1976) Language development programme with older SSN children. Paper presented at the National Conference on the Language of the Mentally Handicapped, Edinburgh.

Overview and Conclusions

Chapter Nine

Broadening the Perspective on Communication Problems

W. I. Fraser and R. Grieve

The contributions to this book are varied in nature, different chapters having had different concerns. Some chapters have been primarily concerned with vocal, some with verbal, some with non-verbal communication. And while the emphasis in some chapters has been on the normal course of development, in others the emphasis has fallen on communication difficulties encountered by retarded children.

However, there are two characteristics common to these various contributions. First, all the chapters have attempted to describe recent research, introduce new ideas, and examine issues and concerns pertinent to the study and amelioration of communication problems. Secondly, another characteristic common to the contributions, although perhaps implicitly so, is that they all reflect the need to broaden our perspective on the study of communication and its difficulties. While we are all well aware that problems in communication may frequently arise from the (normal or retarded) individual's difficulties with receptive and/or expressive abilities, there has recently been a tendency to recognize that such difficulties are unlikely to be resolved simply by confining attention to the individual. How we can help this individual to understand better what is said to him, how we can help that individual to express more effectively what he wants to convey — these are relevant concerns which deserve attention. But they are not the only concerns, for as the psychologist and educationalist Jerome Bruner has recently reminded us (Bruner, 1978), the essence of communication is dialogue. Thus if we fail to tackle problems of communication within their appropriate context, which is social in nature, we run the risk of failing to meet with anything other than very limited success. Communication is not so much concerned with the *expression* of thoughts and feelings, as with the *exchange* of information on the feelings and ideas of those involved in the communicative process. If communication is viewed as the exchange of information, and communication difficulties or disorders are viewed as barriers to the effective exchange of information, adoption of such a broader perspective directs our attention to important aspects of the communicative process.

This has been illustrated by the contributions to this book. Thus in the first section, the chapters on crying emphasize the need to consider not only the overall dynamic patterns of infants' cries, but also how caregivers respond to these patterns. In the second section, the chapters on verbal development try to indicate that language and its development should be considered within its social and communicative contexts, not within a linguistic vacuum. Likewise, the third section on non-verbal communication inquires why retarded individuals respond as they do, as a result of the social circumstances in which they find themselves. And in the fourth section, on therapeutic procedures, the importance of the individual's abilities to communicate across a range of contexts, with a wide variety of people, is given due emphasis.

Of course, while each of the individual chapters has tried to adopt a broad perspective, to some extent it is inevitable that they have looked at aspects of the problem with a close-up lens, for it is necessary to attend to the fine detail of the processes of communication and the difficulties or disorders that may arise. However now, in this concluding chapter, we wish to change the lens and the focus. Here, we wish to look at the problems with a wide-angle lens, and try to broaden the perspective even more. We do so by considering six topics, all of which, to our mind, require examination. The first is concerned with the prevention of linguistic handicap. If prevention fails, then there is a need to identify those who need help. In providing help, the identification of realistic targets and the delivery of effective services need to be considered, as does the removal of obstacles to intervention. Finally, we briefly consider new lines of research that might usefully be pursued, and indicate contributions that various professions can make to the enterprise of understanding and alleviating communication problems.

The Prevention of Linguistic Handicap

As everyone would agree, it is preferable to prevent linguistic handicap occurring, than remedy it once it has occurred. But how does linguistic handicap arise, and how can it be prevented? These are not easy matters, for while most children have the good fortune to begin learning to communicate in helpful, accepting environments, others do not. Children at risk are those born into already large families, accommodated in ghetto housing areas, where, for example, the mother's conscious awareness may well be restricted by fatigue, and perhaps alcohol, to a repetitive commentary on local dereliction and the inadequacies of public transport to allow escape. What are the restrictions placed on language development in early childhood by minds numbed and dulled by such endemic chronic depression?

What are the effects on a child who gets 'a bad start' in turn-taking dialogue because the mother has difficulty in forming an attachment? The mother may have had a request for an abortion rejected, she may have had poor maternal care herself, she may have had a previous child die in infancy. She may be very young, unmarried or undecided as to whether the child should be adopted, or she may have a puerperal psychosis. Alternatively, the child may require prolonged incubator care or repeated surgery, or may be physically stigmatized. Can a child who misses out on early communicative dialogue ever catch up? Individuals mildly retarded from subcultural origins also have a high incidence of neurological defects, which may remain undetected before it is too late. Mothers such as those described above are particularly unlikely to attend antenatal clinics until the last month of pregnancy, and may not benefit from postnatal care. As a result of public housing policies, such mothers often no longer have their own more experienced mothers to hand to detect serious illness in infants. Housing planners do not seem to be aware that grannies can stop brain damage.

Three aspects of retarded cognitive functioning recently highlighted by Feuerstein (1977) are: (1) the child's genetic constitution, (2) deviations in the child's neurophysiological substrata and (3) the child's interaction with the environment. While the last of these is distinctly modifiable, the time of intervention is important. Yet when is retarded performance, produced largely by early deprivation, most reversible? It used to be held that intervention had to occur within 'critical' periods. However, over the years this has gradually been modified from 'critical', to 'sensitive', to 'optimal' periods, for in some disorders, considerable vocabulary acquisition may occur long after the end of the so-called 'critical' language learning periods. But what are these critical, sensitive or optimal periods, and why can learning occur outside them?

An important factor may be improvement in motivation. But, unfortunately, the 'subcultural' child may not even try. Unless education and training can be seen to be relevant, to the child and to his parents, motivation is unlikely to exist, far less improve. So a web of deprivation— brain damage—helpless inarticulateness may develop.

Nevertheless, attempts can be made to rescue the most vulnerable victims of this web. For example, in a project conducted in Milwaukee with disproportionately vulnerable mothers, Garber and Heber (1977) motivated and trained the mothers to improve their early dialogue skills, resulting in two-year language 'gains' in their offspring. Thus teaching the mother — the child's first 'teacher' — is one step that can lead to improvement in the communicative performance of children who have fallen behind, or to prevention of delays occurring in the first place. However, if such remedial or preventative measures are to be taken, the early identification of children at risk is essential.

The Identification of Those Who Need Help

The Milwaukee project referred to above picked up children at risk; in Wirz's words, the 'lucky ones', on whom many resources were focused and whose environment was radically changed. This of course costs money. However, in a finite economy, particularly one determined by government cash limits, rather than such resources being made available they are customarily diverted from other care activities. Thus here the problem is not simply one of detection of remediable mental handicap, but also prediction of which profoundly handicapped infants will benefit most from scarce resources.

The neonatal paediatrician has several clinical signs which help him predict which children are likely to be severely mentally handicapped. For example, the premature infant, who has suffered severe hypoxias, has probably suffered massive structural damage, whereas the full-term child who has been deprived of sufficient oxygen will possibly have suffered only moderate damage to his cortical watershed areas and hippocampus, the resulting language and memory deficits being possibly specific and partially remediable. Yet we still do not know which infants most need, or can benefit from, early intervention.

However, the future of early testing for potential seems promising. For example, Kearsley (1979) can test the mental ability of infants from 3 months of age. To avoid biases introduced by the neuromotor handicaps, Kearsley records changes in the heartbeat, while two hidden observers watch and record the child's facial and physical responses as the child watches brief puppet scenes, in which the child's expectations are built up and then violated. The speed with which the child responds to changes in routine provides a measure of mental ability. Quantitative electrophysiological batteries, including not only EEG readings but about 30 other measures of the brain's electrical activity, may soon also be used to measure intelligence in infants. Such tests include the brain's response to interruptions and clicks, giving a distinct measure that can (with reservations) be statistically compared with data from normal children. The prediction of which profoundly handicapped infants might benefit most from language therapy will gradually become more sophisticated as evidence accrues from paediatric electrophysiology.

It is also known that infants can utilize acoustic information in a linguistically relevant manner as early as 1–2 months of age (Eimas et al., 1971). Important implications for diagnosis may well arise from looking for developmental sequences in perceptual capability. The study of more complex cues available from cry analysis (particularly latency of cries) may also help predict those infants, during 'silent periods' when neurological examination cannot help, who will benefit most from particular attention being paid to their social interaction.

The Identification of Realistic Targets

It has recently been claimed that 'in the past twenty years we have achieved a breakthrough in the feasibility to teach some language to all children regardless of their functioning' (Schiefelbush, 1979). To examine this claim realistically, it would be necessary to consider the cost-effectiveness of teaching methods, a matter that is beyond the scope of this book. While there is no doubt that the efforts made in recent years to fit the handicapped into the community have meant that the mentally handicapped have a better chance to practise communication and to receive from ordinary professionals the education and therapy available to others, it is still the case that the mentally handicapped often need specially designed methods. Again, the question at issue is what resources are to be bound up in which method? However, if teaching methods' cost-effectiveness and resource commitment cannot be considered here, there are other aspects which can be commented on.

For example, any form of treatment which is not subjected to measurement is in danger of being terminated, for its existence will be dependent on funds subject to direct, indirect and opportunity costing. Language programmes must not go the way of perceptual training, which is now considered as little more than 'a busy work manoeuvre, a parent palliative ... which has digressed training into irrelevancies and mispractice. ... It is time we returned to training children in the skills functional for their living' (Mann and Goodman, 1976).

One difficulty here is that the lower the developmental level, the less valid are standard measures. Yet we must try to determine quantifiables. Many teachers and parents of profoundly handicapped children keep a diary of events which are function-based. Such records may well have great utility and, moreover, be amenable to quantification and allow measurement. For example, such a function-based approach takes account of an individual's ability to exercise a skill or process which is under observation. With regard to use of voice, for instance, the practitioner may be helped by knowing that the client can use his voice to draw attention to himself, but is not yet at the stage of being able to imitate the vocalizations of other people. There are similarities between this approach and one which is based on developmental milestones, but for treatment purposes the function-based approach is more flexible. It does not make any assumptions about the expected time of appearance of a skill, but regards that skill as something towards which the client is progressing, or something which he has attained already. Additionally, it avoids the problems of trying to align developmental 'ages' and skills, and of trying to predict the appearance of one skill in a hierarchy from the history of the appearance of earlier skills in the hierarchy (although knowledge about such a hierarchy can be helpful to staff). We should not be overconcerned about trying to estimate an individual's location on a continuum of milestones. That practice can too easily degenerate into unproductive completion of checklists. A function-based approach is also preferable to an approach which uses tests that refer to norms. For example, intelligence tests are inappropriate measures of change in a retarded population 3–5 standard deviations below the norm.

Language therapy thus can be seen as part of a package of measures to help the child's progress along a continuum of decreasing dependence. Certainly there are degrees of independence, and the client may show no progress or even deteriorate. But if function-based skills can be assessed and quantified, at the very least objective evidence is being provided for inspection, and as a measure of maintenance (Gilbert Mackay, personal communication).

Specific objectives in treatment can be set. With each sub-area of a scheme, the practitioner will be able to draw up programmes of treatment which will help to consolidate skills acquired already, and which will facilitate the attainment of higher levels of competence. Treatment thus becomes open to inspection at three levels:

1. at the level of the individual programme, which may or may not have been appropriately constructed;
2. at the level of the choice of objective, which may or may not be in accord with the developmental framework (patchy deficits and islet skills may cause developmental vagary);
3. at the level of the framework itself, which may or may not be a satisfactory conceptualization of the area in which treatment is being applied.

This approach to treatment can claim to be more stringent than most, in that each of its aspects is readily accessible to scrutiny. Of course it also has to be borne in mind that certain time limits on interventions may be required, and that the professional will have to be prepared to impose these, or have them imposed by certain factors (e.g. economic) which are often outside the professional's immediate control.

The Delivery of Effective Methods

This has two aspects. The first is concerned with the education of staff in direct contact with people with language problems, the second is concerned with facilitating the work of such staff, by minimizing unessential paperwork and meetings. Here the shibboleth 'multiprofessional team approach', which has been much bandied about, but examined little, and practised even less, requires close consideration, so that the problems of leadership and responsibility that Wirz discusses can be resolved. Services should be appropriately delegated to those closest to the child — the natural deliverers of communication techniques. As Mittler (1980) has pointed out, we have to train the semi-skilled to undertake this task, and one device that semi-skilled staff can use has been provided by Wirz.

Excessive formality in education, and rigid behaviour intervention, typical of the past, have now been rejected. But in teaching children to communicate, the speaker input to the child should be reduced naturally, rather than artificially simplified or altered. It should also be recalled that speech must have consequences for the child. The child must also have opportunities to listen clearly to his own utterances, and to the utterances of another, in the presence of a person who is speaking only to him, and such learning has to pervade his daily routines. Unfortunately, there is evidence that the more backward the child is, the less people talk to him. As Mittler and Berry (1977) have pointed out, we do not demand enough speech of the mentally handicapped, and we often fail to provide them with opportunities to use certain parts of speech such as verbs and prepositions. We can both waste the opportunities that everyday settings provide for acquiring language, and fail to provide sufficient experience of such everyday settings.

These comments are largely concerned with organizational and managerial issues. Medical, nursing and educational managers need to heed staff reports which relate how much better retarded children communicate in the holiday home, or beach caravan, compared with the classroom, ward or residential school. Here it is not simply the case that staff ratios are better, but that organizational time is saved, for at the holiday home direct-care staff do not need to 'keep ahead' of work or meet deadlines. Managers should also elicit what staff objectives compete with improving the child's language, including career, personal and interdisciplinary ones, and seek ways of removing or reducing the conflicts of interest. Managers should discover their staffs' perception of their own role, and the role of other professions in helping children to speak, in order to identify the discrepancies in expectations that different professions have of the same child or group of children. Not least, managers should know, or find out, where children are happiest, for this is where they communicate best.

The Removal of Obstacles to Intervention

Environmental obstacles to intervention have already been discussed. Here we consider emotional obstacles, whose removal can be much more difficult.

The commonest obstacle to the psychiatric diagnosis and rehabilitation of the disturbed mentally handicapped person is his verbal unresponsiveness. The number of psychiatric referrals of the following sort is large. Mr A. (aged 45, IQ 40) is seen at the request of the local court. He has repeatedly been fire raising, but cannot describe his motives. Master B. (aged 12, IQ 65) has been hurting other youngsters in the school lunch queue. His teacher says that he is impossible to get to know. Mr C. (aged 27, IQ 45) has the fetish of stealing any items of silk. He has proved resistant to behaviour therapy and discussion of the matter, and has been placed in semi-secure care. Mr D. (aged 48, IQ 47) is found throwing breakfast rolls at visitors in a seaside resort in morning mist. He settles after a few hours of excitement. He cannot explain 'what came over him'.

Miss E. (aged 45) becomes tearful at her parents' golden wedding, as if she suddenly appreciated their ageing. She groans for weeks saying she has a pain, but investigation excludes a physical cause. She does not respond to antidepressants. By contrast, Mr F. (aged 59) is a Down's anomaly of IQ 54. He is suspected of dementia (to which Down's are prone). Unlike the previous individuals, he is highly articulate, able to express emotions, and his talk reveals depression. However most mentally handicapped individuals deny the doctor the verbal raw material of his trade, even when they have the potential competence to be explicit.

In the chapter by Leudar, it is proposed that there are several kinds of communication, and of communication withdrawal, which are socially functional. The manner in which retarded people choose to affect their audiences depends on their social relation to those audiences, and in particular, on the distribution of power in a relationship, its reciprocity, and negotiability. Leudar distinguishes four types of communication:

1. *Overt communication,* in which the sender of a message affects his audience by making them aware of what he intends to convey.

2. *Covert communication*, in which the sender attempts to affect his audience, but by covert means. He does not wish the recipient of the message to recognize that he (the recipient) was affected, nor how he was affected.

3. *Actual communicative inertness,* where the retarded person does not originate messages, and ignores messages directed at him.

4. *Aggression,* a type of 'communication' which is both similar to, and different from, covert communication. It is similar in that the sender avoids reciprocity in communication, and attempts to control the behaviour of his communicative partner unilaterally. It is different in that in covert communication, the sender seeks to avoid a conflict, while in aggression he begs it. Departures from overt communication such as those in (2), (3) and (4) are potential reactions to distorted social situations. Thus, largely on social grounds, mentally handicapped individuals may distort or withdraw from communication, making things difficult for themselves and their therapists.

With children, the problems can be even greater, involving not only verbal unresponsiveness and distortions of communication, but a retreat into isolation syndrome, where the child abandons vocal and non-vocal messages. Isolation syndrome, with self-mutilation, is a combination of sensory deprivation and a maladaptive response which requires a powerful form of intervention. Skilled professional advice sufficiently early can prevent it, and replace it by adaptive communication systems, such as Makaton and Blissymbolics. Even when it is fiercely engrained, vigorous treatment can result in the reappearance of vocal signs, or even a return to speech. One problem is that severe isolation syndrome is often susceptible only to aversive techniques, which can be particularly distasteful. And as Tierney has shown, although the elimination of common mannerisms can be achieved relatively simply, the introduction of signals, not previously present, is often not practical.

It should also be noted that the removal of verbal unresponsiveness can have undesirable, non-verbal consequences. In the Milwaukee project referred to earlier, for example, although intense effort and engineering of parental motivation led to significant gains in children's language, these linguistically improved children subsequently showed increased behaviour problems. Thus their language test results improved more than their linguistic usage, suggesting that it was their linguistic skills that were helped, rather than their skills in communication.

Questions therefore remain. They include whether strategies can be identified which will enable the therapist to relate to individuals who are verbally unresponsive, or who distort or withdraw from communication. Also, given improved knowledge of the causes of communication withdrawal, can health education teach or foster a communicative mode which will forestall behaviour disturbance? Health education units, schools television and BBC television have experience of producing programmes of self-help skills. Here one can envisage the utility of educational TV vignettes, depicting upsets and 'reversals' in everyday life, and demonstrating how to cope, verbally or otherwise, as opposed to retreats into mute helplessness.

The Pursuit of New Lines of Research

This book's aim is not just to report research, but to try to stimulate further research, both fundamental and operational. With respect to fundamental research, we look forward both to further developments on the topics introduced in this book, and to new developments. For example, a topic that is currently receiving considerable attention in the literature on normal language development is that of the child's awareness of language, for it is recognized that linguistic awareness has highly significant implications for the nature of the child's cognitive and linguistic functioning in particular, and for the child's education in general (Donaldson, 1978; Gelman, 1978). While a start has been made on the study of linguistic awareness in the normal child (e.g. Sinclair et al., 1978; Campbell, 1979; Hakes et al., 1980), and on means of detecting awareness (e.g. Clark, 1978; Clark and Anderson, 1979), there is clearly much work to be done. However, we anticipate that the next few years will also see attempts to consider the problem of awareness in the mentally retarded child, for the cognitive, linguistic and educational implications are enormous.

With respect to operational research, we have already referred to various problems that need to be examined. Thus there is a need for administrators and managers to examine multiprofessional relationships, and to identify environments which maximize opportunities for language development. Developmentalists and paediatricians need to investigate ways of increasing the precision of early diagnosis and estimation of potential. Therapists need to identify what measures should be appropriately delegated, and which are effective in terms of both cost and results. Psychologists need to examine how their techniques and technology can be most effectively brought to bear on the early origins of language, and how the transition from early turn-taking 'dialogue' in the pre-speech stage to subsequent verbal expression can be best effected.

Here the problems of learning, training and education are paramount. There is a need to identify the most appropriate ways to teach skills to the severely and profoundly retarded child, and a recognition that with such children methods may have to be varied by comparison with those employed with children who are less retarded. We must also be realistic about education. While the notion that some children are 'ineducable' requires constant examination, we need to avoid offering false hope. For example, we must be clear that in the present state of knowledge, our ability to teach a child with a thin rind of cortex, or with a hippocampus and colliculi as ravaged as those of an adult alcoholic with Korsakow's defect, is minimal. More generally, there is a need for collaborative research between psychologists, neurophysiologists and neuropathologists on the study of learning and transfer of learning processes, as these relate to brain activity, especially in profoundly retarded individuals.

The optimal times for training also need to be identified, as we have already mentioned. Here we have to recall that with retarded individuals, we cannot expect to wait for skills to appear, nor wait until the child is 'ready' to acquire a skill. That may be never. As Brinker and Bricker (1980) make clear, waiting is not an option: 'Time has already failed to do for the mentally retarded child what it seems to do for normal children.' But as they also point out, this immediately raises problems as regards intervention: 'On the basis of the available literature, no sequence of language behaviours has been empirically validated as the efficient road to language intervention.' We need to find out not only when best to train, but what it is that needs to be trained.

We also have to remember the importance of adopting a wider perspective, and avoid concentrating exclusively on linguistic communication. As indicated above, there are urgent needs to study vocal and other non-verbal aspects of communication, including the expression of emotion, overt or covert, in the mildly, moderately and severely retarded, through cries, facial expressions and bodily gestures. How can underlying emotional states be reliably identified, and how can such identification procedures be readily used by personnel from a wide range of backgrounds? Here it is going to be perhaps useful, perhaps essential, for interdisciplinary research collaboration between ethologists, psychologists, psychiatrists and educationalists, if effective answers to such questions are to be found.

Finally, it is perhaps appropriate to reflect for a moment on the purpose of this hubbub of fundamental and operational research activity. To some extent, this way of putting the matter is of course misleading, for there are several purposes to the work, rather than a single purpose. However there is one purpose to which we particularly wish to draw attention in conclusion. It might be considered food for thought to observe that even in comparatively rich areas such as Europe, North America and Australia, there are regions where one child in six never gets the chance to learn how to express himself. But it is not simply food for thought. It is a reason for action, and we trust that this book provides sufficient indication of where some of our activities might be usefully directed.

References

Brinker R. P. and Bricker D. (1980) Teaching a first language: building complex structures from simpler components. In: Hogg J. and Mittler P. (ed.) *Advances in Mental Handicap Research*. New York, Wiley.

Bruner J. S. (1978) The role of dialogue in language acquisition. In: Sinclair A., Jarvella R. J. and Levelt W. J. M. (ed.) *The Child's Conception of Language*. Berlin, Springer Verlag, pp. 241–255.

Campbell R. N. (1979) Language acquisition, psychological dualism and the definition of pragmatics. Paper presented at the Conference on Possibilities and Limitations of Pragmatics. Centro Internazionale di Semiotica & Linguistica, Urbino, Italy, 9–14 July, 1979.

Clarke E. V. (1978) Awareness of language: some evidence from what children say and do. In: Sinclair A., Jarvella R. J. and Levelt W. J. M. (ed.) *The Child's Conception of Language*. Berlin, Springer Verlag, pp. 17–43.

Clark E. V. and Anderson E. S. (1979) Spontaneous repairs: awareness in the process of acquiring language. Paper presented at the Symposium on Reflections on Metacognition, Meeting of the Society for Research in Child Development, San Francisco, 15–19 March, 1979.

Donaldson M. (1978) *Children's Minds*. London, Fontana.

Eimas P. D., Siquelana E. R., Jusczyk P. et al. (1971) Speech perception in infants. *Science* 171, 303–306.

Feuerstein R. (1977) Medicated learning experience. In: Mittler P. (ed.) *Research to Practice*. Proceedings of the IVth IASSMD Conference. Baltimore, University Park Press.

Garber H. and Heber F. R. (1977) The Milwaukee project – indications of the effectiveness of early intervention in preventing mental retardation. In: Mittler P. (ed.) *Research to Practice*. Proceedings of the IVth IASSMD Conference. Baltimore, University Park Press.

Gelman R. (1979) Cognitive development. *Annu. Rev. Psychol.* 29, 297–332.

Hakes D. T., Evans J. S. and Tunmer W. (1980) *The Development of Metalinguistic Abilities in Children*. Berlin, Springer Verlag. (In press.)

Kearsley R. (1979) cited by Rice B. The brave new world of intelligence testing. *New Society* 50, 63.

Mann L. and Goodman L. (1976) Perceptual training. In: Schopler E. and Reichler R. (ed.) *Psychopathology and Child Development*. New York, Plenum, pp. 271–291.

Mittler P. (1980) Strategies for manpower development in the 1980s. In: Mittler P. (ed.) *Frontiers of Research*. Proceedings of the Vth IASSMD Conference. Baltimore, University Park Press.

Mittler P. and Berry P. (1977) Demanding language. In: Mittler P. (ed.) *Research to Practice*. Proceedings of the IVth IASSMD Conference. Baltimore, University Park Press.

Schiefelbush R. (1979) Early language problems and procedures. Paper presented at
   the Vth IASSMD Conference, Jerusalem, August 1979.
Sinclair A., Jarvella R. J. and Levelt W. J. M. (ed.) (1978) *The Child's Conception of
   Language.* Berlin, Springer Verlag.

Author Index

Subject Index